Changing Sk.

For
Alan
and
Beatrice

With
Best Regards
Evor.
Bruce
2008

Changing Skies

BRUCE PURCHASE

STEELE ROBERTS
AOTEAROA NEW ZEALAND

to Sara

The front cover author portrait is by Paivii Makarinne Crofts. Photos of Bruce as Dr Johnson (cover, pp 257 and 258) and the portrait on page 1 are by Jon Churchman. Thanks to Jon for technical wizardry, and to Seth Rankin for production assistance … and more. Thanks to Lynn Peck for cover design, and Matthew Bartlett, Sarah Bolland, Michèle Clarke and Christine Tilyard for publishing assistance.

The title typeface is Michelangelo, inspired by the artist's handwriting, and the cover is based on a Magritte sky.

Sunny Young Printing Inc, Taiwan.

National Library of New Zealand Cataloguing-in-Publication Data
Purchase, Bruce.
Changing skies : an actor's life / Bruce Purchase.
Includes index.
ISBN 978-1-877448-29-4
1. Actors—New Zealand—Biography. I. Purchase, Bruce. ll. Title.
791.45028092—dc 22

STEELE ROBERTS PUBLISHERS
Box 9321, Wellington, New Zealand
info@steeleroberts.co.nz • www.steeleroberts.co.nz

Contents

Foreword

I FIRST MET BRUCE PURCHASE IN 1980 when the Royal Shakespeare Company was beginning rehearsals for *Richard II*. Alan Howard was to play King Richard; I was to play Bolingbroke; Bruce to play Northumberland. But it was not until *Troilus and Cressida* in 1981 that Bruce and I really made true contact. By that I mean literally — we had to kiss each other! Bruce was playing Hector and I was playing Achilles. I won't elaborate on this piece of stage business. Certainly Bruce has not referred to it in this book. Suffice it to say that, from that moment on, I could never understand how anyone could possibly enjoy kissing a man with a beard!

After leaving the RSC, Bruce and I met up again in 1983 with the BBC TV production of *The Life of Freud* when he was playing Dr. Nothnagel and I was playing Freud. Both times I enjoyed working with Bruce, finding him not only an excellent actor but a person with a great sense of humour, a capacity for searing wit and an inexhaustible love of language.

In 2007 we met again in a new play, *The Last Confession*. Not only was it a great pleasure to be working together again, but to be able to pick up where we had left off.

Reading *Changing Skies* has allowed me to know Bruce even better. This is no ordinary autobiography proceeding systematically through his life. The reader is thrust straight into his experiences at the National Theatre of Great Britain, entertaining one with wonderful anecdotes about the great man himself, Laurence Olivier. One is then taken on various journeys and experiences touching on his childhood and relationships in New Zealand. Through his professional experience as a theatre, television and film actor, he introduces us to actors, directors and friends in such a way that we are drawn into the lives of others as well as that of Bruce himself. But this is typical Purchase: a man ever interested in other people and curious to know more about them. It is this great observation of life which makes him such an interesting actor.

It was only during our times together in *The Last Confession* that I discovered Bruce's talent as a painter. Recently, I had the great pleasure of going to an exhibition of his paintings. His talent, I am told, is natural; he has never had a formal lesson in his life. And his paintings are extraordinary. Not only are they skilfully executed in different media but they cover a wide range of subject matter. The paintings were filled with bright colour. Bruce doesn't just paint what he sees but how he sees. Similarly, in his book Bruce paints with words. His life and his fellow travellers are not seen in ordinary terms. Always there is wit and humour; those individuals he enjoys and those he doesn't. Here is a man who writes as one obsessed with life and people.

In *Changing Skies* the reader travels through the gamut of emotions from the elixir of overwhelming success to the pain and disappointment in certain areas of his personal life. It kept me gripped. The book ends with a note of hope and thanks — "More to come perhaps? Much to be grateful for."

I pray there is much more to come.

David Suchet OBE, FRSA
London 2008

"Clutching a programme from the production …"

I

Coat of many colours

"**H**ow's your mother?"

Caught off guard by the question and its timing. What game is this, I thought before replying.

"She's well, thank you, Sir," my mind on alert, for 'Sir' has never met my mother. Why this question?

"Do give her my love." The older man walked away slowly down the 'back passage' as it was always referred to at the Old Vic Theatre in those distant days.

A few seconds prior to this exchange we'd passed in that narrow passageway with me standing to one side to let my elder pass. "Good morning, Sir," I addressed him. Self-absorbed, my employer vaguely acknowledged me *en passant*. Having taken only a few steps, I heard my name called.

But the tone had changed for now it was barked out … as an order!

The great man had played this trick before, so when I turned to him I did so with trepidation. Oh God, what have I done wrong this time?

The brief 'How's your mother?' conversation then took place. With no explanation of the 'why' of the question, my boss then ambled off. The year was 1964. I was left contemplating what the heck it was all about. My mother had never met him and she lived twelve thousand miles away.

A dutiful son long absent from my homeland, I wrote at least once a week to my parents in New Zealand. In my next letter I made mention of the strange encounter with my boss, the revered and feared Great Man.

In the ten-day gap before my mother's reply I'd half guessed the truth. But only half! Her comments confirmed my worst fears. She had written to my employer — and what horrified me — he had replied!

I had first clapped eyes on the Great Man when as a lad of ten I'd stood outside a stage door in Auckland in 1948. I'd just watched Shakespeare's *Richard III* in which he starred. Clutching a programme from the production (which I still have and treasure), I stood alongside my mother and other playgoers on the pavement, ready to catch a glimpse of the GM and his wife, who also appeared in the play, when they exited the theatre.

Laurence Olivier — photo by Angus McBean, from the 1948 programme.

The GM's wife appeared first. A hush in the crowd as this famous actress passed to a car at the kerb. Light applause and muted comments, "Well done," etc. An excited woman in the crowd cried out, "Isn't she beautiful?"

As these words were uttered the Great Man himself came out of the stage door. Overhearing this tribute to his wife, he said quietly to the woman who'd shouted, "I think so too," before he, dark and handsome, joined his wife in the waiting car.

This wide-eyed, starstruck kid of ten could not have dreamt that fifteen years after this event the dark dazzling actor/manager would be his boss.

In her reply my mother wrote in 1964 … "Soon after you joined the National Theatre, darling, I wrote to Sir Laurence to see how you were settling in. He replied by return of post …"

Oh my God! My worst fears confirmed. "Wanting to check if I'm eating properly and washing behind my ears, I suppose. I'm twenty-six years of age, Mother."

But mother continued: "Since when, we've kept in contact. He says you're doing well. It's sweet of him to take time to write."

Sweet? Oh Gawd. When next I saw my employer I blushed. Sir

Laurence merely nodded sagely, asking if the All Blacks had won their test match at the weekend.

A few weeks later the National Theatre took its first annual break. The young Kiwi actor made a brief return journey to see his family for the first time in four years. His mother showed him the letters she'd received from Sir Laurence. He blushed again.

Sir Laurence's first communication read like a headmaster's report. In later missives, however, a more characteristic, florid style emerged.

After saying "Give her my love", Sir Laurence must have chuckled to himself as he wandered off, leaving me puzzled. Rooted to the spot.

In 1963, at twenty-five, a year after completion of studies at RADA (the Royal Academy of Dramatic Art), this mother's son had been chosen to join a band of actors at the newly established National Theatre of Great Britain. Its initial base was the Old Vic Theatre on the Cut at Waterloo, and its founder artistic director, the already legendary Sir Laurence Olivier, the already attributed … Great Man. The National began a golden age in British Theatre.

I remember Olivier's first pep talk. The public dress rehearsal had been blighted by a number of technical disasters. After curtain-down, morale in the ranks was low. The whole company exhausted. The following night was press night with all the critics attending. After this ropy performance the actors needed rallying for the official beginning of a brave new venture, long-awaited. The opening production was *Hamlet*, with the glamorous Peter O'Toole, fresh from his success in David Lean's *Lawrence of Arabia*, playing the title role and Laurence Olivier directing. Standing in the well of the auditorium of the Old Vic, Sir Laurence gathered his exhausted cast on stage to address them. How to raise their spirits? He had a go.

"Don't be nervous tomorrow. We've a good show on our hands."

Not strictly true. Although the production included fine ensemble playing from such luminaries as Michael Redgrave, Rosemary Harris, Robert Stephens and others of equal magnitude, it was, despite this stellar combination, cursed with a technically flawed set, and the play's uncut version ran too long, at four and three-quarter hours. The show began at 7pm and curtain-down was quarter to midnight.

The only respite was one twenty-minute interval. It was to open the first season more with a whimper than the long anticipated bang.

But this was the evening before. Echoing the St Crispin's Day speech from his film *Henry V*, Sir Laurence faced the serried ranks attempting to embolden them for battle on the morrow:

"I beseech you — don't be nervous tomorrow. You have no need. I'm reminded of a recent trip to Paris to see Marlene [Dietrich] in her solo show. Before the performance I met with Noel [Coward] and enquired of him how Marlene was feeling. Was she nervous?

"Noel replied firmly, 'Good Lord, why should she be nervous?'

"I responded — 'Noelli, the last time I saw you doing your one man show you were so bloody nervous the microphone was shaking in your fucking hand!' "

Here laughter from the tired bunch of actors, standing about on stage. As the laughter faded, Sir moved to the climax of his tale.

"But Noel riposted, 'Yes, it was then I decided my nerves were getting in the way of the audience's enjoyment. I've never been nervous since'."

Another amused response from the group on stage, and then Sir L rounded off.

"So, dear boys and girls, don't be nervous tomorrow eve. Come out on this Old Vic stage bravely. All will be well. Now off you go. Well done, everyone. Leave me to sort out the few remaining technical problems. Sleep well. You've earned it."

The weary group began to leave the stage. When the area had all but cleared, a panicked shout from the Upper Circle. "The theatre's on fire!" a voice from the Gods announced. Smoke was indeed billowing out from on high. I was standing near the edge of the stage, close enough to witness Sir Laurence's reaction. Revealing

After arriving in London, 1960.

his own feelings of tiredness and despondency, Olivier glanced up in the direction of the smoke.

"Let it burn," he muttered. He picked up his briefcase and turned to leave the theatre.

Thankfully, the fire staff rapidly doused the flames with hardly any damage incurred.

Hamlet opened the following eve to muted cheers, for the audience, having endured four and three-quarter hours, by evening's end were more exhausted than the actors. An inauspicious opening was soon forgotten as other impressive productions entered the repertoire. The National Theatre was on its way.

The next time Sir Laurence talked to me it was about 'old cheese'.

A new production was being cast, with the mercurial Franco Zeffirelli about to commence rehearsals, directing Shakespeare's *Much Ado About Nothing*. This production became one of the National's huge early hits.

I'd just completed an in-house audition for the part of Balthasar, first having sung a song for Franco, as a singer/actor was required.

"Okay," Zeffirelli said teasingly, "now go outside, but come back in immediately and do something to make me laugh." Outside the rehearsal room for barely half a minute, I decided to reprise the audition speech that had secured my acceptance into the company the year before. My reasoning? Well, Franco hasn't seen me do

Outside National Theatre 1963.

13

it. Sir Laurence isn't present — and I know it's funny! But can I still remember the lines? Had to make Franco laugh. I re-entered. Luckily I did remember the words. But as further non-luck would have it, enter Sir Laurence, as I commenced. Afterwards he gently chided me.

"Your performance is now really very ripe, Brucie. Getting to be like a slice of old cheese. Gorgonzola perhaps?"

Junior members like myself, Mike Gambon and others of our age, mere beginners, were in those early days called on to do lots of 'cover' work, understudying the experienced principal actors. Mike Gambon has gone on to have an illustrious career earning a well deserved knighthood, as have so many others from those early years: Jacobi, Stephens, McKellen and Hopkins, and on the girls' side damehoods for Maggie Smith and Joan Plowright.

One of my early understudy chores was covering Anthony Nicholls' performance as Warwick in Shaw's *Saint Joan*. Although neither Tony Nicholls nor I were destined for 'gongs', we were awarded another prize — although Nicholls was a good twenty-five years older than me, and it was long after his death — we became co-grandfathers to a child, named Oakley.

During a matinée performance, early in the first season, I was on my own in the rehearsal room running through my understudy lines as Warwick. To avoid missing my next entrance onstage, in a minor role, I had one ear cocked, listening to the performance broadcast over the theatre's internal tannoy system from the stage, several floors below. My cue to go and change costume was when the heroine sang her prayer. The title role was played by Joan Plowright. She played the young peasant girl using her own native north country accent in a performance of clarity and power. My cue came as Joan sang, "Dear child of God ... Dear child of God."

Bursting through the rehearsal room door onto the landing, where stairs led to my dressing room one floor below, I stopped dead in my tracks ... for there, a few feet away — I nearly crashed headlong into him — stood Joan Plowright's husband, the Great Man himself. He was leaning casually against a wall, calmly smoking a cigarette. As I'd shot out of the door I'd been loudly re-interpreting Joan's sung prayer with the voice of a favourite character of mine,

Bruce Purchase as Balthasar in Franco Zeffirelli's *Much Ado About Nothing.*
Also pictured: Albert Finney, Gerald James and Ian McKellen.

Neddy Seagoon from the Goon Show. The words froze on my lips. Sir Laurence, although he showed no sign, had surely heard me send up his wife's performance, although malice was not intended.

Sir L, usually immaculately attired, was in an old shirt, jeans and well worn plimsolls. Unbeknown to me he was working that afternoon alongside the theatre technicians, up on the fly floor, helping to raise and lower scenery by ropes for the matinée performance. The only thought in my head was whether he had heard my send-up. I felt my old familiar blush rise like sap.

In a voice markedly higher than normal, I blurted out, "Good afternoon, Sir." Olivier, it seemed, was in a world of his own, unaware of anything untoward. He idly blew a couple of smoke rings and drowsily murmured a reply, "Hello, Brucie." To fill the pause that followed, I tried to strike up a conversation. My voice squeaked out, "How're rehearsals for *Uncle Vanya* progressing, Sir?" Eyes hooded behind his specs, Olivier once again responded sleepily to this inane query: "Well … rehearsals are going … well, thank you Bruce."

He didn't seem to be remotely aware of his young employee's acute embarrassment. I edged past him and made swiftly for the stairs. I was two steps down the stairs when Olivier called to me. With precision timing the old man commenced my comeuppance, with beguiling gentleness.

"Brucie," he said very softly, and this Brucie turned on the stairs awkwardly to face the GM.

"Sir?" I mumbled.

Sir Laurence ambled across the landing, decorously stubbing his cigarette out with one foot, on the way. His demeanour serene. Although on the level I was the taller, now two steps down, Olivier towered over me. Precision timing, for now I was effectively 'upstaged'.

The giant, placing his hands on my shoulders, mellifluously enquired, "You've changed your hairstyle, have you not?"

His prey was held lightly in his grasp. "Yes, Sir," voice faint, face crimson.

"That's correct," the Giant's voice, lulling and reassuring. "Yes, you had a parting, there …" he momentarily released one shoulder and drew his finger across the left hand side of my head before replacing his hand again on my shoulders, tightening the grip as before.

"Yes, you had that parting when you first joined us. When was that, Brucie? A month ago? Or was it six weeks?"

"Six, Sir." I was unsure which direction to look in as the Giant leaned in closer, nose to nose, eyes behind his specs mesmeric. The grip on both shoulders tightened perceptibly into a vice-like clasp.

"Most becoming, dear heart," the Giant purred.

I was, *mano-a-mano*, caught like a startled rabbit in the headlights of the Giant's gaze. Through the long pause that ensued my blush intensified. Suddenly, and unexpectedly, the Giant performed his *coup de grâce* for I was swiftly released from his grip, lost my balance, teetered dangerously on the steps, lunging out for the handrail to steady myself, as Laurence Olivier, hands held high in the air, took two rapid paces backwards on the landing, a look of utter disdain on his face, as if to say, why had this colonial upstart been standing so close to him?

Without another word, Olivier turned, exiting smoothly to the fly floor to resume his afternoon task. Brave Dumb Show. Without a direct word he'd indicated to his young apprentice — *Don't dare send up my wife's performance, boy.* And then exited.

With my proud Kiwi feathers singed, I raced to change for my now very pressing appointment on stage. Another year was to pass before that next encounter of "How's your Mother?"

At the end of the first triumphant season at the Vic all members of the company, high and low, in all departments, received a personal handwritten letter of appreciation from Laurence Olivier. A task which must have taken him weeks to accomplish, tucked in against his various chores: acting, directing, administration, and of course time for billets-doux, sent airmail to my Mama. These thoughtful communications were another aspect of his extraordinary attention to detail. This amazing actor, manager, director, carried a bag of many colours — a technicolor armoury, for use both onstage and off.

In those days at the Vic there was a room adjacent to the fly floor door and the rehearsal room, at the very top of the building, lit by a skylight. Earlier it had been used as a Green Room, where actors repaired for R and R — its walls still hung with oil paintings depicting illustrious theatre figures of the past.

But in 1963 it had been designated the Prop Room, and was crammed with large, interlaced cane 'skips' containing properties for current productions. Never in use in the early evening, it became for me a private place, where after the rigours of rehearsal and before supper and the evening performance, I'd go to read quietly on my own. A haven — a sort of private Green Room — away from my shared dressing room and the general hustle and bustle of the rest of the building. I'd also often spend time looking up at the old oil paintings and imagining the lives of those personalities from the past — Edmund Kean was one. Coleridge once said of Kean, the greatest actor of the nineteenth century, that watching him play Shakespearean roles was "as if reading it by flashes of lightning".

In the far corner of this very packed room, on an old plush sofa, probably a relic from its Green Room days, I was never disturbed … that was, not until one winter's evening, the light fast fading from the skylight, as dusk fell …

It was time to go and have supper in the basement canteen. I'd just set aside my current book and was about to rise from my corner seat when, on the far side of the room, the door opened and Sir Laurence entered the fast darkening space. Not appearing to notice me, he carefully circumnavigated his way around the skips and, taking up a position in the centre of the room, with his back turned to me, looked up at the portrait of Edmund Kean. I'd always thought he likened himself to that great nineteenth-century actor. John Gielgud, when Olivier played *Richard III*, presented to Sir Laurence the sword Kean used as Richard. This thought delayed any notion I might have had about announcing my presence. "Too late," I thought. I therefore sat silently and still, lest the springs of the sofa should creak, hoping he would soon turn and go.

Minutes passed as he stood very still looking up silently at Kean's portrait, the room nearly dark. Out of the gloom he began to speak, his voice very low. For a split second I imagined him to be speaking to himself, but no … he had spotted me in the corner when he'd entered. "Do you realise, Bruce, this is the only full-length portrait of Edmund Kean in existence?" he murmured.

In the now pitch-dark room the mood seemed almost reverential. Picking up his tone, not wishing to break the spell, and feeling as if by a trick of the eye in the darkness that Kean was also looking down on us, I replied, "No, I didn't know that, Sir."

Sensing he'd come to the room, like me, to be alone, I got up carefully and discreetly made my way to the door. Supper beckoned. I turned back. I could barely see him by the ambient illumination from the skylight, but from my POV (point of view) he was seen now in profile, still looking up at Kean.

"Shall I switch the light on, Sir?" I said quietly.

"No thank you, Bruce. Leave it off."

I closed the door gently after me, leaving the actor of today looking up at an actor of yesterday in a darkening room. A twentieth-century master, staring at his nineteenth-century forbear.

The 1948 programme included, as a principal illustration, a picture (not this painting) of Kean playing *Richard III*. I wondered about Coleridge's definition of Kean's playing of Shakespeare as I descended the stairs to the basement. Was Sir Laurence there in that darkened space pondering, trying to divine, just how Kean's 'lightning' had worked?

Every month a company meeting took place. Olivier would preside. All members of staff attended and general company matters were discussed. An egalitarian concept, Olivier's own, everyone was to be privy to future plans. At one such assembly, a subject, at the time creating a furore in the press, among literary historians and the acting profession at large, was raised. Should Shakespeare's tomb, in the church at Stratford-Upon-Avon, be opened? Some were in favour, others against. Those who advocated disinterment believed it might prove conclusively whether or not Shakespeare was responsible for the works attributed to him. Other historians argued that another writer of Shakespeare's era might have been the real author and there were several contenders in the ring.

"What did Sir think?" someone in the group enquired. "Yes," another added, "what are your thoughts on this subject, Larry?"

His response, offered deadpan, amused us. "I'd really rather it were left unopened. Wouldn't you all here prefer the theatre at Stratford to retain its present title? The Royal Shakespeare Company at the Shakespeare Memorial Theatre? *Quelle horreur* if it had to be renamed, for the sake of argument, to the Royal Bacon Company at the Bacon Memorial — no rasher decision, to my mind, could be imagined!" One of the contenders for the title, Francis Bacon, was thus knocked over the ropes and out of the ring by the Great Man.

His ripostes could be almost lethal in effect. We'd all been told before the read-through of *Hamlet* that the play would not be cut, but performed in its entirety. Peter O'Toole had played Hamlet years before at the Bristol Old Vic. Peter's performance had been much praised at Bristol, and here, with Olivier directing this time, he was to attempt the role again.

The read-through commenced. It went smoothly until Peter O'Toole made an unplanned cut in the text. The rest of the cast looked bewildered. Not so Olivier. Without lifting his head from the script on the desk in front of him, he calmly interjected, "Those lines are still in, Peter."

"But Larry, we …"

"No buts — they're still in." Head not raised.

Five or so minutes later Peter made another cut in his own lines as Hamlet. Olivier, still not looking up from his page: "Those lines will also be performed, Peter."

O'Toole, once again thwarted, went back and read, half-heartedly, the lines of his latest 'cut'. On with the read-through, the cast waiting for this Hamlet to have another go. He did.

Imperturbable as before, Olivier, head still inclined, responded once again, soothingly, "Those words will also be spoken, for as with the other cuts you've made, dear chap, they've not been excised. May I reiterate for the last time, we're doing the *whole* play," his voice pleasant and easy.

However, I did note that Olivier was slowly twirling a pencil in one hand. It looked like a small dagger, ready to be drawn should he deem it necessary. And Peter, fobbed off once too often, came out of his corner with his mitts up, ready to punch it out with his senior. There was tension in the air as he threw his first punch.

"Larry, old boy, when we first met to talk about the play, you yourself agreed we'd elbow this section. The play's too long. The other bits should go too."

There was a dangerous beat. The pencil in Olivier's hand ceased its movement. His head came up slowly off his script as almost dreamily he replied, "Perhaps you're thinking of when you played this role so memorably at *Bristol*, Peter?"

O'Toole made no further cuts. In performance the production, with just one interval, ran an intolerable length with the audience racing off to catch their late-night transport. If only Peter had succeeded with his commonsense editing, the show would have been much improved. If only …

My desire to learn *everything* and all at once, having travelled 12,000 miles from New Zealand to fulfil my dream on the British stage, was a constant driving force. I was always asking questions. I must have often been a right pain, but I remember Sir Laurence as always tolerant towards his greenhorn from the antipodes.

One of my many questions: "What central requirement, Sir, or discipline would you say all actors should have?"

His reply, accompanied by a bemused smile, "Breath, Bruce."

"Breath, Sir?" earnestly pressing.

"Yes, Bruce. Breath, breath, breath and more breath. You can't have too much of the damn stuff."

Incidentally, as he answered me in the canteen over a coffee, he was smoking a cigarette, taken from a pack on the table, branded Olivier. Like that earlier star of stage, Sir Gerald du Maurier, Sir L had a brand of cigarette named after him. But whereas du Maurier's brand lived on long after that actor's demise, Olivier survived his own brand, as it came off the market some thirty years before his death. It just hadn't 'caught on', as they say in the trade.

Another question from the gauche young me elicited a brief, inspired reply. Same question, different answer.

"An actor, Bruce, should in performance always strive to have relaxed feet."

Brilliant! For if an actor's feet are relaxed, the message having emanated as an instruction from the brain — hey presto — the whole body between head and feet is also relaxed.

On the other hand some advice was unsolicited and arrived at odd, often surprising, moments. For instance in the première production of Peter Shaffer's over-rated *The Royal Hunt of the Sun* I played the small part of a Peruvian chieftain. The role required covering most of my spindly frame with a light tan make-up, commonly referred to as 'bowl', applied using dabs of water with the aid of a sponge straight from the Max Factor pan. I had to use so much of this make-up that the small water-based pan only lasted two performances before a replacement was needed. After each performance I'd wash this off under the shower in my shared dressing room, using a larger sponge and bar of soap. The door to this shower was a saloon-style wooden slatted half door, so there was not much privacy. To get the damn stuff off necessitated a lot of hearty rubbing.

One day, after a matinée I was merrily soaping myself under my shower whilst booming out an aria to amuse myself — and one other person, as it turned out. With water splashing everywhere, I heard a voice, and turned … my aria came to a swift termination. Through the splashing water I saw Sir Laurence peering in over the low gate.

"What do you …?" The teeming water drowned out his voice.

I fumbled the tap, turning it off. My naked skinny frame was drenched from top to toe. In this unprivate state, I said, with a plaintive squeal, "What, Sir?"

"I was just enquiring as to what you use to remove the bowl," he smiled mischievously.

Holding soap and sponge unnecessarily high in the air for him to see, "This, Sir," I squeaked.

Othello was in the repertoire, so Sir L, playing the Moor, was also using a darker shade of bowl. It was said that after application he polished it with silk, for added sheen. Over the shower-gate, like one nattering old farmer to his neighbour, he offered me the following advice as I stood dripping in the closet: "Try Fairy Liquid." With that, he was gone.

I took his advice. Using that particular brand of washing-up liquid plus me old sponge I was able to discard the bar of soap, for the bowl now came off in a flash.

A third and final sample. This question was asked him at a gathering in colleague Terence Knapp's Mayfair flat.

"Sir?"

"Yes?"

"If you had to name just two actors …"

"Oh, I think I can name more than two …"

"No, two — only two — you've most admired."

"Most admired? Only two?"

"Two, Sir. Who would they be?"

"Oh, without a doubt — Wilfred in the theatre, and Spencer in the cinema."

Both Spencer Tracy and Wilfred Lawson were masters of the craft, and although I only saw him in old age Lawson was close to genius.

This re-introduces my mother. She was born in Manchester and was brought up in her grandparents' house in north Wales, emigrating to New Zealand where she met my father. As a child, around 1948 again I guess, my mother took me to see the film of *Pygmalion*, which starred Leslie Howard, Wendy Hiller (a dead ringer for my mum) and Wilfred Lawson. She explained that Lawson had played in rep (repertory theatre) in Colwyn Bay when she was a young girl, and he always lodged with my great-grandparents. Mother had known Lawson.

His talent was magical; you could not see how he wove his spell. Some of his mystery was maybe fuelled by his alcohol consumption — one drink or two, too many and too often — but, pissed or sober, his work was always thrilling to watch. I'll speak of him elsewhere and at length.

Olivier's capacity for hard work, and painstaking attention to detail, was formidable. When I worked with the company he was at his very peak of fitness and command. I did not know him in old age, but by all reports his phoenix-like ability to fight off a succession of debilitating afflictions was truly remarkable.

One last sighting of Lord Olivier was at a distance, in the auditorium named after him, the Olivier Theatre in the National's theatre on the South Bank, not far from the early triumphs at the Old Vic. The occasion — a celebration of his 80th birthday. A light-hearted concert was performed, culminating with a delightful gesture. LO's daughter, Julie Kate, leapt out of a specially constructed 'cake' which had been wheeled onto the stage. Julie Kate walked to the edge of the stage and looked out to where her father was, surrounded by family and friends. "Happy Birthday, Dad," she said, simply, and for the audience most movingly.

Long before then he told me, "You must now take wing and fly." The year was 1965. I'd served two years at the National. This was the old maestro's way of softening the blow, by not openly saying to me that my contract was not to be renewed. It was time to seek pastures new. I'd had a good time there and my share of success, within the ranks. Time to go.

So 1966 saw me on Peter O'Toole's old stamping ground, the Bristol Old Vic, where I remained for a year. It was a very special year — the theatre's bicentenary season, with an excellent bunch of actors assembled: Richard Pasco, Barbara Leigh Hunt, Paul Eddington, Jane Asher, among many, plus visiting directors like the towering talent of Sir Tyrone Guthrie. Sir Laurence sent a congratulatory telegram, the first of many I'd receive over the coming years. A further development following Bristol was a move into television and film work. But theatre always called this jobbing actor back, and often there were reminders of Sir Laurence.

1971. Press night at the Mermaid Theatre, Puddle Dock,

23

Blackfriars, in the City of London. Brainchild of Bernard Miles, the Mermaid was the first new theatre built in London in 300 years. Bernard, knighted in the early 1970s and later 'canonized' as Lord Miles of Blackfriars, was another extraordinary actor-manager. A self-created eccentric, he hid his considerable intellectual powers behind the assumed persona of a simple countryman, a yokel in fact. This provided a camouflage behind which he could avoid that old British criticism of being too clever by half. This first night was the press opening of a production of *Othello*, with Sir Bernard ("call me Bernard") Miles as Iago, and myself in the title role as the Moor.

A few hours before curtain-up I was already fully dressed and made up as Othello, rarin' to go but with hours to wait. We'd had a photo-call for the press and, although armed with my trusty Fairy Liquid, I was unwilling to wash off the bowl, then later have to re-apply the coating of dark make-up for a second time in one day. So I had time to kill. My wife Elspeth and toddler son Reuben had just left, after a supportive visit which had greatly cheered me. When I lifted Reuben up into my arms he'd not appeared to notice that his father was darkly made up and wearing most un-Dadlike clothes. It was Reuben's first visit to a theatre, and perhaps some of my make-up rubbed off on him for he too worked as an actor for a time.

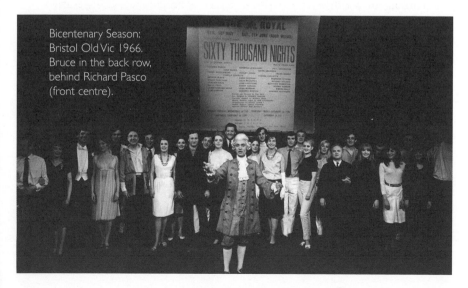

Bicentenary Season: Bristol Old Vic 1966. Bruce in the back row, behind Richard Pasco (front centre).

After they'd left, the stage door keeper delivered to my dressing room a few good luck telegrams and postcards, wishing me well. One telegram was from the Oliviers, signed Joannie and LO. Ah, those great days when the Post Office delivered both domestic telegrams and international cablegrams, and if the message was urgent they telephoned the contents on ahead of the hard copy. It was thrilling to receive an affectionate, encouraging message from the Oliviers, but just before curtain-up Sir Laurence went one better.

Half an hour before the show was due to begin the ever-attentive stage door keeper carried a heavy surprise package to my room. As he later explained, he'd earlier in the day received a phone call from Olivier, who'd given him specific instructions about the exact time I should receive this gift. On no account should it be given me before the half-hour call. A note was attached, which when left alone again I opened.

"Yours is the first *Othello* to open in London since mine. From my experience in this difficult, yet rewarding, role, I know you'll need a good drink after the show …"

The box contained half a dozen bottles of fine champagne, the Maestro's favourite tipple. The acute timing of this delivery had the effect he'd intended. With three of the half dozen bottles safely chilling in the fridge, I walked onto the Mermaid stage bravely. After curtain-down, Elspeth and a few friends gathered in my room. We popped the corks and as they toasted me I asked them also to remember Larry. As I sipped, another champagne occasion sprang to mind …

The method guru, Lee Strasberg, had hit town. Founder of the famous Actors Studio in New York, Strasberg had brought a group of acolytes, his students past and present, to perform Chekhov's *Three Sisters* at the Aldwych. This was Strasberg's contribution to an annual event of the '60s, the World Theatre Season when Peter Daubeny invited productions from around the world to showcase their wares to a London audience. With plays often performed in languages other than English, it was a great idea. One week you might see a Noh or kabuki play from Japan, the next a Greek tragedy — or comedy — from Athens, etc. Now it was Strasberg's American turn, with his method-style interpretation of a Russian classic. His cast

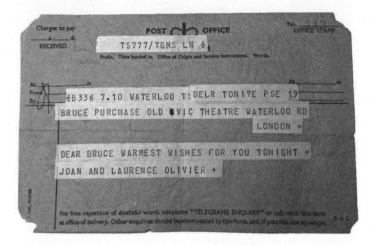

included that fine American film actor George C Scott in the pivotal role of Vershinin. The London critics slammed the production, savaging most of the performances that included his daughter Susan Strasberg. The Americans were devastated.

"Our American cousins need cheering," Sir Laurence announced. "We'll have a party for them on Saturday night after curtains down on our respective shows."

Olivier was host, this party paid for not by the taxpayer but by him — and when he threw a party the champagne was guaranteed never to run out. An excellent band was hired, good food ordered, and crates of champagne brought to the party space, the rehearsal room at the top of the theatre.

The Americans arrived. Still feeling the scars inflicted by the London critics, they looked forlorn as they trooped in. George C Scott, the collar of his overcoat (which he never took off) turned up as if to hide, looked embarrassed when introduced by Strasberg to Olivier. I think he departed early, but as our company with unbridled enthusiasm took to the dance floor, 'our American cousins' soon relaxed, joining in the festivities, knowing they were among friendly colleagues. The music, good food and champagne provided the rest of the cure; the evening was a big success, with friendships forged.

I overheard Strasberg, the event now in full swing, say to Olivier, without either a trace of irony or humour, "Larry, from what I see

26

here tonight, your actors don't appear to need psychotherapy."

Larry responded, nodding pleasantly, as with misted eyes and barely concealed pride he viewed his company dancing vibrantly before him — at play now, not at work.

But Larry (I never dared call him that) was not always as urbane, as laid-back. His very nervous showing as Father Christmas, thankfully not reviewed by the critics, was a case in point. This brave appearance remains unsung, except by the fortunate few, mostly children, who attended a one-off performance.

LO had been strong-armed, possibly by his wife Joan, into playing the white-bearded character at a party for the children of National Theatre staff, a few days before Christmas. The rehearsal room at the Vic had been cheerfully decked out with Christmas decorations and before Santa's arrival the children were buzzing with anticipation.

Joan Plowright whispered to me at the door, "He'll be up in a minute. He's climbing into his costume now." She chuckled and dashed away to help her husband. The children didn't hear this exchange. For them the casting of this role was irrelevant. They were excitedly awaiting Father Christmas himself! "When, oh when, will he arrive?" they chorused.

For the grown-ups present, myself included, there was an entirely different sense of expectancy. What would Sir's St Nicholas be like? Definitive, we hoped. The actor Robert Lang had arrived with his film camera, ready to capture on celluloid a historic event.

The great moment arrived. This emissary from Greenland came in through the door. Lights up! Action! Cue, sound! But it was not an authoritative entrance. Unstar-like, almost shambolic, Santa appeared before us. Head down, body stooped with the weight of presents on his shoulder, he stumbled into the room. The children were ecstatic. "He's here," they screamed. It was only the grown-ups who were instantly aware that Santa was stricken with nerves, his voice when he finally spoke tremulous. Also, and most disappointingly, we could not see his face because of his stooped posture.

But for the children 'suspension of disbelief', an essential ingredient in the attitude of audience to player, did not apply. Here was Father Christmas, and once they'd spotted the bag of presents they quickly crowded around the bringer. Bob Lang, film camera at the ready, was upstaged as the kids rushed in. He attempted, by spreadeagling himself on the floor, to achieve an under-and-up POV, but couldn't get close enough and failed in his objective.

To the best of my knowledge the following is the only 'review' of the performance:

SANTA CLAUS AT THE OLD VIC

Laurence Olivier's performance, which opened for only one single matinée, was Victorian in style, very Bransby Williams, for the reader old enough to recall that actor's Dickensian manner on black and white TV in the 1950s. Questions from Father Christmas to the children in attendance were startling.

"Have you washed behind your ears, my lad?" and "Let me see if you've scrubbed your nails, little lass." These unusual queries puzzled the kinder, but their excitement was such that they probably interpreted them as some curious form of archaic 'Greenlandspeak'. Santa Claus, head inclined with figure stooped, targeted his young audience perfectly. The others in the room, mere grown-ups, taking a secondary, collective role at this charming theatre of the absurd, stood at the back, grinning approval, as the miniatures in the audience joined Santa, centre stage.

No — not by Kenneth Tynan, NT's resident dramaturge, for he was not present. I remember the performance with pleasure, hence my review. Not in spite of LO's nerves but, affectionately, because of them. It was a moving appearance and a wonderful experience for the kids. Sir Laurence, probably forewarned by Joan that there was a movie camera on site, cleverly pulled his red hood low over his brow, so that only the children crowded at his feet got a clear unobstructed view of his face. We grown-ups never got a look in.

"Hard cheese," the Great Man may have uttered.

On occasion he assumed other, off-stage personas. This man of many colours, oft-times as unpredictable as the British weather he was born into, had contrasting moods, different combinations; like the climate, hard to outguess. His demeanour could change in a flash, from easy bonhomie to a temperature so cold one could believe it might even freeze vodka. His tunnel-visioned will drove him, so forcefully at times that he seemed even a stranger unto himself.

With Chekhov's *Uncle Vanya*, he directed and also played the part of the country doctor, Astrov. It was a superb production, with ensemble playing from a splendid cast that thrilled audiences. Michael Redgrave's Vanya was breathtaking, and together with Joan Plowright's Sonya, their final scene was heartbreaking. I've never seen another version since that got within a mile of being as good, and I have it on video in black and white to remind me of that excellence.

At the technical dress rehearsal a few days before Vanya opened to the public I spent some hours at the back of the stalls, adjacent to the sound and lighting box which is the epicentre, the technical command post for a show.

The 'tech', as it's known, is a slow, painstaking process which can take a day or two, sometimes longer, depending on the complexities of any given production. Lights need fixing, adjusting and focusing for each scene. Set positions are exactly placed, sometimes flown in and out from the fly tower above the stage. Costumes are worn for the first time, and any problems solved by the wardrobe department. Entrances and exits are precisely fixed. Sound cues are timed and appropriate acoustic levels balanced. All this and much more — myriad details addressed, allowing, in the end, a show that will run smoothly before the paying customers. If, heaven forfend, an audience witnessed a tech they'd find it as interesting as watching paint dry. But if you're in the 'biz' this approach to the minutiae of a production is fascinating, although exhausting for all involved.

On this particular day I was merely an interested observer, free to come and go as I wished. If it got boring I could up and off. LO was on stage in his Astrov costume, but in his dual role as director, timing a sound cue.

Nuala Delaney, a young red-haired ASM (assistant stage manager) was in the sound box off to my right. In those pre-digital days, Nuala was ready to switch on a tape at the precise moment required. Nuala, this her first job with the company, became a very capable assistant to her immediate superior, the redoubtable Diana Boddington, who as stage manager was in overall charge of the technical aspects and general running of the production. Diana was at Nuala's elbow, ready to cue her assistant when LO signalled from the stage. Once plotted exactly to the satisfaction of Olivier, a move would be incorporated into the running instructions for the show in performance.

Diana Boddington, doyenne of the stage managers within the

company, was much admired, one of the best in the business, a pro to her fingertips. She'd been professionally associated with LO for many years and he trusted her judgement and skills implicitly. Diana, on the other hand, knew her employer extremely well — all his many colours, shades, shadows, cross-currents, crossnesses, dark clouds, blue skies, calm waters and flash floods. Diana handled LO's complex nature with firm, yet affectionate, kid gloves. She could give as good as she got.

Olivier signalled, Diana cued her assistant, but Nuala mistimed it. LO called out calmly from the stage, "Let's try that again, please."

Nuala had a second stab at it but failed to hit the precise nail on the head.

"Again," said LO from the stage, but this time through gritted teeth, for he was feeling the strain of the long day's tech. Nuala, this her first show at the National, nerves no doubt surfacing, blew it, at this third attempt.

LO on-stage erupted like Mount Vesuvius. He danced in fury, voice booming, piling one colourful expletive upon another. I sat horrified, yet fascinated. What would happen next?

Diana, without a split second's hesitation, rocketed out of the sound box. She stood in the aisle next to me, hands on hips, glasses askew on her nose, her diminutive though ample frame rocking with an anger all her own. She shrieked out across the auditorium to the madman on the stage.

"You great big bully!" then repeated for good effect, "You great big bully! Just *who* do you think you *are*?" Diana would not tolerate anyone berating a member of her staff. No matter who!

How would the Great Man react, I thought. He fell silent, rocked backwards and forwards on his heels several times, then replied sheepishly, "Sorry, Diana. Sorry, Nuala my dear. Let's do it again and again and again until we get it right."

Diana's scorching admonition had done the trick. Tension diffused, Nuala, her protectorate guaranteed by the amazing Diana, quickly solved the problem and the rest of the day passed without further incident.

The National was well into its second year of operation, success following success, morale at a high. Yet out of this, suddenly a spot of bother. Two old companions had a falling out, and one was to leave the company prematurely.

The colleague was leaving under a cloud. Why, I did not know. It couldn't be because of a quarrel over 'billing'. Let me explain …

Max Adrian, a superbly gifted performer, equally at home in comedy, light revue, or dramatic roles, was a wickedly funny raconteur and wit. He had a deliciously sinuous way of delivering lines. Splendid as the professor in *Uncle Vanya*, very funny as Polonius in the long-winded *Hamlet*, and witty in *The Recruiting Officer*, his contribution in those early days was considerable. I particularly remember his laser-like Inquisitor in *Saint Joan*: a performance of great clarity, quiet and powerful, illuminating the Shavian lines effortlessly.

At the first assembly of National Theatre players in the Aquinas Street rehearsal rooms, Max announced to all and sundry, "I note, dear colleagues, with great satisfaction, that I'm top of the bill!"

Laurence Olivier, Max's old chum, and the rest of us laughed for we already knew that all players' names on playbills, posters etc. would by decree be listed alphabetically, regardless of title or place in the pecking order. There was to be no star-billing — no 'top of the bill'. But yes, Max's surname, Adrian, began with A so he was, at least alphabetically, top of the list. Olivier's name, alphabetically, along with the likes of Plowright, Purchase, Purnell, were middle of the list and Redgrave (Michael), Smith (Maggie) and Stephens (Robert), to name but a few of the original fifty players in the company, way down at the end, with Wynyard (Diana) as tail gunner. Another egalitarian concept born out of the provincial repertory system and adapted by companies like the Royal Shakespeare Company and still current with both the RSC and the National Theatre.

Max's comment we found amusing, for then the sky was bright blue and the sun shone down on the lot of us. Barely eighteen months later, however, there was definitely a hard frost on the ground, with Max Adrian — as far as his old mate Larry was concerned — beyond the pale, *persona non grata*.

Max announced a farewell party for his last night with the company. LO, it was assumed, would not attend.

"There'll only be champagne served," Max, in the canteen, shouted with zeal. LO's tipple!

The party, he said, would start before the show, carry on during and wind up after curtain-down on *The Recruiting Officer*. To have a party before and during a performance was an unprofessional notion, but by then Max didn't give a damn.

No takers either before or during the performance, of Farquhar's play, but that didn't deter Max. He became his own party, tippling on champers whenever off-stage, in between his scenes. LO, also performing as Captain Brazen, was furious.

In spite of these shenanigans, the evening's performance went without hitch, Max on alcohol-infused auto-pilot. By curtain-down he was visibly sozzled.

After the show, colleagues drifted in and out of Max's dressing room to say farewell, LO noticeable by his absence. I called to say goodbye to this naughty man whom I so admired for his many talents, his insouciance and sheer devilry.

When I arrived there was a brief lull in the party, for attendance in Max's dressing room by members of the cast was sporadic. Some members of staff had been conspicuously absent. Sensing a new and captive audience, Max handed me a flute of champagne and neatly danced me into a corner. He was ready for a chat — a chat, as it turned out, in monologue form.

"I've known Larry for tirty-five years," the monologue clicked into gear. "Oh, he wass a darlin', darlin' man and a darlin', darlin' friend to me." Here he took an enthusiastic gulp of champagne.

This Irish-born actor, of Jewish descent, once he had drink on board assumed what I imagined to be the accent of his parents, who'd hailed from Vienna. He pressed on with his tale, his champagne flute waving in the air as he illustrated each point.

"Yes, Bruce, I've known Larry, this darlin' man for tirty-five years. So long. So long." I was effectively trapped, my back to the wall, escape difficult, well nigh impossible in fact. "I do not work wizz him till I go to Chichester."

Olivier had gathered the nucleus of his company over a two-year period, with summer seasons at the new Chichester Festival Theatre, prior to the commencement of the National at the Old Vic. I'd joined at the very end of the second Chichester season with an appearance in *Saint Joan* at the Edinburgh Festival, *en route* for London.

Max's accent now took on an even more exaggerated, Viennese colour, very 'mittle' European. A sudden shout: "No! ... No! ... Wait a minute. I work wizz 'im on the film *Henry V* ... you see it? You remember ...?"

"Yes, Max ..." but I was swiftly cut off.

"... I play the Dauphin in that wonderful film. You remember?"

"Yes, Max, I ..."

"Then I go to Chichester. Such fun. Such fun." A flurry of his arms, champagne flying in the air.

"But Larry ... oh ee wass a darlin', darlin', man and a darlin', darlin' friend to me."

Here I try to take a sip from my glass but he grips my arm to prevent me, possibly thinking this a form of interruption to his flow.

"Unfortunately, Bruce, people 'ave told 'im ee is Great ... please, please, do not mistake me ... ee iss a very good actor. A very, very good actor. But, oh ee wass a darlin', darlin' man and a darlin', darlin' frenn to me!"

"Yes, of course, Max, Sir is ..."

Not a chance for me as Max presses on. "Unfortunately, ee believes this. Ee beliefs ee is Great. This is very sad. But, *oh*, ee wass a darlin', darlin' man and a darlin' darlin' frenn to me ... but now eez a *sheet!*" Other colleagues entered the room at this point and he whirled around, chuckling, to play mine host. I slipped away.

Whatever the quarrel between Max and LO, their friendship was soon re-established, but he was never to rejoin the company. With Max's untimely, early death, nine years later, LO mourned the loss of "this *diseur*", his "dear friend".

The National's reputation for excellence went from strength to strength, over the years, due largely to LO's ability to lead from the front, his choice of colleagues in all departments, and his contributions as both player and director. Among his early performances, my own favourites were his Captain in Strindberg's *The Dance of Death*; another captain, Brazen, in Farquhar's *The Recruiting Officer* (with Max); and his role as Tyrone in O'Neill's *Long Day's Journey Into Night*.

Although I didn't care for his *Othello*, I didn't much rate my own attempt six years later at the Mermaid Theatre either. Comparisons can be odious, and in my case perhaps impertinent! But today it would be unusual if a white actor were cast in the role of the Moor. A contradiction? Acting is surely acting? It is certainly barmy to contemplate a white man putting on black bowl as Othello, only to see it rub off on the pearly white skin of Desdemona as the Moor strangles her at the end of the play. When I played Othello, a black actor colleague, Rudolf Walker, sent a good luck card. It was a photograph of himself with PTO written across his face. I did so. On the reverse side of the photograph of Rudolf, he'd attached black Leichner grease paint, with careful direction as to how to apply it. Well said. Justifiable bitterness? Well perhaps … for he was clearly pointing out that *he* hadn't been given the part. He did later get his chance and gave a fine performance. The critic Kenneth Tynan had a great idea — a white Othello, with all other parts played by black actors. Patrick Stewart, of *Star Trek* fame, did this in the States, but it was Tynan's idea 34 years before Pat Stewart did his version.

I appeared briefly (blink and you miss me) in the film version of *Othello* with Olivier as the Moor and Frank Finlay as Iago, but I was not in the earlier stage production. I was, therefore, able to attend the press night when it opened at the Old Vic. This occasioned one moment of deep embarrassment for me. I was halfway down in the stalls seats, alongside me my agent's wife. Philip Pearman was my agent at the time. He was married to the most formidable actress I ever had the terrified privilege to meet. A fine player, also gifted with a lacerating wit. She was the unique, irreplaceable, Australian-born Coral Browne. If you were the butt of her wit, as I was upon occasion, Coral could terrify; but she was always funny, memorably so.

We were in the packed stalls, Coral next to me on my right, and Philip to her right. LO's performance was extraordinary, but let's not dwell on that, for much has been written by others.

As the interval lights came up at the end of the first half the audience erupted into vociferous applause, but I noted Coral did not clap, sitting stonily alongside me. As the applause faded, there was a lull, a quietening in the auditorium, before the audience began to buzz with chat and start to rise and go to the bar to busily discuss the show.

34

Into the brief void between fading of applause and start of excited chit-chat, Coral spoke, her voice projecting effortlessly across the stalls and probably as high as the dress circle. Her clarion call may have even reached to the gods of the upper circle and, courtesy of the amplification system, God help us, even into Olivier's very lair, his dressing room. Using her inimitable Australian drawl, Coral said piercingly,

"What the fuck does Larry think he's doing?"

"Hush, Coral," said Philip. Heads turned in our direction. As a member of the company, surrounded by colleagues in the stalls about us, I felt like melting into thin, thin air. I sank as deeply into my aisle seat as my tall frame allowed.

Shirley Bassey, Cardiff-born diva of West Indian descent, was heard in the interval commenting every bit as caustically as Coral on Olivier's ludicrous, Caribbean style performance.

"Darling, it's *me*, in *drag*!"

If Browne and Bassey had met that evening they would have been a fine double act. But I saw how hard it was for a white man to play the Moor: maybe I shouldn't have tried.

Others shared Max Adrian's opinion that Olivier was good, but not great. I once asked Cyril Cusack why he and LO were not on speaking terms even after Lindsay Anderson brought Cusack into the National for his production of Max Frisch's *Andorra*.

I came out with it boldly while sipping whiskey at the Irish Club.

"Why does Sir Laurence not speak to you, Cyril?"

"Ah, that's a very interesting story," in Cyril's soft velvet delivery, "a very interesting story indeed." His eyes twinkled briefly, as he took a slow sip from his glass.

"Many years ago I was appearing with Vivien Leigh in the West End. Such a lovely girl, really quite enchanting. Well, one evening I rather disgraced myself," Cyril purred, "and Sir Laurence, who as you know was married to the adorable Vivien, said I'd never again work in the West End!"

A casual puff on his cigarette, as he held the pause, then, "and I never have."

Cyril took another sip and looked thoughtful, before winding up.

"But Sir Laurence is a very good actor, isn't he? A very good actor," he added for good measure.

He then flickered a slight, almost bleak smile, before courteously enquiring if I'd join him in another drink.

"I'll get these," I said and headed for the bar, but Cyril appeared at my elbow. "They won't let you order, for you're my guest!" He grinned broadly.

Ten years after my conversation with Cyril at the Irish Club I was invited to a friend's 60th birthday party, at her son's house next door to us in the village where I lived, Ascott-Under-Wychwood.

Lindsay Anderson was also present, for our mutual friend, the birthday girl, had financed Lindsay's first film. A chance for me to dot the final i's and cross the last few t's to round off this saga, or so I thought.

Lindsay listened attentively as I recounted my conversation at the Irish Club, though his expression was unreadable. Anderson, son of a General, had a patrician air and was himself a shrewd tactician. He heard me out.

"What an interesting story," was Lindsay's bland acknowledgement. "Well, of course Cyril was right. Larry is a very good actor." His expression revealed nothing.

Olivier's command of many aspects of his craft was supreme and bred a unique loyalty among crew members in those early days, but it's a curious British tendency first to create heroes and then to destroy them. When, in his own turn, Olivier was forced to take wing and fly, the manner of his departure was handled clumsily by others. His departure was a classic breakdown in communication in a profession specializing in that art. It's what the job is all about — communication. Even in the early days, a couple of cannonballs were lobbed at the National. While in no way intended to kill our commander, the careful discriminations between 'good' and 'great' were definitely supposed to dent his healthy ego.

I was no longer the callow skinny colonial boy from the early 1960s when I had a final meeting with LO six years before the 80th birthday celebration. It took place in a theatre foyer, twenty years after I'd first worked with the GM and thirty-five years after I'd first clapped eyes on him outside that theatre in New Zealand.

Baron Olivier approached across the foyer, the crowd recognising the old chap and parting in deference to him and his equally distinguished companion, the ageing film star Douglas Fairbanks Jnr. These two charismatic stars of yesteryear, walking arm in arm, were deep in conversation. Both were elegantly attired, for it was a full dress occasion. One of them was wearing a handsome, beautifully tailored dark cape, its red silk lining flashing intermittently like neon, as the two troubadours from way back sauntered as if in slow motion towards this portly, middle-aged New Zealand born actor ... me.

As they drew ever closer, recollections raced through my mind ... how after completing my original audition before Olivier in 1963, when interviewed by the Great Man, I was so nervous, my knees so wobbly, I'd sat on the floor at Sir Laurence's feet. That created a precedent, I guess, my mind flashed at me ...

... How I'd seen Olivier changing from costume to street clothes in a corridor backstage and exiting by a fire door, in a state of panic — all this because with his ex-wife in the audience he'd muffed his words and couldn't face Vivien Leigh after the show. The fire door slammed after him. Seconds later Ms Leigh appeared and said to his dresser, "Where's Larry?" ...

... How Bernard Miles had described the young Olivier on the first rung of the ladder he climbed to such giddy heights: "He was an actor who combined all the vitality and virility of the old, with the sense and subtlety of the new, in a fresh and vigorous blending ..."

... How the GM stood with a pint of bitter in his hand, ending a year of self-imposed abstinence. This in the pub that stood then next door to the old Waterloo Road stage door. How he'd said to me and the actor John Stride that he was so stressed in his job he wondered if it was all worth it. "I'm away from home so much that when I return, my children barely recognise me ..."

... How Olivier had called our colleague Jimmy Mellor to his dressing room and urged him not to drink so much. "Look what liquor has done to me, James." I remembered how my old mate Jimmy laughed as he recounted the details of their meeting (Olivier and Fairbanks now almost level). Yet, I recalled, Jimmy was dead a few years later, still a youngish man of middle years, his liver wrecked by booze ...

The two venerable old gents now level. I noted LO was a shadow of his former self. Would the old boy recognise me?

"Excuse me, Sir?"

The elderly thespians, chuckling over some shared memory, stopped and turned towards me. Fairbanks' face open and instantly friendly, so typically American. Olivier's expression by contrast was cross. Why had he been interrupted in mid-flow, his demeanour indicated.

"It's Bruce, Sir," heart sinking under the Baron's basilisk stare. "Bruce Purchase, Sir," I added lamely.

The GM looked blankly up at this tall bearded stranger, before replying politely, albeit warily, "My dear fellow! How are you?"

It was clear he didn't know who the hell I was. Demoralised, disappointed, I quickly exchanged mere generalities. "What a good show it was," etc, before excusing myself to beat a hasty retreat.

Once decided on departure, like many a tall and heavy man I moved lightly away, fleet of foot. With relaxed feet, I hoped, smiling grimly, blush in evidence as of old. But I'd only taken a few swift steps when I heard Olivier call out to me. I whirled around to face the Great Man again. Ten feet now separated us. What's the old devil up to now? I thought, but answered aloud, "Sir?"

LO looked like his younger self again. "Brucie?"

"Yes, Sir?"

"You've grown a beard."

"Yes, Sir."

"I barely recognised you."

"It's good to see you, Sir."

"The beard — it suits your present role."

"Yes, Sir."

"Most becoming."

"Thank you, Sir."

One last question from the Great Man, delivered in the sweetest voice imaginable:

"How's your mother?"

Figures in the crowded foyer now moved through the space between us.

"Do give her my …" but more of the chattering classes came between LO and me, obliterating the last of the Great Man's words.

A second before Lord Olivier and Fairbanks were swallowed up in the crowd, I caught the old man's expression. A broad and wicked grin lit up my old employer's face.

II

On the Coromandel

O UR ORIGINS, IF TOLD US, may often surprise ...
There was an urgency in my mother's voice. Putting aside
my task, I quickly joined her at the front of the shop as she gazed
out into the bright early morning light. It was summer, 1957, in
Auckland.

"See that man in the middle of the road?" I saw only the back
of a tall, thin man, waiting for the traffic to clear. The stranger was
dressed like some Auckland businessmen of that post-colonial period
in a striped short-sleeved shirt with tie, drill shorts and long beige
knee socks with smart brown leather shoes.

"Yes, Mum — but who is he?" Her voice when she answered
seemed unusually soft, barely above a whisper:

"He's the man I came to New Zealand to marry."

My eighteen-year-old self was startled and in the pause that
followed I stared sharply as my mother looked out through the large
window towards the man in the street. When I glanced back to the
busy suburban scene the stranger had disappeared. Still in shock
from my mother's revelation, I asked: "What do you mean?"

Breaking from her unexpected reverie, Marjorie Purchase turned
to face me.

"I met him in North Wales in the mid-1930s. He was a New
Zealand engineer working for a year in Colwyn Bay. We became
engaged, planning to marry in Auckland a year later. He returned
to New Zealand and for the year that followed we wrote ... endless
loving letters. I sold my business and eleven months after his
departure I too came here by ship ...

"Via Suez and Colombo, in Ceylon?" I'd always known that part
of Mum's history ...

"Yes … the ship berthed in Auckland after a six-week voyage and I was thrilled to have arrived. I looked from the railings at the large crowd on the wharf below. My fiancé stood with his family smiling up at me. But I knew in that instant that I would not be marrying him."

"How?"

But she pressed on with her tale, for my mother definitely had an instinctive — some would say psychic — side to her.

"As we were due to marry a week after my arrival I had to tell him that day, hours after my arrival. We broke off the engagement and because I'd only money for the one-way journey I applied for several jobs and was offered one as manager of Adams Bruce [a café famed for the quality of its chocolates and ice cream sundaes] where I worked for a year before being transferred to Rotorua."

There a year later she met a young man in his mid-twenties … Grenville William Richard Hinton Purchase, a technician working for the Post Office. They became engaged and married a year later. Purchase was known as Bill. He was a tall handsome man with a strong build and a beguiling gaze from the brightest of blue eyes. Marjorie, fairly tall, with a good figure, a fine face and dazzling smile, was blessed also with a serene nature and a formidable will. Photographs show them as a glamorous couple. Shortly after their marriage Bill was sent to a new job in Thames, a town on the Coromandel Peninsula, east of Auckland. Within a year their first of two sons was born, and duly named William Reginald Bruce.

Eighteen years after my birth in Thames on the Coromandel Peninsula, standing in my mother's shop in Auckland as she recounted her tale, I responded:

"So I'm just an accident of fate, eh Mum?"

In the role of a baby, in Thames, NZ.

She didn't reply but looked gently up at her tall son.

At this moment the door of the Greenlane Paint & Hardware opened to admit her first customer of the day and she adopted her finely honed shopkeeper persona. I quickly asked her:

"What is his name?"

"His name was Jack."

I crossed the shop floor to continue my earlier task. Behind him I heard my mother's voice:

"Good morning, Mr Wyllie. How can I help you?" Her voice sounded calm That's fine, I thought, Mum's good as gold again.

Talking of gold, Thames had a population of only a few thousand during the time I grew up there in the 1940s, but seventy years earlier the population had been five times larger. The reason for this was the discovery of gold.

At the Shotover Claim on 10 August 1865, gold-mining began in New Zealand. Other excavations rapidly followed and thus began the Thames gold rush. The opening up of the land where gold-mining took place was made possible by persuasion of the iwi (local tribes) by a Ngati Paoa chief, Haora Tipa, a wise mediator who was influential in the Hauraki Gulf area. We know what he looked like (a handsome man, his entire face decorated with deep double-cut tattooing), for he was painted by the German-born artist, Lindauer.

The two original settlements at either end of the two-mile long, half-mile deep plain, finally melded into the one town named Thames. Gold drew thousands to the area, all needing roofs over their heads. A member of the British Royal family, the Duke of Edinburgh, visited briefly in 1870. He bought shares in the very successful Long Drive mine. Yes, even the UK Royals cashed in!

Dozens of hotels were rapidly constructed to cater for Thames's sudden growth. At one time there were over a hundred, all doing a roaring trade. Hotels with names such as Munster, Digger's Rest, Ancient Briton, Rob Roy, Karaka, Crown and Provincial, Nil Desperandum, Brian Boru, Brian Borihme, Shellback etc.

After a hard day's work in the long dusty drives and shafts of a mine the workers were desperate to slake their thirst. The many hotels provided that necessary service with ales produced by two breweries that sprang up … Ehrenfried's XXX from the Phoenix Brewery at the northern, Grahamstown end of the plain and Lampieres to the south in the original settlement known as Shortland.

At the end of a day the miners came, post haste, from the diggings: the Moanataiari Claim, Golden Crown & Cure, the Waiotahi, Nonparells, Black Angel, Alburnias and many more. The Caledonian Mine was the most productive.

History would have us believe that Thames was never a lawless place like the Hollywood-depicted American Wild West. Oh no, the Thames men were not gun totin' blokes. Rather we're told they were peaceable 'gennellmen,' who could 'hold their likker'.

Court records sometimes tell a different story, but on the whole the two settlements grown to one town and linked by a two-mile long main thoroughfare named Pollen Street was a law-abiding community of, at the height of the Boom, over 15,000 souls. In 1871 alone, gold to the value of £1,188,708 was produced.

In 1876 the owner of the Commercial Hotel advertised thus: "Albert Butler begs to intimate that he has entered into possession of the above old-established house." He also adds, referring to his restaurant:

> … it has where he hopes, by keeping only the best brands of ales, wines and spirits, to receive a fair share of patronage now been re-opened under the supervision of Mr Pollock whose reputation as a chef-de-cuisine needs no puff.

In 1882, another hotelier, Tom Herron, says that in his 'Commercial Rooms:'

> …there will be supplied Home and Colonial Papers and Sporting Telegrams will be posted in the Club Room," and goes on to say: "… my experience as a gold assayer of long standing will be at the disposal of my customers," finally assuring his clientele: "Pure Whisky … No headaches.

But by the turn of the century, the boom was tailing off. Hotels began closing and many buildings became shabby as the population diminished.

However over a period of 85 years the Thames mines produced £28,000,000, only closing down in the 1950s. 'Tis said, there's still gold in them thar hills.

Fine architecture from that period remains. The verandahed shop fronts in the long main thoroughfare and other equally excellent examples of colonial 19th-century architecture (e.g. '1868. W Culpitt, Sadler') still exist throughout the town. A tangible reminder of the glorious days of the Thames gold rush.

At the height of the gold boom in 1874 the Thames Temperance Society had tried without success to close over thirty hotels, but in my childhood the Licensing Commission cancelled the licences of six of the remaining ten. Today, of the four that remain, my favourite is the Brian Boru which was owned in the halcyon days of the gold rush and for ninety years by one family, the Twohills.

A Thames pub crawl on 13 March 1951 was a sight to behold, when most of the adult male population took part. I saw my father wheeling a barrow down Pollen Street. In it was a man who looked fast asleep … One pillar of local society pushing a wheelbarrow carrying another pillar, seemingly toppled. Was it a Mr Brokenshire, a Mr Arbury, or maybe a Mr Danby, grocer Coakley, even garage-owner Donkin asleep after a hard day selling new Austin motor cars. Supine in the barrow like a beached whale, who was that other grown-up? … Could it perhaps have been Mr Jacomb the optician; or Mr Bongard the chemist? On second thoughts, maybe it was a Mr Zedin who sold bikes, or Mr Batson where I bought my first bedside radio (a Philco in the Art Deco style), or even Tony Voykovich, the greengrocer. Perhaps either Bateman the butcher or maybe even the long-serving mayor of Thames, Syd Ensor?

Who was it?

Could it have been Robert Twentyman, builder, contractor and funeral furnisher? Mr Causley who sold dahlias and tomato plants? Definitely not Mr CY Lee. No, not him. For on my regular visits to 'the pictures,' it was at greengrocer Lee's that I always bought a choc-ice before entering the King's Theatre. Thrills! Adventures! Indians! Dana Andrews in Kit Carson, Tim Holt in *The Arizona Ranger* … or Tigers! Leopards! Panthers! Crocodiles! with Sabu in *Song of India*. In those politically innocent years of the 1940s and '50s the choc-ice I'd always buy on my way to the flicks was called an Eskimo Pie. No, I'd definitely have remembered if it'd been Mr Lee, because the sleeping man trundled along Pollen Street by my Dad was definitely of European extraction and kindly Mr Lee was Chinese.

Whoever he was, he looked peaceful as he quietly snoozed. And crowding the street other townsfolk walked from closing pub to closing pub, all six.

An emotional farewell ... at least for the men of our town.

"Everything's tickety-boo, son." Dad grinned at me as he weaved past me, erratically.

Thames in the 1950s was not a one-horse town and certainly not a one-pubber.

At the start of the Second World War my father joined the Auckland East Coast Mounted Rifles (a cavalry regiment) and later went to the war with the 2nd New Zealand Divisional Cavalry, serving not on horseback, but as a tank commander. He was away for many years. I was eight and my kid brother Grenville six when he returned. Our mother had been a solo mum to two young sons and single-handedly run a busy general store. Gren and I were both grocers' sons, for shortly after I was born my parents had purchased an old wooden general store at Parawai, to the south-east of the town. It'd been there since the 1860s and the sale included the land the shop stood upon, a good-sized section. They bought the land from the Ngati Maru tribe. Our new property had originally abutted a marae (a place of meeting), used by the local tribe. Until the late 1920s a fine old carved meeting house named Hotunui had stood there.

By the early 1920s Hotunui had fallen into disrepair, but with intercession between Ngati Maru leader, Eruini Heina Taipari and the Native Land Court, the house was restored to its former glory. It now stands in the central court of Auckland's War Memorial Museum, where it was unveiled in 1929.

Eruini Taipari I remember as a popular and respected figure in the Thames area. His grandfather, chief of Ngati Maru, had remained neutral during the Maori/Pakeha wars in the 1860s, thus avoiding having their property confiscated. By leasing, not selling, land they made a tidy fortune, especially up the Kauaeranga Valley during the gold rush and logging days. When I knew Taipari he was still farming his land and successfully racing thoroughbreds.

Our land deed has many signatures of the elders of the hapu

(sub-tribe). Because our folk had bought the property directly from Ngati Maru, my brother Grenville and I were always welcome on their land behind our place, where their ceremonies still took place — tangi (funerals) and more festive occasions. We grew up feeling very connected to the Maori community. We'd often attend their hangi feasts, where the food was wrapped in flax and sack-cloth and placed in a hole on a bed of river stones (white-hot because a fire had been lit over the rocks beforehand). The wrapped food was then covered over by the earth previously dug, and left to cook in the earth for several hours before being unearthed, unwrapped, and consumed with gusto. In a Maori oven there may be whole lambs, baby suckling pigs; wild boar and vegetables (including the uniquely flavoured sweet potato, kumara, now available at Sainsburys in the UK). All of this was a feast fit for a king, certainly for a chief and his tribe.

On their land I broke my arm when I was ten, swinging, as Tarzan, from branch to branch of a big old rimu tree. I miscalculated one mighty leap, missed my grip, fell to the ground. I ran home … yowling. Around this time, with my arm in a sling, I was deputed every morning to carry a steaming bowl of hot porridge with brown sugar and fresh cream on top, across the road to a wooden house that stood on that Maori land. Old Nuka Merriman, who had only one arm, would receive one-handedly, with a solemn nod to me, the porridge from my one-armed self! He'd then re-enter his abode and disappear down a short dark passageway. Made by my mother, this morning delivery was for Nuka's bedridden wife.

Life cannot have been easy for our mother during the war when Dad was away. As the elder son, I was encouraged to be the man of the house. This role I took seriously but was glad to relinquish when Dad returned. During his absence Mum and her two young fellahs lived in small but comfortable quarters directly behind the shop. The living room led directly into the old, Colonial-style, general store, with its large folding out wooden bins of loose sugar, flour (whole-meal and plain) and salt. The interior of Parawai Store should have been preserved, like Hotunui, in a museum for posterity.

In those days Kiwi kids walked barefoot and the soles of our feet were like leather. Only if we travelled out of town did we put on shoes and socks. Oh, and if we had photos taken, intended for Mother's mother, our Welsh 'Nain'. If Nain had seen her grandsons barefoot she'd have assumed we were below the poverty line. But in the New Zealand of the 1940s, going barefoot, even to school, was considered normal. It did make for the occasional accident ... running through long grass, a dangerous gash caused by stumbling over a collapsed barbed-wire fence or, stepping on an unseen rusting nail, necessitating a rapid journey for yet another tetanus injection— the threat of lock-jaw averted once again.

Our mother was a good solo parent and although she was always busy we never felt neglected. We were always encouraged to be self-reliant. Grenville and I made much of our own entertainment. When I got a bit older I built hutches on our large property for my white Angora rabbits, and cages for pet canaries and budgies. All for sale. I had a sales empire and was a keen gardener too; new potatoes and radishes were among my special crops.

There were also jobs to be done helping our mother. From an early age I did the bread round after school, mounted on a big old bike, with a small front wheel ... its huge basket filled with fresh loaves in brown paper bags. Gren and I also helped in the shop itself, serving behind the counter or humping heavy sacks of flour, sugar and salt.

When I was eleven I was sent by bus one day to Auckland to order goods for our store. In my first pair of long trousers (yes, and wearing shoes and socks for this special outing) I visited warehouses in the big city ... Nathans and Gordon & Gotch were two on my list. I felt very grown-up. I'm sure my parents had forewarned them of my impending visit, as normally these orders would have been phoned through. Gren and I also aided post-war food-rationing in the UK. We achieved this by melting lard or dripping in large tins then waited for it to cool. Before it was completely set we then submerged fresh eggs into the soft goo. The lids were finally firmly pressed on and the tins ready to be sent 12,000 miles by ship to the UK, to assist the poor old Poms with their cooking. The fat they nestled in protected the eggs against breakage *en route*.

Because of the stringent rationing of food in 'the old country,' in New Zealand, meat and butter coupons were saved for later dispersal as 'product,' to post-war UK. I note that on my eighth birthday in 1946, the saving of butter coupons in the Thames area alone, provided 67 lbs weight of butter to be sent to feed the food-deprived folk in Britain.

Our Nain included too of course!

I further note that on that day the local weather was unfavourable and high tide in the Firth of Thames was at 12.24pm. At the flicks Charles Starrett was starring in *Trail to Laredo* and in the local paper there was an announcement on behalf of the Thames Chess Club: *An innovation. Coffee will now be served at half-time. Mr Basil Ludwig serves café noir, café au lait or café any old way"* ... Eat your heart out Starbucks.

During the war years, Grenville and I were mainly in the company of women and old men, for most of the younger ones, if fit, were away serving in the forces. One old cove who was very supportive of our family, in those days without Dad, was the local Catholic priest, Father Lyons. Much to the delight of my kid brother and me, he kept a talking parrot on his verandah. When I was very young I thought this priest's name was 'Father Lions,' for his charismatic nature seemed lion-like to me.

Our paternal grandparents would sometimes visit us and in the summer holidays we boys would travel by bus and train to holiday with them at their place in the far north. Those weeks of glorious sun-drenched days were bliss.

One other main school holiday destination was by train from Auckland. We'd leave early evening heading southbound, in the direction of the capital, Wellington. The powerful Limited Express was pulled by a big steam-driven locomotive called a KA. These were exciting journeys. When the train pulled into Taumarunui in the central high country of the North Island, far from the sea, after midnight our Uncle Tom would be there to meet us. He'd drive Gren and me in one of his big American cars, or his old truck, at high speed along the narrow, winding gravelled road, up over the Big Hill, usually killing either a possum, rabbit or hare as we sped through the night. The vehicle's sweeping lights illuminated the vegetation on both sides of the road as we careered around the corners. We prayed no car or, perish the thought, massive tusked wild boar would

Great-grandparents from Berlin:
Wilhelmina and Emil Zander.

approach from the opposite direction. But, intelligent animals that they are, they heard us coming and were always back in the safety of the thick native bush by the time we hurtled by.

Half a century later, in a hotel bar in the tiny town of Owhango ('Or-fung-or') some twenty-five miles from our uncle's farm, a Maori guy wearing a beautiful carved greenstone pendant around his neck approached me and asked: Where you from in England?" By then I'd lived some forty years in Britain and as an actor, do sound a bit like a Brit.

I replied: "I was born here in New Zealand. I'm a Kiwi."

"No you're not."

"Yes I am."

But he was adamant that he knew I was a Pom. So I added:

"As a kid I spent my holidays on an uncle's farm at Otunui."

"What uncle?" still disbelieving.

"Tom Runciman."

Startled, but delighted, he proceeded to tell me a story that in turn delighted me.

"We used to call your uncle Tom Big Car, 'cos he always drove those big American cars. Do you remember his monster Chevy, the two-tone red and white?"

I did indeed remember that big flash Bel Air and told him so.

"Well, years later, long after Tom was dead and the car had been sold to another guy, it was converted [stolen] and after that was used in a bank heist by the Mongrel Mob."

This a reference to Maori fellahs who sometimes get up to no good. I was amused by this yarn, though I suspect our Uncle Tom would *not* have been amused.

Besides being a successful sheep farmer in the King Country he was also a much respected Justice of the Peace.

In Thames on VJ day I was allowed to take my turn with the celebratory ringing of the town's fire bell in Pollen Street as the populace gathered to celebrate the end of the war with Japan. I also remember as a lad, the sighting during that war of a low-flying Japanese plane over our town. It flew in regularly to photograph two factories (Chas Judd and AG Price), prior to a planned attack by Japanese forces. That attack never happened, but in those dangerous years that plane, with its pilot clearly visible, swept in regularly, low over the town. Its approach was from the east and came I guess from a Japanese aircraft carrier far out in the Pacific. But there were no big guns in Thames to have a go at bringing the plane down and it never shot at us.

Fifty years later, however, the Japanese had won a war — an economic one. Japanese cars were being put together in a factory in Thames and the country's roads were crowded with second-hand Japanese vehicles.

Dad returned from his European war in 1946 and Grenville and I travelled with Mum by train from Thames to Hamilton to meet him. This stranger, after his long absence, appeared to his sons a dashing figure, dressed as he was that happy day in his smart army officer's uniform. On the train back to Thames Gren and I sat opposite our parents, staring with incomprehension at our beloved Dad. There was a lot to be taken in. He held hands with our mother as she smiled happily at him and then across to us, sharing these precious moments with his two sons ... I was eight and Gren six. Not yet demobbed from the army, our Dad spent only a week with us before returning to Papakura Army Camp, near Auckland. But by then we knew we'd see our hero again soon.

His next return to us was thrilling for he came accompanied by a few of 'his men'. They arrived outside the Parawai Store in a big army tank ... Huge caterpillar tracks and, protruding in front, its long dangerous-looking gun-barrel. Parked behind Dad's tank were two motorised Bren-gun carriers with smaller but nonetheless impressive weaponry. Our mates joined Gren and me as we stood in awe. I was so bloomin' proud I was fit to burst.

Dad encouraged our school friends up onto the tank, tactfully suggesting to his sons that we ride in one of the Bren-gun carriers. This disappointed us but in thinking about it now, Dad was right. He didn't want his sons to 'get above themselves'. Once aboard, our convoy headed off, with the tank in lead position. From neighbouring houses, grown-ups and other children came out to wave and cheer us on our triumphant journey … around the block!

… … … … … … … … … … … …

PARAWAI STORE
Greetings for 1947
To all our customers, both Mrs Purchase and myself extend our sincere good wishes for Christmas and the New Year. Rationing has never extended to the goodwill and friendship existing between our customers.
Call and see us or ring 288.

… … … … … … … … … … … …

We sold just about everything in that shop of ours: all fruit, including ripe bananas from Fiji; fresh wholemeal and plain breads; Zambuk, "for tired feet"; Hellaby's prime meats; Dr Morse's Indian Root Pills, "for great relief from constipation"; Kremelta, "for all cooking purposes"; Sunlight Soap and, coarse to the skin, Sand-Soap too; Kruschen Salts for "keeping you on your toes"; Amber Tips tea and Choysa too; comics, newspapers and magazines, which included the *Woman's Weekly* and *Best Bets* for the horse races; large slabs of dark cooking chocolate; pins and needles; Wrigley's PK chewing gum; Chesdale cheese; salt, sugar, spices, eggs, flour; Bycroft biscuits (with the image of a little boy running with a biscuit and, inside that image, the same boy running with a biscuit and inside that, etc, ad infinitum). You name it … that which was needed by the locals and Parawai general store certainly sold it.

Mention of the Bycroft biscuit tin with the image of the boy running, rings a definite bell in my memory. Betting on horse races was a strictly government-controlled thing. You were only able to lay bets on-course or off-course with the TAB … the Totalisator Agency Board. But our Mum, respectable Thames businesswoman that she was, had a profitable though illegal sideline — as an off-

"On the train back to Thames Gren and I sat opposite our parents, staring with incomprehension at our beloved Dad."

course bookmaker. On a Saturday I was deputed to guard a big Bycroft biscuit tin which, empty of biscuits, became full of betting slips. The phone would ring and a bet would be placed. The slip was then put by Mum in the biscuit tin. I was instructed to do a runner, up 'Jacob's ladder' (steps that led to the bush behind our property) if there was ever a police raid. As everyone in the town, the police included, used Mum's services, this possible raid by the authorities was not very likely. But our good mother took no chances.

"It might be a raid by the police from Auckland."

Mind you, I would have risen to the challenge ... me as a boy running with a biscuit tin, helter-skelter in the direction of the bush, pursued as I imagined, by a crowd of Keystone-like cops ... straight out of a film. What fun that would've been!

Darn it, the raid never came.

At our store, apart from our day-to-day customers, deer and pig hunting blokes would arrive on horseback, accompanied by their dogs. They stopped to fill their saddle-packs with provisions before riding to the bush for their hunting sprees. Our cat Patch knew the exact boundary of our unfenced land and woe betide any dog or un-tethered horse which wandered from the road, for Patch would protect our property with ferocity, biting into the lower lip of a dog and not letting go until the offending animal had ceased its trespass. On one occasion, it taunted an errant horse by leaping to its mane and holding on with one paw whilst scratching its neck with the other. We didn't want to lose trade, so dear multi-coloured Patch was sent to live with friends twenty miles away.

Three days later as we were having lunch, in through our back door entered a familiar-looking cat. Yes, it was our Patch. In spite of his natural fierceness towards animal trespassers he'd got the message and from then on attacks against the hunters' horses and dogs ceased, so we never gave Patch away again.

Dad was now out of the army and truly back with us. He'd served with distinction during the war. It was said that on one occasion, had another officer been present to witness our father's brave action, he'd have almost certainly been awarded the Victoria Cross. As it was, Dad being the only officer present, he won a Military Cross (MC). Damn fine thing anyway.

… … … … … … … … … … … …

Hamilton City Council
To have the honour of meeting Their Excellencies
the Governor-General Sir Bernard and Lady Freyberg,
the Mayor of Hamilton, Mr Harold D Caro,
requests the pleasure of the company of
Mr and Mrs W Purchase …
on the evening of Monday, 31 May 1948

… … … … … … … … … … … …

Dad was awarded his MC that night and we were there to witness the event. General Freyberg had been Dad's commanding officer during the Second World War.

A proud moment.

My father died aged 58. His early death was caused primarily I believe by his war wounds. At the funeral I was approached by a woman who had nursed him through two serious woundings.

"On both occasions we never thought your father would last the night but he pulled through, twice," she said. "Bill had a strong character. We were so proud to have known him."

A fellow soldier on that same day said: "Bruce, your father was literally shot to billy-oh!"

When his cortège set off from the church on his last journey there, standing to attention on either side of the road, were dozens of his former comrades-in-arms.

"Tall and straight both in stature and character ..."

"A good listener with deep and penetrating eyes that rarely left the speaker's face ..."

"Unhurried and ... deliberate in both movement and decision, a trait of character which stood him and others in good stead when under enemy pressure."

These were just a few comments I registered through my grief on that painful day in 1968.

After his miraculous return to us after the end of the war we'd begun the process of melding together again as a family. At times this was not easy. Once I heard Mother say to him when she thought I was safely tucked up in bed asleep:

"Don't treat Bruce and Gren like soldiers, Bill. They're only little boys."

The soldier in him took time to ease back into civilian life, for he'd spent too many years in the company of men, and with them witnessed much brutality and pain. But ease back he did, for he was a wise and kind man. Many who knew him remarked on the steady gentle gaze from his clear blue eyes. He helped me improve my swimming style by building on what my grandfather had taught me. Dad was a fine swimmer and he coached me in the Australian crawl, the freestroke style that keeps you fast and low in the water. By age eleven I was competing well at junior championship level.

He set about building us a new home to replace our dilapidated old quarters behind the store. Still a splendid house, it afforded us more space and even had underfloor heating, relatively unheard of in the late 1940s. The system was called pyrotenax ... copper piping with heating wires inside which were disconnected in the summer. One aspect I did miss, however, when we moved into our new home is one of the strong memories of my childhood — tucked up in bed on stormy nights, the sound of thundering rain on the corrugated-iron roof above. This was the safest sound in the world. In our new place with its tiled roof, the rain fell almost silently. Dad demolished our old home along with the old general store and in its place constructed a new building which housed both a dairy and a new grocery shop.

The days of a general store were over.

The memory of war was fast fading, as were recollections of the days when Thames was rich because of the gold discovered deep in the quartz. It was said that some of the gold seams contained more gold than quartz in each recovered block brought to the surface. The Thames gold rush made many rich but left many as poor as when they'd started. As a boy I knew a number of old miners and other old blokes who remembered the gold days. Two spring to mind: Joe Bolland and Mr Onions.

Both were small men (it was easier to crawl along those dusty drives and lower yourself down precipitous shafts if small) who lived in tiny shacks. Mr Onions, a customer on my bread round, lived in a two-room shed built entirely of corrugated iron nailed to a wooden frame. It had no insulation … hot as hell in summer and even in the relatively mild winter in Thames, cold inside in spite of a wood-burning stove going full pelt. I always coincided my drop-off of his daily wholemeal loaf to time with Mr Onions having his 'tea', his early evening meal. He would always eat before nightfall to conserve the kerosene in his lamp, for he had no electricity in his shack.

Mind you, in the 1940s even my rich farming uncle, Tom, didn't have electricity on his large farm at Otunui. That, as with modern mechanisation, like tractors, bulldozers and haymaking machines spewing out bales of hay 'from their innards' came much later. Uncle Tom and my Aunt Nell and family lived in 'the backblocks' far from the nearest electricity supplied town.

It was a joy to watch Mr Onions eating. His dinner always consisted of two lamb chops with boiled potato, peas and the newly delivered loaf. This food was accompanied by a big tin mug of tea. He was a tiny, portly chap with neatly brushed thinning white hair and a moustache that overhung his small mouth. Before eating he diced his food into precise cubes and removed the crusts from his buttered bread, cutting slices into tiny squares. Having completed this everyday task he commenced eating.

He was then away like a jack-rabbit, flicking the tiny cubes through the air with a fork. I was mesmerized by this eating technique. The hurtling pieces of meat, potato, bread and peas, miraculously entered his mouth which was almost hidden by his white moustache. It was amazing. All the while, with mouth full, he chattered away to me with an occasional break as he lifted his mug of tea to his mouth and took a gulp which washed the food down his gullet.

Many years later, as an actor in Britain, I was playing an eccentric character who had an eating scene on stage. I remembered Mr Onions' unique eating method and attempted to emulate it. I practised for hours at home, making a frightful mess, but never succeeded in getting the Onions style off pat.

Old man Onions talked and talked of the good old days of the Thames mines, and spouted old poems too …

There's a Manukau butcher, you all know his name …
    [Scraps of food thrown to his mouth]
He throws down his cleaver and shuts up the shop,
And would laugh at you now if you asked for a chop.
There's a baker as well, who no longer kneads bread,
He doesn't sell French sticks, but gold bricks instead
    [More scraps of food to the mouth].
And a young farmer too, who his time now devotes,
Not in reaping the crops, but in sowing wild oats! …
    [a gulp of tea from his old chipped mug]

"By crikey, that farmer must've been a jolly old scoundrel," Mr Onions would chortle, rocking back in his chair, his eyes to the heavens.

The other old chap from my childhood, Joe Bolland, was entirely different. Small, thin and wiry with a deep-lined face, he was also very stooped. A quieter man than Onions and a gentler soul by far, he was employed by Dad to do simple tasks about our property. I now see Joe as rather like the ancient character Firs in Chekhov's *The Cherry Orchard*. He had a face like the American actor, Joe E Brown … Remember him in Billy Wilder's classic film, *Some Like it*

Hot? He has the final line in the film when Jack Lemmon, dressed as a woman, confesses he's actually a man. Brown, from his position behind the wheel of the speedboat, replies with that memorable line: "Well, nobody's perfect." That's the face Joe Bolland had. A classic Irish face.

Joe had been a gumdigger in his youth, hard yakka digging the resin deposits left by kauri trees, which bled off the amber gum into the earth.

Felling of the huge kauri in the Thames area began at the end of the 19th century at the mouth of the Waihou River. Kauri resin was used in the manufacture of polish and to fashion decorative objects. At the wonderful kauri museum at Matakohe in Northland there's a large collection of *objets* made from kauri gum.

The room glows with the stuff.

In 1950, fifty years after Bolland had last been in Auckland, Dad drove him there to see the modern city. This proved a revelation. Where the big Civic cinema now stood in Auckland's main thorough-fare, Queen Street, had in his youth been a cattle-market. Dad shouted him lunch at Auckland's Northern Club. To cool his tea in the dining room of that establishment Joe poured some of the liquid into his saucer, raised it to his lips and gently blew upon it. "There's milk if you need it, Joe," Dad suggested, but Joe continued pouring tea from his cup to his saucer unabashed, and slurping noisily. If this embarrassed the other diners it didn't my father, who later fondly described this scene to us. Dad pointed out that Joe in his early years would have made his tea first by boiling a billycan over an open fire, then sipped it in his own fashion out of a tin cup. Joe didn't need to learn the manners of the genteel classes for he had his own.

The gold rush lured gumdigger Bolland to Thames with his pick and shovel, in search of a fortune never found, but I'm certain that Messrs Bolland and Onions had their share of the good times. They were both sturdy, optimistic blighters, even as old men. They'd at least survived their long, hard-working lives. Some unlucky blokes didn't even have the chance …

A monument at the Grahamstown end of town remembers Kiwi troopers and gunners who died during the South African Boer War (1899~1902) *In the Empire's hour of need.* It names Thames citizens

Donkin, Farquar and Forbes and the inscription below reads 'Erected by the residents of Thames Goldfields. December. 1902'.

Although the golden era of mining was fast fading there were still reminders for me and my schoolmates. In the hills behind Thames where we played Cowboys & Indians were many old boarded-up mine workings, and an old water race made of corrugated iron with wooden supports. In the early days of settlement this narrow viaduct brought water for the town from the Kauaeranga Valley, near the big pool where Thames kids swam in the summer. But in our childhood, as with the old mines, it was out of use and filled with fetid water.

We lads took big risks at times: boating on flood-swollen rivers in canoes we built with the ubiquitous corrugated iron, sliding down precipitous inclines near Shortland cemetery on home-made sledges, or daring each other to enter the closed-up mines. This was a dicey pastime. We'd prise off a board or two at the entrance and scramble through the space. Then with torches or candles we'd light our way along the dark, dank caves (drives as they were called), eventually reaching the dangerous edge of the deep mine shaft itself. In the barely illuminated damp we'd drop stones down the hole, guessing the depth by the seconds counted. Our projectiles mournfully echoed as they hit the water-filled shaft far below. A stupid game, but having survived these daring escapades of childhood, a vivid memory.

In the 1890s a Thames boy recalled: "… there were hills to climb, and wild goats to chase with bows and arrows, though I cannot recollect even one goat permitting itself to be struck. There were glorious mud-fights on the flat near the Shortland wharf at low tide. The Thames was truly a boy's paradise — in those good old days of the 1890s."

Life for lads in those reported days in the 1890s was little changed by the 1940s. I'd add sailing in wooden dinghies with the Thames Sea Scouts, out on the Firth of Thames along with the joyous 'dancing' dolphins … learning sailors' knots too; swimming out to rocks on the coast north of Thames, a tack hammer in my togs to tap oysters off the rocks while treading water and eating *al fresco* these tasty morsels; fishing for eels with my mate Tau Abraham on the riverbank near home, hauling out big slimy specimens and cooking them over a wood fire before tucking into this delicious kai.

Other local characters spring to mind. Miss Dunlop: prim, elderly, very much like a spinster from an earlier age, her dress almost Victorian. By contrast another character, Mrs Fortune, a flighty woman … scattiness personified. But my, she didn't half play the piano. "Come along, Colonel," she'd call from the piano stool in front of our upright grand. "Come and sing."

Miss Dunlop taught me at Sunday school at Holy Trinity Church at Parawai on the bank of the Kauaeranga River on the way to the racecourse. This wooden church had been built by Ngati Maru in 1886. Queen Victoria made a personal bequest of a bell which is still in the bell tower. I was very fond of Miss Dunlop, who taught me the Gospels. I shall always be grateful for her gift of stories. Listening to her and to other old folk, Pakeha and Maori, who had good stories to tell made an impact. That I became an actor with 'stories to tell' perhaps had much to do with this early nurturing.

"Come on, Colonel!" — Mrs Fortune always called Dad that; he'd been an officer, yes, but not that rank — "Do come and sing."

She'd commence playing, head low over the keyboard, her protruding teeth mirroring the ivories that her bony fingers skittered across. Dad would put out his untipped Senior Service cigarette and amiably cross the room and there at her side, obligingly sing whatever Mrs Fortune had chosen:

"Come into the garden, Maud, for the bat black, Night, has flown" … his baritone filled the room. The piano was a fine upright grand built in Dresden and brought out in 1886 from Berlin by my Jewish great-grandparents, Oscar Emil and Caroline Wilhelmina Zander.

I remember saying to my mother in her shop that day in 1957, when she told me her story about the man called Jack:

"And here's another coincidence, Mum."

"What's that, son?"

"Our Koch & Sohne piano."

"Yes?"

"Another accident of fate."

"I'm not following you …?"

"Well, Mother dear, if that piano hadn't been brought to New Zealand from Dresden it would probably have been destroyed by the Allied bombing."

"Your great-grandparents would most certainly have perished if they hadn't come to New Zealand." Mother looked at me with a steady gaze.

Führer and his States …

I feel for you, the Führer said, I deeply sympathise.
With sobs and tears he sorted out, states of convenient size.
Holding his pocket handkerchief before his longing eyes.
"May we now live in unity?" "May we now live in unity?"
But answer came there none, and this was hardly strange because,
He'd eaten every one.

Written in the style of Lewis Carroll's 'The Walrus and the Carpenter' and published in the London *Daily Telegraph* in 1939.

As a five year old I tried to persuade my mother to let me get the bus to Auckland and then a ship to Jer-menny to let me kill the Few-rerr, because I told her that Daddy would then be able to come home to us from the war. It puzzled me at the time that Her Hitler was called a Her when I just knew he was a man.

I have often described my mother (who died in 1984) as 'the Perle Mesta of the South Pacific'. Mesta was a society hostess in Washington DC in the 1940s. After the war, as American representative in Luxembourg, she was the inspiration behind the central character in the American musical, *Call Me Madam*. Mother, like Mesta, was a generous hostess and on those sing-along evenings she always provided lavish food.

Fashionable fodder of the period. At these nocturnal feasts there were usually: "Tasty saveloys make ideal suppers. Be sure they are from Lairds of Pollen St … mini-sausages too"; cheerios and chipolatas, placed with cubes of pineapple on toothpicks; club sandwiches — delicious multi-layers of buttered bread interspersed with contrasting flavours, then pressed overnight under a board and heavy books placed on top, then the crusts cut off and the sandwiches sliced into narrow fingers; cold meats, salads and hot cheese scones; an array of flavoured jellies served with lashings of whipped cream; slivers of cooked beetroot, suspended in plain gelatine; trifles flavoured with sherry and piled high with whipped cream, then decorated with hundreds and thousands, those gritty dots of coloured sugar.

And no gathering of goodies was complete without several pavlovas, that ubiquitous pudding so beloved of most antipodeans. For folk who don't know the 'pav', it's soft meringue made with egg-whites, rich and gooey inside and then decorated on top with whipped cream and fruits of the season ... Chinese gooseberries (now called kiwifruit), raspberries, strawberries, passionfruit. You name it, Mum flaunted it.

"Well, I'll be jiggered," the men would chorus. "Delicious," the ladies murmured. Then regardless of their girths they all tucked in, feeding on the sweetness of it all until they confessed they were all stonkered. (The stonker was a huge First World War German cannon ... if it had you pinned down by its fearsome barrage, you were finished.)

This sweet fodder was accompanied by equally sugary drinks: sherry, Drambuie, *crème de menthe*, Pimms, and locally made fruit liqueurs from nearby Tapu. For wowsers, an equally sugar-drenched product in a bottle: Lemon & Paeroa, manufactured in Paeroa, also near Thames. It's no wonder most New Zealanders of that period had false teeth at an early age, and that their dentists were so very good at their profession! There was never beer served on these occasions; beer was a pub-only drink, and hotel bars where it was served were in those days the sole preserve of men.

At those food-centred gatherings of the 1940s and early '50s the (pre-TV) topic of conversation was radio drama. The wireless was always on. At just such a gathering one beak-nosed woman was wittering on about a hero of hers in a radio 'soap'. It was then everybody's favourite. *Dr Paul* ... a story of adult love.

At age eleven I was already well into elocution lessons with Mrs Val McCoombe and winning prizes. So I thought I knew a thing or two about radio acting too:

"I think he's awful," I said. The beak-nosed fan turned and gave me a 'children should be seen but not heard' withering look.

"What would you know about acting, young man?" Being a right little whipper-snapper, I became incandescent with rage and retorted:

"Anyway I think that actor's a queen." The room fell silent. Mrs Fortune put down her plate of hot cheese scones and hurried to the piano. She commenced a jaunty jig, no doubt a diversionary tactic. But Miss Cox, who gave me after-school lessons in arithmetic, was first to speak. Her voice sounded somewhat croaky ... like footfalls on gravel. As Mrs Fortune hit the ivories this maiden lady said hoarsely:

"It's all right, Bruce doesn't know what that word means." She was dead right but nevertheless I was poised to reply ... that I did know. But my saintly Father smoothly interjected:

"Out into the garden, son. Go play with your brother." He winked at me. I reluctantly obeyed and carried my peevish fury out onto the front lawn where, to work my steam off, I trounced my kid brother in a savage game of knuckle-bones.

At age five, when asked by a neighbour, Mrs Hetherington, what I planned to be when I grew up I answered confidently: "An actor." This surprised people, for I'd not seen a live play or even been to the cinema, and television in the home still lay in the future. By seven, however, I'd at least caught up with the magic of film. On 1 January 1946 I saw Abbott and Costello in *The Naughty Nineties* at Thames' Regent Theatre. I soon became a regular picturegoer, attending the Saturday morning Children's Picture Club. These sessions always included serials with gripping cliffhangers. Along with the likes of *The Three Stooges* and Laurel and Hardy, there were also songs to be sung. Our responses were guided by an image of a bouncing ball moving in time above the words on screen. We sang our hearts out — all this pleasure for only 1/9d. One firm favourite at these kid's matinées was comedian Leon Erroll in his one-reelers full of corny gags. Leon Erroll did one bit of business that greatly tickled me. He tried, without success, to attach his hard-fronted shirt by a stud at his waist but it repeatedly rolled up to his neck. This comedy had me rolling hysterically in my seat at the flicks.

Rolling again, but some twenty years later, on that occasion in a theatre seat, when the great actor Alistair Sim repeated Erroll's comedy-business in a London production of *The Magistrate*. I wondered then if that lugubrious genius Sim had, like me, seen Leon Erroll. With immediate recognition of this bit of 'comedy-bizz,' I was the single strident laugh during that live matinée in London in the 1960s. Good ideas are often 'stolen'. In a television interview in

2004 Sir Anthony Hopkins admitted he stole a bit of 'bizz' from Charles Laughton. Tony and I were classmates at drama school in London in the 1960s and shared digs in Kings Cross. An esteemed colleague, I'd be flattered if he's stolen anything over the years from me, for I certainly have from him.

In theatrical terms, aged ten, I witnessed a startling manifestation of the craft of stage acting. I'll talk of that baptism a little later into this book, because it profoundly influenced me as an emergent performer and, serendipitously, became an important part of my early life in London. Nevertheless, aged five, I'd stared in fascination into my grandad's big amateur actor's make-up box, filled with its sticks of Leichner greasepaint and powder, spirit gum, etc. At five, the attraction of acting was clearly not the roar of the crowd, for at that tender age I'd not yet heard any such roar! But I had experienced the smell of the greasepaint!

Thanks to my elocution teacher I did become extremely proficient at recitation, pursuing it single-mindedly as a craft. But hubris set in and on two occasions I was rebuffed from what I deemed my natural path to glory.

The first such put-down was much deserved; the second less so. The first was at a concert in Thames, where I'd just 'given my Puck'. As I exited the stage with the applause continuing, I thought it'd been definitive. Alas, as I reached the darkened wings, the next act — a group of girls in long dresses, supported in their width by bamboo-hoops beneath — commenced their entrance. The last girl in the line was holding her hand spread out at arms length as she entered upon the stage. Her hand looked so very, very, beguiling as it floated by. This was too much — I grabbed the girl's hand and re-entered the stage and took another bow! At the end of the evening I was duly chastised. But by then I knew I'd blown it.

On the second occasion I achieved hubris of a high order. In Standard Six at Thames South Primary School I took overall charge of the school play to be performed at the end of the year. This was to be my swan song from the small town of Thames, for I was soon to be off to the big smoke ... I had secured a place at Auckland Grammar School and thought this very prestigious move was a well-deserved achievement. An incident after the one performance of this school production, however, caused me to retire for several years from acting.

The play at the end of that primary school year was *Old King Cole*. Perhaps it was a subconscious audition for an anticipated greater role to come, the role of King Lear (which after forty years of acting still eludes me). At twelve years of age I elected myself not only to design both set and costumes but also to cast the other parts and direct the production. If this was not vanity enough I finally cast the central character in this children's play. Yes, you've guessed correctly … Old King Cole, the starring role, was played in 1952, by Bruce Purchase.

But as my dad said to me when one day I rushed home from the hills clutching a rock that I imagined to be suffused with gold: "It's fool's gold, son. It has no value." My teacher, Mr Menzies, whom I had greatly liked, reviewed the performance of *Old King Cole*. With all the parents, pupils and teaching staff present he praised everybody involved except for one: twelve-year-old me. A powerful lesson which I took to heart, and chose not to perform again for the next five years.

There is a cheerful coda, however. Over half a century later (in 2003/4) while performing a stage play in New Zealand, a member of the audience asked to speak to me afterwards. He enquired if I remembered him from Thames.

"I think I recall your face."

"I was in Standard Six with you, for the last half of the final term." When he told me his name I remembered him clearly.

"I've never forgotten," he said, "one particular moment in the school play at the end of that year." My ears pricked up and I enquired cautiously:

"And what was that … moment?"

"It was when you took off your coat and turned it inside out and it became a coat of many colours. For fifty-two years I've never forgotten that moment."

I thanked him profusely, for he'd broken a spell.

III

An old Southern gentleman

I STOOD ON THE PAVEMENT OUTSIDE the Cambodian Consulate as the door slammed shut behind me.

"No journalists allowed," the clerk inside had said.

"But I'm no longer a journalist. I'm an actor."

"Not believe. It say journalist."

"It's been altered. Can't you read, for God's sake?"

"No visa for journalist. You go now!" Other figures had then appeared, ready to eject me.

Let not a push become a shove, I concluded and headed for the exit. In the street outside the consulate it was stifling hot. God, how I hate Singapore.

Two days earlier I'd stood before a much friendlier official, in Auckland, my New Zealand passport open on the desk in front of me. "Problem is," I'd explained, "I want to visit the temples at Angkor Wat, but the airlines told me the Cambodians don't welcome western journalists. For the past six years I've worked as a professional actor in Britain. Can you issue me with a new passport indicating my change of profession?"

"When are you leaving?" asked the friendly Kiwi.

"Tomorrow."

A new passport couldn't be processed in the available time. However … "We can score a fine line through 'Journalist' and add 'Actor' alongside."

"It'll still be visible."

"Yes."

"I don't think they'll accept it."

"Possibly not. Which way are you flying?"

"Via Singapore."

"Hmm. There's a Cambodian Consulate there. Let's make the alteration anyway and see how you get on."

The answer was as badly as I'd feared.

At Changi Airport, after rejection at the consulate, I mulled over what to do next. An hour later, decision taken, I was heading west.

"To hell with Cambodia and Angkor Wat. I'll see the temples at Isphahan instead and also look up Edwin!"

Edwin Leane, a former colleague, had married an Iranian and now edited an English language newspaper in Tehran.

Eight years after leaving New Zealand to study at RADA I'd returned home because my father was seriously ill. After his death I was on my way back to the UK, returning to work, though God knew what.

On New Year's Day 1969 I arrived in Tehran, which was cool, though bright and sunny. A contrast to the heat and humidity left behind in Auckland and Singapore.

"Can you advise me of a cheap hotel?" This at the tourist desk in the terminal. The young man on duty smiled and pointed to a coach parked outside. "Take that bus."

The coach took me to its sole destination, which was the Hotel Intercontinental.

This must be an Iranian practical joke, I thought. Never mind, I'll stay one night and find a cheaper hotel tomorrow, for I knew funds back in the UK were low.

After settling into a room I clearly couldn't afford, I phoned Edwin. A woman's voice answered: "He's in Rome. Back at the end of the week," Edwin's wife on the line informed me. "Let's meet up when he gets back." She rang off. Damn, I could do with a drink!

In the hotel bar I ordered a large gin and tonic and settled into a comfortable armchair to study a tourist guidebook and plan the coming week.

I was alone in a dark-paneled cocktail bar but for one attentive waiter who swiftly delivered my order, placing a bowl of nuts on the glass table in front of me. I glanced at the map of Tehran and was about to take a sip when the peace and quiet of the bar was disturbed by the arrival of another customer.

A small elderly man entered the room at speed. I observed him, a sort of Jimmy Cagney look-alike. The stranger achieved several things in a short space of time. As he ordered a dry martini he swept off his winter coat and beret and threw them in a pile on a chair. Simultaneously his eyes swept the bar, taking in my presence. "Mind if I join you?" and joined me before I could reply, taking a handful of nuts from the bowl on the table.

All this was achieved smoothly in a matter of seconds. He threw the peanuts into his mouth, began munching them as he introduced himself. "Hi, I'm Al Kaufman. Who are you?" He spoke with an American accent of the southern states but his delivery not a southern drawl, more like a machine gun.

Al Kaufman received his martini and carried on munching, signed the bar bill and — in the characteristic way all Americans have — repeated his new acquaintance's name several times, placing it securely in his memory. The old American then set about finding out all about me with rapid bursts of questioning as if there was no time to be lost. He quickly learned a lot as well as offering up facts about himself. He was a lawyer visiting Tehran, giving free advice to young voluntary members of the US Peace Corps based in the city. He was married and had a son who owned a rope-making factory, adding he'd also been mayor for many years of St Louis — one of the biggest cities in the southern USA. By now the lawyer knew I was an actor in the UK. Al Kaufman ordered us both a second drink.

"Do you know Curt Jurgens?" he asked.

"I know who you mean."

"D'yah know Elke Sommer?"

"On screen."

"D'yah know …?" Naming a well known German film director.

"Yes, I've heard of him."

"Let's sit at the bar." The older man leapt up and I obediently followed. Kaufman jumped nimbly up onto a high bar stool.

"Telephone." He barked at the waiter and turned to me. "They're making a film here. You oughta get in on it."

Before I could point out it was surely a German film and I was an English-speaking actor, the phone was on the bar and the lawyer lifted the receiver. "Get me the Hilton."

"But, Mr Kaufman!"

"Call me Al." He spoke again into the phone. "Hello, is that the Hilton? I'd like to speak to Curt Jurgens. Yes, it's Kaufman speaking … What? Well get me Elke Sommer on the line. Uh huh. Well then, …" naming the German director, "When? Uh huh. Well how can I get there?" A muffled voice at the other end of the line as Kaufman listened intently. By now I was amused but also full of trepidation.

"I see …" the powerful old American ploughed on relentlessly: "Well, in that case this is what I want you to do for me. Phone American Express on my behalf — yes, it's Al Kaufman speaking. Get them to order up a plane for me …"

My eyes popped.

"Tell Amex we'll be around in …" glancing at his Rolex "… half an hour. Thank you." He slammed the receiver and turned triumphantly towards a very startled young actor.

"Come on kid, drink up. We're away."

"But away … away to where, Mr Kaufman?"

"I told you to call me Al," he growled.

"Al … Can you tell me …?"

"We're off and away to the jolly old mountains of Iran," Al Kaufman gleefully announced.

I told my newfound friend the impossibilities as I saw them. The old man listened intently as the information was presented to him: "You see Mr — I mean Al, it's quite clearly a German film. If they're casting parts it'll either be for other German actors or, maybe, Iranian extras. They'll need a British actor like they'll need a hole in the head. It won't work … Al?"

The tough old man was silent for a few seconds. He finally responded.

"But we've got a plane," he said softly.

"So it would appear."

Another silence as he mulled over what he'd been told. Then:

"Can you speak German?"

"No."

"Iranian?"

"Nope."

A further pause as Al looked at the phone in front of him. He suddenly arrived at a decision and picked up the receiver once again.

"It's Kaufman. Get me American Express."

I breathed a sigh of relief and took a sip of my drink before lighting a cigarette. Al eyed me sideways.

"Those things will knock ten years off your life."

"As long as it's the last ten," I grinned.

"Hello, is that Amex?" Back in high gear.

"Well, it's Kaufman speaking. The Hilton have phoned you?" Brief pause as he listened.

"Good. Well there's a slight change of plan."

"Is there?" Me startled.

"Yes, but we still need the aircraft."

Do we? my silent query.

"We'll be around in ..." looking at his watch again "... twenty-five minutes. Tell the airfield there's a change of plan. We'd now like to go to Damascus."

I stood eyes wide open. Mouth agape. Cigarette stubbed out in alarm.

"Yeah, that's right — Damascus." Al, elated, slammed down the receiver. "Pack an overnight bag, kid. We're off."

"But ..."

"No buts. Move your ass." With that, he jumped lightly off the high stool, deftly swept up his coat and beret and made for the door, shouting back over his shoulder ... "Put those drinks on my room and order a cab. See you in ten minutes. Remember your passport." With that he was gone.

An hour after first meeting we entered the offices of American Express, with its Iranian manager waiting for us just inside the front door. He approached and was clearly extremely nervous.

"Mr Kaufman ...?"

"Have you organised it? When do we leave?"

"Mr Kaufman," the manager repeated in an urgent whisper as if afraid of being overheard. He urged his client not to travel to Damascus. But Al was already in mid-flight.

"My British actor friend here," he said firmly, "and I have always wanted to go to Damascus. We've yearned to go ever since we were kids, haven't we, Bruce? The *Arabian Nights* and all that bullshit."

The manager, in a high state of panic, interrupted Al's flow, beads of perspiration visible on his brow. "Mr Kaufman," he pleaded. "Don't go. It is dangerous for you to go there."

"No journalists allowed," I added ruefully.

Al Kaufman's demeanour changed in a flash. He became very cross, clearly not accustomed to having any plan of his thwarted.

"Why, for chrissake?" he barked.

His voice cracking with tension, the manager quickly explained: "The Israelis today bombed Beirut Airport and the Syrians are hanging suspected Israeli spies in Damascus."

Al, now suddenly attentive, listening hard. He finally replied: "You amaze me."

The manager continued. "And begging your leave," he croaked, "Americans at present are very unpopular in Damascus."

"You continue to amaze me," his eyes popping in mock incredulity, "Americans unpopular?" He assumed gravitas, pacing slowly up and down, 'milking' the pause. A natural actor, I observed. The manager stood silent, sweating profusely.

"Well, I never," Al ruminated if to himself, "Americans unpopular." Changing tack, he turned on the hapless manager.

"Okay! Okay!" he enquired. "But we've got this aeroplane. Where, in your ever so humble opinion, can we go?"

I did get to see some temples after all. A few hours later on 2 January 1969 we landed at Isphahan. Who'd want to go to Angkor Wat, when they could go instead to Isphahan, I thought as the plane taxied in on the runway.

Over the following weeks Al and I became the best of buddies. An unlikely duo, the charismatic elderly southern gentleman and his young Kiwi mate, the actor. Al and Bruce. Definitely an odd couple.

Doors in Isphahan and back in Tehran opened easily. Everyone seemed to know my old mate. We were welcomed by our various hosts with considerable hospitality, although I became aware that Al was always greeted with wary deference. It was something I noted he seemed to expect, certainly enjoyed and, was I mistaken, even demanded. It did occur to me to wonder why this should be so but with the momentum of our travels, and having such fun, I brushed the thought aside.

One time, in pride of place at some traditional local dinner, I was offered by our Iranian host my first ever, though not my last, sheep's eye.

"You have to accept it and eat it. It's an honour," Al gleefully explained. It was an honour, however, which he himself was willing neither to accept nor to digest.

Back in Tehran after Isphahan, we walked a lot. He was a keen walker and although I was much the taller, he set a mighty pace and I just had to keep up. "Walking's the best way to discover a place."

He gave me a great gift — teaching me an instinctive way to discover a new city. He was a natural intelligence officer, gaining knowledge on the ground, fleet of foot. I had to be alert to his every whim. "Not that way, kid. This way," leading me off down some dubious, nay, dangerous alley. Nevertheless he was invariably on the ball and we'd discover some treasure no mere tourist could ever hope to see.

After Isphahan I'd moved to a cheaper hotel, but we met up every day over the following week.

"Come on up." I was phoning from the hotel foyer.

Minutes later I knocked politely, although the door to his suite was open. He shouted for me to enter.

"Shall I close the door?"

"Nah, leave it open. I'm expecting someone," he said mysteriously. "Pour yourself a drink."

On that occasion he talked about his advisory legal work for the US Peace Corps. "Doing it for nothing. Costing me a fortune. Naïve young kids," adding cynically, "most of them dodging the draft back home."

The Vietnam war was still raging. I also learnt he was a friend of Richard Nixon and was to be an invited guest at Nixon's upcoming presidential inauguration.

"Why on earth do you support that crook?" I exclaimed. This a long time before Watergate. It only occurred to me, many years later, that Al had perhaps been sent by Nixon or his like, to investigate rather than advise the members of the Peace Corps.

One day in a dingy basement bar he'd introduced me to an American who owned the dive. Afterwards I'd asked Al, "What's he doing running a seedy bar here in Tehran?"

"CIA," he'd cheerily replied. "It's a cover." I could see him relishing his use of a favourite American myth.

As we chatted that day in his suite there was a knock at the door. He bellowed, "Come on in, it's open for chrissake." A pretty dark-haired Iranian maid appeared in the doorway.

"Later, later," he'd spoken gently and she'd turned and left.

I was puzzled. "What's that all about?"

He explained that, on his second day in the hotel, he'd been reading a report while reclining on his large double bed. The same young girl had entered the bedroom, unannounced, although the suite had already been serviced. He read on as she aimlessly pottered about, eventually approaching the other side of the bed and plumped up the spare pillow. He'd flashed her a glance and she'd then looked directly at him and smiled. The penny had then dropped. "Oh, I see what you mean," he said. "Trouble is, she comes every day if she knows I'm here. Sometimes twice."

"But never thrice?"

"No, never thrice. But I'm an old man, for chrissake. I'm seventy-two years of age, you'd never guess?" his eyes glinted as he recounted his tale.

"Would you prefer if I left?"

"Certainly not. I'm an old man can't you see? She'll be back later anyway," he sighed, as if resigned to his fate.

"She never came to my room when I stayed here."

"Maybe you lack a certain charm."

"Or money."

"You're learning, kid. You're learning."

Coincidentally, that day his wife had phoned from the States, instructing him to buy some Persian rugs. He had me along for a second opinion.

After our arrival in the largest carpet shop on Ferdowsi Avenue, the staff locked the front door and wheeled out a large drinks trolley. They'd been expecting this VIP, for the US Embassy had phoned ahead. We had the place to ourselves, attended by two salesmen.

Though the Shah was still on his Peacock Throne and the laws were somewhat slacker than after Khomeni came to power, I guessed they'd locked the front door to keep out any passing cleric who may have chosen to look in.

Al spent thousands of dollars, driving a hard bargain on each carpet he chose. After an hour he called it a day, but they nonetheless presented another carpet just in case he should change his mind. It was a beauty and I said so.

"Well then, you buy it. I've got enough."

Embarrassed, I whispered I didn't have the funds.

"Whaddaya want for that one — in British sterling?"

The salesmen who'd already sold Al a Shah's ransom, quickly exchanged glances. The old shopkeeper spoke.

"A hundred pounds." Even I knew it was a bargain at that price but hastily whispered to Al I didn't want to buy a Persian carpet. I didn't need a Persian rug.

"Give them a cheque for chrissake. Will you take a British cheque?"

"Of course." I was being cornered. Al pressed on.

"Will you take a £10 deposit and the balance post-dated?" he thundered.

Both salesmen chorused they'd be happy with that arrangement.

I blurted out in panic, "But I can't take it on the plane." Al again. "Can you deliver it, no extra charge, to London?"

"We can," another chorus.

He turned to me. "There! Now buy the goddamned rug." *Fait accompli.* Negotiation complete. It arrived on my doorstep in London three weeks later. Incidentally several weeks before the post-dated balance was due for clearance.

We ate out together every day and took turns to pay. "It's your turn to buy me lunch, Bruce," adding, "I know the very place." I was not blind to the fact when it was my turn to pay he'd choose a cheap café, and when he was buying we'd end up in a smarter, often much more expensive establishment.

It was now the end of the week. "I'm leaving tomorrow," he announced, adding, "The maid's wearing me out." He was planning to go home via the East and left early the next morning.

I spent my final day in Tehran with Edwin, back from Rome, and met his wife. The next morning I flew to Athens, stopping for a day with Greek friends and then onwards to London.

A week later the phone rang. It was Al. He was in London, he told me. Where he'd been for the previous ten days I was never told.

"Are you free? I'll take you to the theatre. I hear *The Mousetrap*'s good," he bellowed down the line from the Hilton.

"No," I said emphatically. "Let me choose and I'll take you."

We went to see a National Theatre production of Somerset Maugham's *Home & Beauty* at the Old Vic Theatre. Laurence Olivier had just taken over a role in the show.

When Olivier made his entrance I spoke to Al *sotto voce*, "That's the man himself." He, on the other hand, responded by booming out aloud, "Doesn't look like fucking Heathcliff to me." I'd been in the company and as the great actor's eyes angrily raked the stalls for the culprit, I sank low in my seat — Row D in the centre. Afterwards Al wanted to meet the actor and I nervously escorted him backstage.

"Oh, I spotted you, Brucie," Sir Laurence laughed. "Crouched like an All Black forward in the scrum. By the way," Olivier continued, "Why do they call them All Blacks when they have a touch of white on their socks, dear boy?" Al was wide-eyed, quite overwhelmed when I made the introductions. "You have a very carrying voice, Mr Kaufman."

"Call me Al, Sir," he mumbled.

"Perhaps you'd like to join our ranks, Al?" Olivier was charm personified, both rancour and laughter well concealed.

Al visited London at least once a year over the next few years. He was always the same rumbustious cheerful soul I'd first met in Iran. He once came to attend an American Bar Association conference, held that year (1971) in London. He always stayed at the Hilton on Park Lane. He adored having traditional English afternoon tea, served in his suite where he would hold court. Watching him balance cup and saucer as he nibbled on a cucumber sandwich or scone was a sight to behold.

I joined him one day. An American couple were also present but when introduced their names meant nothing to me. After they'd departed:

"Yah didn't like them, did yah?"

"Liked her. Didn't like him."

"Do you known who he is?" he pressed me.

"No idea."

"He's the attorney-general of the United States," my friend proudly announced. It was John Mitchell, who along with Nixon would later resign over the Watergate scandal. Mitchell's wife, whom I'd liked, was at the time of Watergate referred to by the American press as 'Martha, the Mouth'. She sure could talk.

On another cucumber sandwich and clotted cream occasion I'd enjoyed the company of his other guest.

"D'yah know what he does?"

"He's a judge, isn't he?"

"He's the Chief Justice of the Supreme Court."

By the time Al left I'd met a clutch of top US lawyers, some of whom were on the White House legal team.

That same visit I took him to watch a days shooting of a film I was working on at Shepperton Studios. It was a free day for me and I'd arranged for him to sit in on the set and watch the action. Having positioned him in a chair, I wandered off.

"Who's your friend?" The question came from one of the stunt guys, a tough Cockney who'd once been a bodyguard for the notorious gangland brothers, the Kray twins. He'd also been a minder for Frank Sinatra when Sinatra visited Britain, "Because I was willing to carry a gun," he'd told me on an earlier occasion.

"Frank's a great guy."

"Yes, I'm sure he is," I'd replied, respectfully.

"So who is he?" My stuntman/hoodlum repeated his question.

I gave him Al's credentials.

"Has he got a son?"

"Yes.

"What does his son do?" What was this all about?

"He makes rope, I believe. Yes, he owns a rope factory in St Louis."

"Yeah, I thought so," he gestured in Al's direction, "your friend Kaufman runs the Mafia in St Louis. I know because I've been there."

I never checked to see if this might be true, believing I'd encountered one of the myths that surround the American rich, but something occurred on a subsequent visit which made me reconsider what I'd been told that day at Shepperton Studios.

This time Al had a small entourage, a group of five in all. He was travelling with his wife and three friends. The other man was younger — probably in his sixties, a big burly Irish/American, Emmet Concannon. He was a tough, self-made millionaire, his wealth coming from haulage which led me rapidly to think of Jimmy Hoffa and corruption. The other two were Emmet's wife and their daughter, Mimi.

Concannon made it clear from the outset he was not going to like me. I could almost hear him thinking "What does this big faggot actor want from my friend Al?"

His wife appeared to be on some kind of medication. She remained silent for most of the time except for one memorable interjection. The subject of Nixon's recent impeachment came up in conversation. Al had commented succinctly, "He should have burned the goddam tapes." Then Mrs Concannon spoke, her sole contribution to the day. She stood and said, "It's not true what they say about liberals in the United States." Mumbling her words, she continued, "There aren't that many. They just make more noise than anyone else."

My eyes must have widened in amazement but I quickly arranged my expression when out of the corner of my eye I saw Concannon glaring at me. He seemed to be indicating "What the hell does this pinko-liberal Brit know about politics in our country?"

His daughter Mimi was all oohs and aahs about their grand tour thus far, but the fifth member of the party was the real surprise.

Mrs Kaufman was delightful. Younger by twenty years than her husband, she was extremely intelligent and utterly captivating. Slim, attractive and elegant. We liked one another and this pleased Al.

All this, however, under the cold malevolent gaze of Emmet Concannon, directed specifically at me.

Later we went out for dinner. "I've booked a table at Stone's Chop House," Al announced. We took two cabs and Al directed me to travel with Mimi and her father. Across from me sat Emmet, eyes narrowed like piss-holes in the snow. We sat for most of the short journey in silence except for the occasional gush from the girl — "Oh my gawd, is that Piccadilly Circus?"

Then Emmet spoke. "Nice to see Al?" he growled at me.

I answered somewhat over-brightly, "Yes we've been friends for years now. It's good to see him again and to meet Mrs Kaufman and, of course, your wife and you, Mimi," (she flashed me a toothy smile), "and ... and, you too Sir ..." My voice trailed off unnerved as I was by Emmet's basilisk stare. He spoke again and this time what he said chilled me to the bone:

"I've known Al for thirty-five years," his voice ice-cold. "Don't cross him." The emphasis was unmistakable.

During the meal the actor performed to the hilt. I felt I was fighting for my life. I played the Court Jester, attempting to prove my credentials as 'Mr Nice Guy' before 'Justice Concannon'. The table was kept 'on a roar', anecdote followed anecdote, witticisms falling as trippingly off my tongue as much as the terror I felt inside would allow. The actor achieved some success. Al laughed loudest and Mrs Kaufman was an attentive and appreciative audience. Mimi laughed mercilessly, not really understanding a single word or reference.

"Oh my gawd, that's just so funny, isn't it Daddy?"

But Daddy didn't find anything funny. He hacked away at a large slab of incinerated steak and stabbed at the peas on his plate, sending them whizzing in the air like little green bullets, mostly landing in the lap of the 'hired entertainment'. For her part, Mrs Concannon shuffled the food in front of her from side to side, muttering to herself and looking utterly miserable.

Al was relentless. "Tell Emmet that one about ..." urging me on to even greater excesses.

The farewells took place out on the pavement as their hired Daimler limousine stood at the kerb ready to take them back to the Hilton. First a gracious adieu from Mrs Kaufman, charming to the last. A dazed half-wave from Mrs Concannon and a final gush from pretty young Mimi.

But something had changed. Hard man Emmet approached and I flinched as my hands were grasped in the haulier's powerful grip. Emmet moved in real close, eyeball to eyeball.

Then came the real surprise of the day. Concannon's eyes were now wide open. His light blue pupils revealing a gentle expression, flecked with tears:

"Forgive my wife, Bruce, for she knows not what she does. She's not a well woman," he spoke softly and hesitantly. He then clasped my hands to his chest. I was stunned.

"I just want you to know," he continued, "that everything Al has told me about you is true." My face did not flinch.

"Thank you," I muttered, uncertain as to how I should respond. But Emmet then released his grasp and, turning away, lumbered off into the limo.

To my left, having witnessed this little scene, stood my old Tehran buddy, grinning widely. My face must have been a study:

"Even a blind shrew will bump into a nut in the forest," Al commented cheerfully. "But what sights we've seen, kid. What sights we've seen."

We embraced and, as he stepped into the limo, he said over his shoulder, "Don't do anything I wouldn't do, kid."

I watched the big black Daimler slide smoothly away from the kerb, its windows darkened, the occupants invisible. As it turned the corner out of Panton Street I muttered, "I promise I won't."

We never met again. Sometimes I look at my Persian rug in pride of place in the centre of my drawing room in London and imagine it as a magic carpet.

Perhaps it'll fly me to Cambodia, or the jolly old mountains of Iran, I muse.

Then I hear Al's voice in my head, "Yeah, that's it kid. Let's fly there. Hi Curt! Hi Elke! Have you gotta job for a young British actor?"

IV

Early travels and living beside the Waitemata

W E WERE OFF TO THE BEACH ONE DAY. I was seven and Grandad asked me: "Do you think you're ready to swim on your own?"

That sunny summer day he was in an over-the-shoulder, navy, cloth-cut bathing costume. I was in kid's togs and we were walking over a wide-planked bridge that crossed a narrow stream.

"Think so, Grandad."

With that he lifted me high in the air and threw me off the unfenced bridge. I hit the water hard. Winded by the impact, I sank deep, but quickly recovered and I kicked myself to the top. As I cleared the surface I saw the bright blue sky above and, lo and behold, found myself swimming on my own. Glancing up at the bridge I saw Grandad looking calmly down at me. He smiled and I grinned back. He'd timed the whole thing perfectly.

Shortly after my move from Thames to attend Auckland Grammar School, Grenville William Edward Purchase, my beloved Grandad, died in an Auckland hospital after a short illness. His death and that first change of location had a profound effect on me. The last time I saw Grandad alive in that hospital, the only food he was having was beer which, for ease of ingestion, was allowed first to lose its fizz. This ale from which he gained some solace is named after Auckland's main harbour ... the Waitemata. When he died, my grandmother was persuaded to sell their Northland home to be nearer the family. It was the end of a happy era. Dreamy summer holidays of childhood, spent at our grandparents' place at Ngunguru in the warm north of the country, were suddenly over. But, back in time ...

Ngunguru (pr. Noong-oo-roo) was an unspoilt backwater in the 1940s. It has an estuary separated from the Pacific coast by rolling white sandhills. This inner harbour with its moored boats is a safe place for children and was where my Grandad taught me to swim.

Shooting wild rabbits with him, or, with young brother Grenville, pretending to be Beau Geste and his fellow French Foreign Legion comrades, in the rolling pampas grass-strewn sandhills, were pastimes we enjoyed in those golden summer days. Fishing too. Grandad would take us out to the entrance of the open sea, by sculling us with one oar in a rowlock at the stern of his clinker-built dinghy. Once the anchor was thrown, armed with lead-weighted handlines, we'd catch a few snapper for lunch or the evening meal. We could clearly view the snapper, eight or so feet below, approaching our bait through crystal-clear water.

Grandad was an English-born seaman and met my Nana, Nellie Janie Zander, when his ship called into Auckland early in the twentieth century. Her Jewish parents had emigrated from Germany in 1886. Grandad jumped ship to marry her. You could do things like that in those days … They had eight children, though the eldest, Charlotte Wilhelmina, died young. Letters she wrote shortly before her sudden death reveal her to have been an intelligent and witty eleven year old. My father became the eldest child in the family, his six siblings Nell Janie (jnr), Harry Zander, Marie Lillian, John Rupert, Katherine Elisabeth and Edna Grace. They all married and, apart from Aunt Betty, had many children, so Grenville and I had lots of cousins close in age to us.

Our grandparents' place became a well-attended family compound during the summer months. And because Grandad built several guest houses, each with its own outside dunny — a deep-drop, chemical latrine — there was plenty of sleeping space for everyone. After his retirement he built another room made of fibrolite, with space for a billiard table, dartboard and table-tennis.

On rainy days this was very much the epicentre of sporting activity for our family and by an early age he'd taught both Gren and me to play billiards, darts and table tennis. He was himself an expert billiard player and sometimes, to supplement his pension, took the local bus, driven by Karl Erceg, one of Northland's many German-born émigrés, into the nearby town of Whangarei. From there he'd be flown by biplane to Auckland city where he'd play hustler in the billiard parlours. He always won enough to pay for the relatively expensive return flight with cash left over to buy presents for his grandchildren. His return was always joyful: "What had Grandad brought back for us?"

To the rear of the property he created a bowling green with clubhouse and flagpole, and designed a flag which was sewn by Grandma. We kids spent many a happy hour pushing a huge old home-made concrete roller back and forth over the grass to keep the green flat. We loved to play too, a sport usually reserved for older folk, though the balls cool and smooth as silk felt awfully heavy in my young grip. Years later when revisiting the area with friends Judith Binney and Sebastian Black, I saw the property and spotted Grandad's old concrete roller parked in the deep-shade overhang of a hedge. It was much smaller than I remembered!

On the front lawn was a quoit court, marked out with a little dispenser box on wheels Grandad designed and built. The liquid inside this contraption was his own mix of water, cow dung and plaster which left clear white lines on the netted court. In those long-gone summers Gren and I, to prevent sunburn, wore colonial-style hard brimmed hats. In old black and white photos we appear like very young British District Commissioners about to do service in Africa.

Our grandparents kept a large vegetable patch and alongside was a hand-pump to raise water from a well. In the early evening buckets of this water drenched the earth parched during the day by the sun. That vegetable patch produced all that was needed and Grandad's sweet corn was indeed as high as an elephant's eye. In the paddock behind the bowling green was a soda well. On days when that big field was not occupied by a fearsome bull, we'd go armed with a pail to draw the refreshing carbonated water. We drank this fizzy stuff with our meals or mixed it with ice-cream to make delicious soda-pops.

On the nearby beach we gathered shellfish, pipis, and in the late afternoon we'd take long blissful walks in the shade of old pohutukawa, the New Zealand Christmas tree, festooned as they are in December with bright red flowers. Their thick strong root tentacles grip, it seems miraculously, both the edge of the cliffs above the sand and above the big rocks at each headland.

One aspect of Ngunguru holidays we didn't enjoy was insistence by the old folks that we endure a siesta after lunch. Siesta was just acceptable on a Friday, after Karl Erceg's bus had arrived in the morning from Whangarei bringing us piles of comics ordered by our generous mum to be sent direct from Gordon & Gotch's Auckland warehouse. The arrival of these comics was fun. *Classic Comics* were my favourite, but having to retire to our beds in the middle of the day was frustrating. During siesta time the sun was hot and we wanted to be out in it.

Other holidays with family at the village of Plimmerton near Wellington were enjoyable too. Uncle Harry and Aunty Jean along with cousins Rosalie and Keith lived there. Their house was near the beach so we could swim in summer or, in winter, sample childhood interests in windy Wellington. On wet days we sometimes played card games and card tricks. Another favourite was Monopoly, which on one occasion became a three-day event. As we played into the third day it became too much for my kid brother who, frustrated, upturned the board and exited out into the rain to watch trains go by. Trains, particularly those driven by steam were and still are a passion for him.

A star-turn holiday for us was on the family farm with Uncle Tom (of Tom Big Car fame) and Aunty Nell, along with our galaxy of girl cousins. Life on the farm was exciting, but often hard work … riding the boundary fence checking for damage by wild pigs, deer and goats, and shooting them too … digging in hefty strainer posts for new fencing … cows to be milked, morning and eve, and cream separated from the milk with the aid of a magenta-coloured machine with its name in gold lettering on the front … calves to be fed a.m./p.m. with buckets of skimmed milk still warm from the cows, 'slurp, slurp', big brown eyes eagerly looking up over the edge of the bucket … pig troughs filled to the brim with yet more skimmed milk … chickens fed corn and bran, their delicious eggs collected in a billycan … digging up paddocks with horse-drawn plough.

We mustered on horseback, with sheepdogs swiftly rounding up strays, then the sheep were docked, shorn, marked, dagged or dipped. During a day of mustering, when the dogs sometimes let the flock spread too wide, our Uncle Tom's language was ripe. This amused us because uttering 'damn' or even 'blast' in the Runciman household was strictly verboten.

When we were sent to the back of the farm equipped with .303 rifles to shoot wild goats, Uncle Tom gave us only one bullet per goat. If you only wounded the animal the final task had to be completed with the sharp knife we each carried in a pouch on our belt. When meat for the table was needed, Uncle Tom would slaughter a lamb in the barn, which we were allowed to witness. Urban children often think meats originate as tightly wrapped plastic cuts on supermarket shelves, but our uncle gave us a master class in what being a carnivore really meant.

Lambing was a busy time in the cold winter months high on that hill country farm. That and many other tasks were all jobs our Uncle Tom set us when we were still quite young. And during the lambing season, back at the homestead in front of the roaring fire, there were always newborn lambs that needed bottle-feeding, after their mothers had died giving birth. Attractive little bundles, baaing for milk. These tasks were not just jobs for the boys. When our girl cousins came home from their New Plymouth boarding school they too were called on to work long, exhausting days.

During shearing and hay-making extra labour was not only welcome but necessary, and other uncles, friends, neighbours, nieces, nephews, all pitched in. There were lots of horses on the farm used during mustering of the sheep or for the pulling of ploughs and the hay-making scythes. No mechanised balers in the 1940s. Instead there were labour-intensive haystacks built high by the menfolk armed with pitchforks — their shirts glistening with sweat. Undried cut grass was also used to make silage.

These busy times demanded plentiful food. With help from the womenfolk, Aunty Nell cheerfully (jokes and jollity six-a-penny) toiled in the kitchen, producing loads of nourishing food for everyone. We kids were responsible for transporting it on horseback, high into the hills to wherever the work was taking place. Tea was made by boiling billycans over fires. When but a few hands were gathered for sorties to far outposts of the farm, thermos flasks and sandwiches were carried in saddlebags. Only the grown-ups had saddles — we had to ride with only bridles and sacks across our horses, held in place by tightly secured surcingles. This was a practical way to learn to ride, for without saddle or stirrups, we had to grip tight with our legs either side of the belly of the horse.

One day I was on a horse behind my cousin Jana, taking food to haymakers at the back of the farm. In my left hand was a billycan of orange-flavoured jelly and in my right, a pail of cream. Without suitable grip, I was perilously balanced and when a rabbit skedaddled by, our mount reared up and toppled me down onto the bone-dry summer earth. The jelly and cream went flying into the air and rained down upon me. I'd landed on my back, luckily with no bones broken.

When Jana finally controlled the steed, she looked down at her ten-year-old cousin pasted head to toe with orange jelly and cream. Now, with frailer bones, I would rather not repeat such experiences, but in my career I would often be called on to ride horses in films. My early experience stood me in good stead, both on horseback or, on occasion, as I accidentally toppled off my film mount as I did once when playing a Scots bandit in BBC TV's *The Borderers*. On this occasion the earth I landed heavily upon was in Scotland.

Auckland is built between the Manukau harbour to the west of the city, which opens into the Tasman Sea, and to the east the city's main port, the Waitemata harbour. This first opens into the Hauraki Gulf, with its many beautiful islands, then to the Pacific itself. In 1952 I was the first of our family to arrive in Auckland from Thames, to start at Auckland Grammar School. The rest of the family followed later, after selling up. For a few months I stayed with my dad's sister Betty and her husband, Gordon Howard. Gordon had only one arm, but he drove cars with style, steadying the wheel with his knees as his left arm swiftly changed gear. I remembered the style twenty years later when in an episode of *The Avengers* I played a one-armed South American scientist who was shot by a poisonous arrow from a blow-pipe. Gordon lost his arm on a duck-shooting trip when he accidentally blasted himself with his shotgun and toppled into the water. He clung to his dinghy for many hours until miraculously rescued from that lonely lake. New Zealand's a wide-open country with few passers-by! Gordon was a tough character, blessed at all times with good humour, and always laughed when recounting the events of his accident.

My time at Auckland Grammar, one of the best schools in the country, was not a great success, but I admired a few teachers and made a few friends. Years later on a return trip from the UK, my former art master Jack Crippen invited me back to my old alma mater and the headmaster, Henry Cooper, offered me a glass of sherry in his study. Also present were members of the staff, including Crippen and a few others who'd taught me. My scholastic achievements were slender, but by that visit in 1967 I'd made my mark as an actor and Henry Cooper had decided I was one of the school's success stories. His newfound charm cloyed somewhat and, gripping my dry sherry, I said:

"The last time I stood in this room, Henry," — he blanched at my over-familiar use of his first name — "was when I was being carpeted by you for some minor, now long-forgotten misdemeanour, on this very mat I'm now standing on." The teachers quietly chortled behind their sherry glasses; Henry Cooper guffawed, rather cheerlessly, clearly not amused. He'd been my French master and was a good teacher, and French was my favourite subject, but he became headmaster when the likeable Mr Littlejohn retired. French teacher Cooper became a very different kettle of fish. Jekyll became Hyde. Mr Littlejohn I'd much respected, but his replacement I didn't much care for. I've been told by some folk that he eventually relaxed his style and became a popular figure. Depends on who you talk to, I guess. Later he became vice-chancellor at Auckland University and was knighted for his services in the field of education.

Also at that gathering was Alan McSkimming, who taught drama. Although I was always willing to get up in class to recite a dramatic text, throughout my time at Grammar I always declined his offer of parts in school productions. Mr Menzies' critique of my multi-contribution in *Old King Cole* at primary school had left me unwilling to tread the boards again. It took several years before I re-embraced my destiny. A pity because in those productions at Grammar, a boys' school, the pupils from Epsom Girls' Grammar just down the road joined in to play the female roles. The lads participating were therefore able to make assignations with the girls. Foolish boy that I was then, I was literally having none of it.

After I left school, at sixteen, I spent two years as an apprentice in a bakery. As a kid I'd worked one school holiday in the Thames Bakery and had enjoyed getting up at 4a.m., the smell of rising dough in the big vats and the cutting, weighing and placing of it into baking tins. Later the scooping of these hot loaves from the ovens with a large wooden pallet and placing this delicious smelling bread onto big wooden trays ready for delivery to shops like ours at Parawai. My interest had sprung from the off-loading of the fresh bread at Parawai Store when I was very small.

In my early twenties, as a student at the Royal Academy of Dramatic Art, I funded myself by working long hours at Dugdale & Adams' bakery on a corner of Gerrard Street in what is now London's Chinatown. So my early experience helped get me through drama school, but in the Auckland days, rising at four in the morning for two years finally palled. I left this honourable craft and was fortunate to get a job as a journalist, which suited me better.

My self-induced failing at Auckland Grammar was replaced by development as a writer. Clive Tidmarsh, my boss at the handsome monthly *New Zealand Timber Journal* taught me about writing, printing and publishing and I learned about the timber industry, attending many conferences. The printing experience came to my aid later when I played the character of the head-printer, Big James Yarlett, in *Clayhanger*, a 26-part television adaptation of Arnold Bennett's novels produced by ATV in Britain in the 1970s.

Another bakery experience also took place in Britain. By the 1960s I'd developed a toe-hold in the acting profession and was living with Susannah Davis, a curator at the London Museum, in those days at Kensington Palace. One day I accompanied Susie to see a bakery at Mornington Crescent, near Camden Town, which had stood on that site for over a hundred years but was about to close. The museum was considering buying its decorative interior and equipment as a perfect example of a Victorian bakery, completely unmodernised. While Susie examined its antiquity I chatted to its owner, the son of its founder. This old man, who was ninety and thought he ought to retire, was fascinating.

"I've had many interesting customers over the years. For instance there was that red-headed Kings Cross councillor who wrote plays."

I hazarded a guess. "Do you mean George Bernard Shaw?"

"Yes, that was him. Then there was that Russki who went back to his country and caused a revolution. He bought his bread here."

"Do you mean Lenin?" My ears now tuned for more revelations.

"That was him. Nice chap, Mr Lenin."

He also told me there'd been a man who owned land nearby at Chalk Farm.

"He went off to Africa and invented a country."

"Cecil Rhodes, who founded Rhodesia?"

"Yes, that's his name," the old baker explained ... and much more.

*

But for certain events after I left secondary school, the career I finally found as an actor could have eluded me, because of the bleak two lost years I spent in the 1950s. The grocer's son might've become a baker. The early perfume of Grandad's greasepaint replaced by the delectable smell of freshly baked loaves ... having not audiences coming into a theatre but hot buns and fairy cakes coming out of an oven!

I drifted back to acting by first being persuaded to join a young group who performed concerts — light revue — at a Presbyterian church near our new home in Auckland. All of it, by association, was very wholesome. This group encouraged me to enjoy once again the process of performance. I was then invited in 1957 to take part in an amateur production of Philip King's play *See How They Run* (recently re-presented in the West End). Although I enjoyed the small role I had, the penny for me had still yet to drop. I'm a slow-learner! However it did drop when a gifted director, Edna Harris, offered me the role of Reverend Hale in Arthur Miller's powerful drama about the Salem witch-hunt, *The Crucible*. Under Edna's precise direction I ended up with critical acclaim. As if scales had been removed from my eyes, I realised what I wanted to do with my life.

A couple of years later I was well on my way. I was by then essaying the role of Moses in Christopher Fry's verse play, *The Firstborn*.

Alongside me was my former drama teacher, Alan McSkimming, who was playing the Pharoah. We were in a theatre dressing room both applying make-up for the evening performance. Alan said quietly:

"I tried so hard to persuade you to act at Grammar."

"I know, I know."

"Why didn't you? Here you are now ... very successful in this small pond, but soon to leave for London with a well deserved Government bursary in hand to help you on your way. Why didn't you accept my offers at Grammar?"

"Can't explain that one, Alan." I could have, but it would have meant being critical of my primary teacher Mr Menzies, who I respected. Talking to this recent teacher of mine I thought it perhaps better not to criticise an earlier one.

Once clear I wished to become a professional actor and to travel to Britain to learn this craft, I set myself a three-year target, which I achieved on schedule. By 1960 I'd secured my top prize — a prestigious government bursary to study in London. To achieve this I'd crammed in as many amateur productions as I could manage and also got into professional radio drama, building this around my day job as a journalist. With not-to-be-deflected determination I'd swiftly developed a reputation as an Auckland actor. This meant working long and demanding hours, day and night, and included the formation of a theatre company, the Company of Four, which played many venues within commutable distance of Auckland. We all mucked in — all sharing the driving and the setting up of lights, sets, props, etc. A hectic schedule, but though we all had day jobs, we never seemed to tire.

There were many encouragements *en route*. A letter dated 31 March 1958, handwritten on the headed notepaper of the Royal Oak Hotel in Wellington:

Anwyl, Mrs Purchase,

Thank you for your delightful letter, and I am so glad your son enjoyed the performance. I should be very happy to see him about quarter hour before the performance on April 17.

Emlyn Williams

Emlyn Williams was as good as his word and was most encouraging. This famous and accomplished actor/writer (*The Corn is Green* and *Night Must Fall* are probably his best-known plays) was on tour with two separate one-man shows, as Dickens and as Dylan Thomas. I enjoyed them both enormously. Mother and Williams had grown up in the same part of North Wales and possibly because of that he was *simpatico* towards me. Nevertheless I'd prepared myself for the meeting by reading Emlyn Williams' autobiography, *George*, so was able to chat to him about his life.

Equally inspiring (and also a result of another letter from my assiduous Mama), an enjoyable meeting with one of the most delightful and formidable actresses of the 20th century, Dame Sybil Thorndike and stage director and actor husband, the elderly Sir Lewis Casson. This at the beautiful old 19th-century His Majesty's, later illegally demolished while under a protection order, a disgraceful action that took place one holiday weekend when the dastardly destroyers knew that everyone else would be away. When we met, Dame Sybil was appearing in that theatre in Enid Bagnold's play, *The Chalk Garden*. I attended a matinée and met them both afterwards. When told I was planning to study acting in London she was effusive but he just muttered darkly: "Bloody fool." Sybil drew him aside and quietly told him off; when he returned, meek and mild, he was utterly charming.

Later, in the 1960s, I'd live for a year or two in the King's Road in Chelsea, opposite the old Essoldo Cinema, which would later house live theatre such as the original *Rocky Horror Show*. Dame Sybil Thorndike and her husband lived nearby and we would occasionally be in the same 'greasy spoon', our local café, for lunch on a Sunday. Whilst reading my Sunday paper I'd overhear their conversation, such as:

Dame Sybil: Murray wants us to go out for dinner with him after our second performance on Thursday.
Sir Lewis C.   Does he?
Dame Sybil: Yes.
Sir Lewis: Very well.
Dame Sybil: But … do you think you'll be up to it?
          (A dangerous, brief pause.)

Sir Lewis:	What do you mean ... 'up to it?'
Dame Sybil:	We will have done two shows.
Sir Lewis:	So ...?
Dame Sybil:	Murray thinks you may be too tired and not up to having dinner after the evening show.

They were both starring at the time in a West End production of *Arsenic and Old Lace* and the Murray they were talking about was their producer Murray MacDonald, another veteran of the time. In the late 1960s, three years after this conversation I was directed by Murray in Arnold Bennett's enjoyable *Milestones* at the Yvonne Arnaud Theatre at Guildford. An excellent production.

Sir Lewis:	(exploding with wrath) Of course I'll bloody well be up to it.

Sybil had succeeded in her mission. She'd chivvied her beloved husband into anger, and as long as he was capable of losing his temper, Sybil knew he was still fully alive.

New Zealand actor Rhys McConnochie told me of a chauffeured drive he shared with them between London and Chichester. Whenever Lewis seemed to be nodding off, Sybil would loudly announce: "Lewis! Lewis! Look! Look!" Waking suddenly, he responded: "What? What?" Sybil then pointed out of the car and shouted with enthusiasm: "The cows! The cows! Just look at the cows in that field. Aren't they beautiful?"

Several years after my first meeting with them backstage at His Majesty's Theatre in Auckland, I graduated from the Royal Academy of Dramatic Art in London. At RADA I'd been awarded third prize at the end of my course (first and second prizes went to Gemma Jones and Martin Jarvis) and the guest of honour who presented the prizes that day, in the summer of 1962, was Dame Sybil. After the awards ceremony the prizewinners were invited to take sherry with this doyenne of the British theatre. I said to Sybil: "You probably won't remember me ..." and mentioning our meeting backstage in Auckland, said that I'd then told her I intended to study acting in London. With her customary enthusiasm for life she launched into a hymn of praise about the landscape of New Zealand, culminating with: "...some of the oldest flora and fauna in the world ... no I

Taken in Auckland just before departure to RADA, aged 21.

don't remember our meeting, but how wonderful that you came."

One disappointment in my theatregoing experience in Auckland in the late 1950s was attending another such matinée at His Majesty's, of a show starring Sir Donald Wolfit and his wife Rosalind Iden. They'd compiled a programme-performance which comprised scenes from Shakespeare. I was dismayed by the so-called performance I saw that Saturday afternoon. It was quite clear to my young twenty-year-old self that Wolfit was 'walking through' that matinée. He perhaps assumed his audience in that Antipodean city wouldn't notice the difference. Such arrogance annoyed me and soon became fury as I considered just how difficult it'd been for me to save the price of my ticket. It was however a good lesson: as a result I've never in my long career 'walked through' a show.

As I ploughed away seriously at acting in Auckland in the late 1950s, several fellow New Zealanders particularly noticed my efforts: my inspiring yet pragmatic drama coach Gil Cornwall; a contemporary, Vincent O'Sullivan, graduate of Auckland University who was also at the time a good local theatre critic; two professors from the English Department at varsity, John Reid and Sydney Musgrove; a new New Zealander, Jewish Russian émigré, Boris Lewin; Cavell Trask and the man she later married in London, English-born theatre director and architect Peter Morgan. These seven, plus the aforementioned director Edna Harris, had an enormous influence on my early efforts and Vince O'Sullivan, who has become a major

New Zealand writer, became a close friend. This important bond and also my solid friendship with Pete and Cavell, founder members too of our Company of Four, have endured since those formative years. In 2004 Pete and Cav stage-managed my one-man show on the life of Samuel Johnson (*Johnson is Leaving*, written by John Wain) when I briefly toured it in New Zealand.

Boris Lewin and the Ukranian family he shared a house with also hold a special place in my heart. They lived nearby but I got to meet them through a girlfriend, Janet Le Lievre, who lived next door to them. Many contented hours were spent with Boris, Mama and Poppa (a White Russian who had been a cavalry officer), their daughter Shura (who taught Russian at Auckland University) and her Welsh-born husband Denys, who tried, though unsuccessfully, to write plays. Also 'Aunty,' who made cheesecake, the like of which I'd never tasted before or since.

Boris saw my every performance and became an important influence on my early life as an actor. He was always sharply perceptive, giving credit when it was due yet always urging me to become better … "Yes, good, but …" He always challenged me to dig deeper in a role, teaching me that there would never be any arrival point in this search. Boris was a natural teacher and a remarkable human being.

Many years later, suffering incurable cancer, he chose a dramatic exit from life. In the garden at the back of their house Boris Lewin poured petrol over himself and then lit the fuel.

Shura came home from work, looked out the back window and saw a charred figure on the lawn that she thought must have fallen from the sky.

At his burial high on a hill Shura told me the day was fine and still, "yet as the coffin was lowered into the ground, a violent wind came from out of nowhere, hitting the hillside with great force."

A tree alongside them bent with the sudden impact almost to the ground, she said. "It sounded as if it was groaning with pain."

Then, as suddenly as it had manifested itself, the mighty gust abated and the tree quickly righted itself. The mourners were left once again standing in stillness, though dazed by their extraordinary experience.

My many visits to their house were my first real experience of being with people from a different culture and I soaked up the atmosphere. At dinners in that happy house there were always ceremonial toasts between the many courses — flavoured vodkas characteristically tossed swiftly down the throat. These sumptuous banquets were always attended by interesting guests; the vice-chancellor of the university was one such. The talk at table challenged this Thames lad to join in with whatever conversation he could contribute, and I quickly learnt to keep up. Walking home after those exceptional evenings I almost floated in the air. Thirty-four years later in his play about the 18th-century man of letters, Dr Samuel Johnson, John Wain has Samuel Johnson say: "Conversation, at one and the same time, a sport, an art … and a path to wisdom."

That says it, I think.

Two events at this stage of my life slightly interrupted my three-year master plan to study in England. The first was when I was called up for compulsory military service in the army. Luckily I only served six months before being balloted out and didn't have to continue part-time over a further two-year period. I served my stint at Dad's old training ground at Papakura army base, near Auckland.

The second detour from my master plan was part of a fall-back plan should I not be awarded the coveted bursary. I decided I had to earn bigger money so left my job as co-editor at the *New Zealand Timber Journal* and got a job at Southdown Freezing Works, a big abattoir on the outskirts of the city. I worked in the freezer, feeding in the freshly slaughtered lambs on rails. In the army my acting had been put been on hold, but though I worked up to eleven-hour days at Southdown, at night I was able to summon up my remaining strength to either rehearse or play in a production for one of the many Auckland amateur dramatic societies. Toiling away in the freezers afforded me mind-space to learn my lines on the job, for the hard work didn't get in the way of my feverish imagination and piling up frozen carcasses in the freezer kept me fit. I was appointed a charge-hand with a small group of men (often 'new' New Zealanders) to whom I delegated tasks.

One was an Estonian who was saving cash before he continued his journey around the world in a yacht, his next planned stop Tahiti. I've often wondered if he made it, for I did visit his tiny craft moored on the Waitemata Harbour. As a yachtsman I wouldn't have dared take it out further than Rangitoto Island in the gulf.

Another guy was a Dutchman, newly arrived in New Zealand, who didn't have much English. Shortly after he commenced work I gave him a list of jobs which I took care to explain slowly and clearly. After I'd completed my instructions he said in amazement: "You haven't once said *ferk*." He was quite naturally surprised, as at Southdown Freezing Works, most of the work-force used the 'f' word, liberally sprinkled between more prosaic words from the mother-tongue. "Fucking this" and "fucking that," was commonplace utterance in that workplace as the poor dead lambs trundled past us on the rails.

One other character in that bestial building was a sheep named Judas. He'd been on duty for a couple of years, responsible each day for leading thousands of innocent lambs from the holding pens below to the slaughtermen waiting for their arrival at the top. Once at the killing point, Judas would simply peel off to his left and return to another pen below and there begin again his unbrotherly task, leading his mates to slaughter, day in, day out. Justice did eventually out. A new slaughterman's assistant mistakenly grabbed big old and valued Judas and hung him on the rail, where the slaughterman himself, not noticing it was charming old charge-hand Judas, promptly slit his throat. I can't help thinking that Judas for a few seconds must have tried, in his sheep-like way, to say to that new young worker:

"Hey! Don't you recognise me? I'm Judas. I work here!"

Being in the army was different. In peacetime we didn't have to kill anyone or anything, we just had to pretend to be trying to do that. As an actor I was up for that aspect of the training and thankfully, being of the lucky generation I am, have never been called up for real battle. In many ways I enjoyed my spell in pretend battle costume, and bayonetting dummies helped strengthen my boxer's punch. I was at the time a keen amateur boxer, first at secondary school, then in the army. After one bout during my army stint I was, whilst on parade, put 'on charge'. I'd injured my right thumb and found it difficult to properly polish my rifle and kit for morning parade. As a result the young officer put me on two charges: dirty rifle and dirty brass. As he passed on down the line my eyes must have ever-so-slightly looked to the heavens and the always alert sergeant-major following spotted this and gave me a further charge ... that of 'dumb insolence'. This is a brilliant forces' concept. You don't have to have said anything, no, just in your head, thought something negative. Throughout my life I've always been able to spot 'dumb insolence' in anyone. Later that day I was marched into my company commander's office. Though this was my first meeting with him I knew he'd served under my father during the war and admired my dad.

Major:	[looking at the list on his desk, then up at me, standing at attention] Three charges. What have you to say for yourself, soldier?
Me:	Sorry, sir.
Major:	Are you by any chance related to Bill Purchase?
Me:	Son, sir.

He looked startled, appalled. He gazed at me bleakly, in silence, then spotted my bandaged hand. A ray of hope?

Major:	What have you done to your hand, soldier?
Me:	Sprained my thumb sir.
Major:	How did you sprain it?
Me:	Boxing, sir. Last night, sir.
Major:	[after a brief pause] Did you win the match?
Me:	Yes, sir.
Major:	Difficult with the injury to polish your kit, I imagine?
Me:	Sir.
Major:	Three days confined to barracks. Dismissed.
Sergeant:	About turn. Quick march. Left, right, left, right, left, right ...

On 22 May 1960 on the steamship *Ruahine* I left Wellington harbour for Britain and my new life. The lad from Thames wept on deck as the ship rounded the Wellington Heads and set out into the open sea on a light swell. First port of call Tahiti, then Panama Canal. A stopover at Cristóbal Colón and another at the Dutch island of Curaçao ... then the sighting of the Azores and finally, four weeks after departure, arrival at Southampton on 22 June. I was twenty-one and it would be four years before I saw my homeland again.

The memories I took with me have stayed with me throughout my life and as an 'intimate stranger' (as Dan Davin told James McNeish he saw himself in relation to the land of his birth) on return visits, the richness of my New Zealand heritage is always re-affirmed. On one such return I took my twenty-year-old son to Thames to show him, for the first time, my home-town. Reuben was born in London but both his parents are Kiwi … his mother the Dunedin-born writer Elspeth Sandys.

As we approached Thames I pointed out the local aerodrome and told him that as a kid after school I'd persuade one of the pilots at the end of his working day to take me for a spin in the two-winged, venerable and dependable Tiger Moth, which had two open cockpits. At the end of that day I'd shown Reuben the town and the beautiful Coromandel coast beyond. We were returning to Auckland when Reuben said suddenly: "Look, Dad." On our right a plane was taking off from the Thames aerodrome. Although it was silhouetted against the setting sun it was still recognisable. A Tiger Moth! The same one I flew in as a kid forty years earlier? You can take the boy out of Thames, but you can't take Thames out of the boy. On a more recent trip to New Zealand, another Tiger Moth nearly entered my life. At a party in the Hawke's Bay in the North Island, Sir Peter Elworthy, a well known New Zealander, invited me to visit him at his home in the South Island.

"I'll take you for a spin in my Tiger Moth."

"Oh, I'd love that."

After his departure a friend who'd overheard this conversation, said to me: "Don't accept that invitation."

"Why not? I'd love to go up again in a Tiger Moth."

"Just don't accept the offer."

Sir Peter Elworthy died suddenly a fortnight after his generous offer to take me flying.

Memories, equally vivid, still retained from my teenage days in Auckland, beside the beautiful Waitemata …

… Sailing on that harbour, up the coast to Kawau Island in a gaff-rigged fourteen-foot T class

… Watching a mighty Sunderland flying boat picking up speed on the water of the Waitemata, then lifting slowly into the air, bound for Australia on its seven-hour flight

… In the wheelhouse of the old Auckland ferry *Kestrel*, which was captained by a great-uncle and allowed to steer it, momentarily, on its journey to Devonport on the North Shore

… Learning how to dance so I could escort a VIP to a ball — that yarn comes later when I talk about performing in a production of *My Fair Lady* that toured for several months, mainly in Germany, but played extensively also in Vienna, Zurich and Paris. Learning to dance in 1956 in Auckland involved, if you've not already guessed, an earlier passion, for another fair lady. At the time she was also, like me, just seventeen.

… Thames memories still vivid too: a lone ten-year-old boy at a Saturday matinée in the King's Theatre in Pollen Street, to see a travelling show which was to include magic, hypnotism and juggling. It was only when the curtain rose slowly and performers came on stage to rehearse for their Saturday evening show that I got the message — they'd cancelled the matinée but forgotten to inform their one paying customer. Me!

I stood up and made a quiet and rather sad exit.

… Other more successful shows though: first, Tex Morton (like America's Gene Autry) an amazing balladeer, trick-shooter and rider; and secondly all the thrills at Barton's Circus, where after I had enjoyed the show, a tethered mule outside kicked me up my backside. Was it anything I'd said …?

… Oh yes, and the races. Waiting as an eleven year old on a corner near our home to see a hero, Grenville Hughes (top jockey 1950-'51) drive by in his swish Chevy two-seater on his way to trounce the other riders at the Thames Jockey Club summer meeting — 'Entrance four shillings for the men, two shillings for the ladies and vehicle entry 2/6 pence'. My hero, who I thought every bit as charismatic as Hollywood's Humphrey Bogart, won the Goldfields Cup that day in 1950.

… Lastly, also in 1950, Miss Grace Deane was the bathing beauty chosen in the Regatta Contest for the Thames coast. She'd certainly have, in my opinion anyway, given Miss Esther Williams, Hollywood's 1940s bathing beauty star, a run for her money.

The life that began in Wellington on 22 May 1960 as my ship

sailed became a very different life from the one I left behind. A patchwork quilt of experience, a life that's taken me, often because of work, to many parts of the world. It's left me pondering, however, what my life would have been if, in the first place, I'd not taken that initial plunge.

V

Almost a film star

"**D**O YOU RIDE?"
"Yes."
"But do you ride well?"
"Sure. Since I was a kid in New Zealand."

It's summer, 1960. I am chatting to a man of middle years in the driveway to a large house in south-west London.

The older man explains his question. He's already elicited that I'm in Britain to study at RADA. I'm renting the mews flat to the rear of his property.

"My Aunt Irene is casting a film and told me she needs young actors who are experienced riders."

"Well, you're definitely talking to the right man, Ronald," I replied.

"I'll give you her address and phone number and tell Irene you'll be in touch. When do you start at RADA?"

"September."

"That's fine then, as filming starts soon. You'll be able to do the job if Irene thinks you right for the role."

The next day I journeyed from Wimbledon to the West End on my newly purchased second-hand BSA Bantam. A tall bloke, I must have looked distinctly odd, perched on that small motorbike. Unused to roundabouts, I had to negotiate for the first time the alarming free-for-all at Hyde Park Corner. For a country lad it all seemed chaotic for there were no traffic lights, as now, to monitor the flow of traffic.

Six weeks earlier I'd arrived off a ship at Southampton. I'd stayed briefly with friends in an elegant rented house in St John's Wood before moving in with two other New Zealand chums to this mews flat at Wimbledon.

The flat was part of a property called the White House which stands on West Side Common, Wimbledon. It had, until his death in an air crash during the Second World War, been the home of film star, Leslie Howard. In 1960 it was owned by his son, Ronald, also an actor — and nephew to the casting director, Irene Howard.

Soon after arrival in the UK I'd spent a couple of weeks hop-picking in Kent. Bob Barr of Church Farm, Horsmenden, always employed Kiwis for this task, advertising annually for conscripts at New Zealand House in London. This was when I bought my khaki ex-army motorbike.

And talking of motorbikes, back to the journey into the West End. I'm careering through the London traffic on my way to my first ever film interview, at the 20th Century Fox building on the corner of Soho Square and Frith Street, to meet Ronald's Aunt Irene, one of the leading casting directors of that period.

I parked in Soho Square and walked confidently into the building but was swiftly intercepted by a uniformed guy whose manner, having done national service, I recognised as clearly ex-services.

"Can I help you, young man?" his tone suspicious. He probably recognised the dress, manner and sun-tan as some colonial lad just arrived in the metropolis from abroad. I told him I was there to meet with Irene Howard. By then with my antipodean accent he did know I was a new boy on the block.

"Have you an appointment, lad?"

"No," then as an afterthought: "Should I phone?"

"No, young man — *write!*" He guided me expertly to the door I'd only just entered.

Out on the pavement I reflected on this ejection: Cheeky bloke, I thought, but headed off to a nearby red telephone box. I was soon, via her secretary, on the line to Aunt Irene. "Ah yes, Ronald told me about you. When can you come and meet me?"

My callow, unpolished, youthful self explained my predicament. "Don't worry, come back in a few minutes," Irene Howard reassured me.

My second entry into the foyer was in marked contrast to my

first, for the commissionaire was suddenly almost a transformed character: "Ah, Mr Burgess, you're here to see Miss Howard."

"Purchase. Bruce Purchase is my name."

"Ah, yes. This way, Mr ... Purchase."

Did I sense a hint of dumb insolence, the splendid military term learnt during National Service in New Zealand?

"Thank you," I replied frostily, but as he wasn't my company sergeant he couldn't put me on a charge of dumb insolence. As I stepped out of the lift, Irene Howard's secretary greeted me warmly and escorted me to the office.

The interview with Irene went well and she instructed me to travel by underground to Uxbridge Station, from where a driver would take me to Pinewood Studios for a riding audition. I left my motorbike in Soho Square and took the tube.

At Pinewood the impressive exterior sets for this film were already in place. Beyond, on the back lot in a field, a horse-master, groom and several horses were in place for my arrival. The riding test that followed was easy, except for the jumps which I'd never cared to do. One aspect of the test I felt at ease with was the fact they called on me to ride without a saddle, only a sack held in place by a surcingle, and no stirrups of course. This was how I'd ridden as a child — saddles were for grown-ups!

The next day Irene phoned to offer me a part — the character, really only a glorified, not walk-on but ride-on role. I would get to work with an idol, Rex Harrison. But before filming commenced the star, Elizabeth Taylor, fell ill and the film was postponed indefinitely.

So, instead, two months later, I took up my place at RADA, for a two-year course.

The next year in 1961 the film project resurfaced, with Elizabeth Taylor returned to good health. Irene offered me the same role and John Fernald, RADA's principal, encouraged me to accept, promising me a place back at the academy after my film contract. But my benefactors at New Zealand House, who were paying my bursary, were adamant: "It will threaten your grant," said Mr Quelch, my paymaster. I was not too upset, thinking at the time such offers of film work were commonplace.

When that film part was first offered to me it was then to star, both the aforementioned Harrison and Taylor and also Peter Finch. It had now been relocated to Rome and with Peter Finch no longer available, his role was re-cast. Richard Burton assumed the character of Anthony and yes — if you've not already guessed, the film was a blockbuster, ran way over schedule and budget, making a lot of money for everyone involved — *Cleopatra.* I would discover that film roles did not necessarily grow on trees and it was another nine years before I was offered a second film job, this, *Macbeth,* with Roman Polanski directing. But back in 1961 I was well into life at RADA and had bonded with my fellow students — the next generation, among a stellar crew, the likes of Anthony Hopkins, John Hurt, Ian McShane, Martin Jarvis, Gemma Jones and film director Mike Leigh, to name but a few.

Polanski's *Macbeth* (screenplay by Ken Tynan) is one of the best Shakespearean adaptations to film. Many European critics praised it but most US critics, on the other hand, savaged it. This, in spite of the National Film Board of America's choice of *Macbeth* as best film of 1971.

Did the US critics react thus because Hugh Hefner's Playboy Club put up more than half the movie's budget, with the balance from Columbia Pictures for distribution rights. When asked for a comment, Roman Polanski responded succinctly: *"Pecunia non olet"* (money doesn't smell).

I met with Roman Polanski in November 1970. Our conversation was interrupted when his secretary entered the office to say she had Jackie Stewart, the racing driver, on the phone.

"'Excuse me," Polanski said, "I must take this call."

Jochen Rindt had been killed in a Grand Prix race the previous Saturday and Roman talked of this loss. He wound up their conversation with a chilling sentence: "Yeah — whad a year — whad a year." His wife, Sharon Tate, had been brutally murdered in Los Angeles less than a year before.

I was hired to play Caithness, which did not involve many lines of dialogue, but did have a lot of screen time, which on film can often be more effective than mere words. I was initially booked for twelve weeks but delays doubled this. Jon Finch played the title role, Francesca Annis as Lady Macbeth, and Martin Shaw as Banquo. At

A scene from *Macbeth* with Bruce Purchase in the title role and Susan Wooldridge as Lady Macbeth. This was the first production of the new Theatre Clwyd, opened by H.M. the Queen in the 1970s.

the start of my contract I was not called, although payments began. I was told delays on filming were caused by bad weather, but I later discovered it also had more to do with Roman's perfectionist zeal. "Thadd's mudge bedder. Fandastic. Okay, let's do it again. Action." Yes, take after take after take, until he got the print he wanted. The filming got way behind schedule and as the budget escalated the insurers tried to get Roman off the film. One morning he walked onto the set at Shepperton Studios waving an airline ticket, as he told us all: "Goodbye. Goodbye, thizz izz my larse day."

But help was at hand and I think Polanski knew it. Later that day Hugh Hefner flew into London in his big black Boeing with its white bunny logo on the tail and upped the budget, which saved the

103

day. Roman stayed on the movie until completion, months later.

Perhaps as a response to Hefner's largesse, Roman shot an extra scene one day at Shepperton. It was on the set of the witches' coven. Adorning the cave, a crowd of actresses of varying ages, all stark naked. We were by now into overtime. Roman shouted 'action' and the women burst into song — a rendition of 'Happy Birthday', sung to camera and addressed to Hugh Hefner. It was included with the rushes which were flown daily to Hefner in LA. Amusing at the time but now in our more politically correct age, viewed as exceedingly tasteless, I guess.

A companion piece to the above: Roman at breakfast in our hotel, whilst on location in North Wales, reading aloud a very funny description of masturbation from *Portnoy's Complaint*. His audience included Kenneth Tynan (at the same table), me at an adjacent table and a rather prim middle-aged waitress at Roman's elbow, there to ascertain if they wanted tea or coffee with their breakfast.

The endless delays enabled me and my wife Elspeth to take short holidays, to France, the West Country and Greece. I'd leave contact numbers with the first assistant director, Simon Relph, but we were never called back early.

One day at Shepperton the unit ran out of fake blood (sometimes referred to as Kensington Gore!), such was the demand. Unfazed, Roman instructed the prop-man to go to the studio canteen and bring back two catering size tins of red jam. The 'dead' bear in the film was then liberally smeared with the raspberry jam. I don't think the pips are visible on film!

And now for some gossip — late gossip, about an event over thirty years ago. We were shooting a banquet scene and I was hoping we'd not go into overtime as I had an interview at the Dorchester Hotel that evening. I mentioned my concern to a beautiful blonde extra alongside me at the banqueting table. I told her I was meeting ... let me refer to him as X — a film star who was to both direct and star in a film to be made in Europe. The blonde laughed when I mentioned X's name. "What a coincidence," she grinned, "because I'm also worried, because I too have an arrangement to meet with him tonight."

"For the film he's directing?"

"No," she smiled again, "I'm his girlfriend when he visits London from the States." Her appointment was 7.30 that evening and mine 8.45pm. It was my turn to laugh. We didn't over-run so I made it to the Dorchester on time.

X greeted me in a towelling robe at the door of his suite. In the lounge area I saw the door through to his bedroom was firmly shut. "The blonde is behind that door," I thought to myself.

Next morning we picked up from where we'd left off the day before and, as per continuity, the blonde alongside me again. She had indeed been in the bedroom during my chat with X, and smiled her beguiling smile:

"When he said," attempting to imitate X's American accent, "you're a very tall British actor. There's a paucity of tall British actors …" She enquired: "What does paucity mean?" I feigned ignorance: "Your guess is as good as mine — a shortage, perhaps," I punned.

X himself was unusually tall, though somewhat bandy-legged. I didn't get offered a role on his film, shot on Malta. Perhaps I was too tall or maybe had become complicit to the dalliance with the blonde. He was a married man and perhaps, between the sheets, the blonde had blabbed.

Another actor on *Macbeth*, a friend at the time of the following event, I'll also leave anonymous, for a different reason. I'll refer to him as Z.

On location alongside Banburgh Castle in Northumberland, the set-up for a battle involved principal actors and hundreds of extras, dressed as soldiers of the period. Preparation was taking a lot of time so Simon Relph suggested we principals, on horseback in the foreground, dismount for a break. We all, Z included, slipped from our saddles and our individual stand-ins replaced us on our horses.

As we hit the ground Polanski was walking rapidly past, absorbed in the minutiae of the set-up. Z imitated Roman's Polish accent, making a comment he obviously thought funny for as he turned away he laughed at his own witticism.

Roman was clearly not amused. He turned in his tracks and approached Z's departing back, at great speed. Having caught up from behind, he punched the actor forcefully in the kidneys. Z gave out a yelp of pain and was nearly felled by this powerful blow from the diminutive, extremely fit and agile director.

That evening back at the hotel I asked Roman why he'd punched Z.

"He was imitating me."

"'I sometimes do that myself, Roman."

"But you are never cruel. He was mocking me in front of the entire unit. Thadd's the difference."

After many months of filming we're near completion — the wrap.

"Charles Jarrot wants to meet you." The voice was that of our first assistant director, Simon Relph (who after a distinguished career as a producer became chairman of BAFTA in 2002).

"We won't need you for at least another hour, so pop across to his office now," Simon gave directions.

There is a widely held opinion that if you go to an interview dressed appropriately as the character you are being seen for, your chance of success is enhanced. This theory can be applied if it's a modern character, more difficult with historical/costume roles. Wearing 11th-century costume on your way to an interview in Soho Square would be somewhat over-the-top, certainly an embarrassment for this actor. But on this sunny day in 1971, walking from one sound stage at Shepperton to the next one I was not embarrassed and perfectly dressed for the interview in my costume as Caithness, for film director Charles Jarrot wished to interview me for the part of Lord Morton in *Mary Queen of Scots*.

As I entered his office he looked up from his desk and I was sure in that split second I had my next role in the bag. At that very agreeable meeting Charles told me an amusing story:

"With an office in LA," he said, "I was in pre-production for this film, when I received a telephone call from a top LA agent. This guy said he had a client who would be perfect for the role of Queen Mary. I enquired who and his suggestion dumbfounded me." The agent had put forward Barbra Streisand as perfect for the role, adding, "for instance did you see Barbra in ..." (naming a modern film of the period) — "where in one scene Barbra dressed up in period costume."

Jarrot cast the divine Vanessa Redgrave, who was indeed perfect in the role as Mary in *Mary Queen of Scots*. Glenda Jackson played Queen Elizabeth with other principal roles played by Patrick McGoohan, Trevor Howard, Ian Holm, Nigel Davenport and, yes, I did get to play Lord Morton.

I very nearly got to work with Roman Polanski again, many years later. It was arranged for me to fly from London to Paris to have lunch with him. I was happy at the prospect — of both lunch in Paris and working with Roman again, for our relationship on *Macbeth*

had been good. But the meeting was cancelled; Roman had decided to cast all the characters in the movie as older, probably because he cast Walter Mathau in the lead so all the other pirates had to be older. The film, *Pirates*, was made in Morocco but was not a success.

Mary Queen of Scots, unlike *Macbeth*, actually came in a week under schedule. I was on the Shepperton Studios back lot, reading a newspaper in between shots and noted our producer, Hal Wallis, had the previous day bought an Impressionist painting at auction in London, for a lot of money. I showed a fellow actor alongside me the article: "Hal Wallis has rewarded himself after bringing this film in under-budget. He's bought a fine painting with the difference."

As Lord Morton in Hal Wallis's production of *Mary Queen of Scots*.

Hal B Wallis, legendary old Hollywood producer, struck me as a curiously dull man. Clever at his job, obviously, but he was not a charismatic individual. Yet here was the man who had discovered both actor Humphrey Bogart and director John Huston. At our first meeting in Alnwick, in Northumberland, I rather naively raised this in conversation with him. "Yes," said Wallis, his voice flat, dull, "both very talented." He could have been talking about soap.

Another event a couple of weeks later showed a further oddity in the personality of Hal Wallis. We were filming in Scotland when the horse Vanessa Redgrave was riding stumbled on a bridge over a ravine. For a second or two the situation looked dangerous; Vanessa might be thrown off and fall to the rocks below. But the horse recovered its balance and all was well.

"Did you see," I said to the American publicity guy standing next to me, "in that instant of potential danger, Mr Wallis's hand went to his heart." The American's laconic reply: "Heart? Hal doesn't have one, and since when does one's heart sit on the right hand side of a person's chest? Hal, my young friend, was reaching for his wallet."

On a free day, Ian Holm (who played Rizzio), his then partner, Bee Gilbert, Maria Aitkin and myself crammed into Holm's MGBGT and headed off for a swim. Although summer, the water was very cold as we plunged into the surf. I said to Ian: "After I finish this film I'm going to play Othello at the Mermaid Theatre. You are an experienced classical actor, me a mere beginner — may I ask your advice?"

"Ask on," replied Ian.

"How should one, for instance, say the line 'Blood. Blood. Blood'?" I imitated Neddy Seagoon, from *The Goon Show*. Ian laughed, gave me no advice and we dived back into the sea with our nubile companions.

Fourteen years later. An office at Pinewood Studios:

"We've never met."

"Oh yes, we have met before," I said.

It was the mid-'80s and I was with veteran American film director Franklin Schaffner, to talk to him about a role in his next film, *Lionheart*. During most of the interview Schaffner sat sideways in his chair and didn't look at me, just listened to my answers.

"Oh, when did we meet before?" he muttered. I reminded him that fourteen years earlier, at Shepperton Studios the actor Michael Jayston had invited me to join him for lunch:

"And you, Mr Schaffner, were also at that table. You were in post-production on your film *Nicholas and Alexandra* [Jayston played Tsar Nicholas]."

Schaffner flicked me a glance. I continued:

"Michael Jayston told a story about you and your producer on that film, Sam Spiegel. Spiegel had announced he wanted everyone in a scene that would be shot the next day to come in early as he intended to re-write it that very evening. The next morning everyone gathered, but instead of handing out copies to the actors so they could read this new version, Spiegel himself read out the scene, playing all the characters, in his far-from-perfect English."

I paused in the telling. Schaffner did not move, his head inclined down in the direction of the floor in front of him.

"And …?" he said softly.

"Well, apparently Spiegel then turned to you, Mr Schaffner, and asked 'How does that sound, Frank?'"

"As Mike Jayston described it, you gave it a beat, Mr Schaffner, before replying, 'Jewish'."

Schaffner now turned slowly in his chair to face me. His gaze was steady and clear.

"You have a very good memory."

My next meeting with Frank Schaffner was a few weeks later in the wardrobe department at film studios in Budapest. I was dressed in armour and Frank had come to view the costume. I had just flown in from London, but he didn't greet me, concentrating instead on my costume. He made a few minor suggestions to the Italian designer, Nana Cecchi, then, as he departed, turned back and smiled warmly at me: "Welcome to the 12th century."

Lionheart was a story about the Children's Crusade. Hungary, in winter, was used as location for scenes set in Paris and northern France, and later in the New Year the film unit moved to Portugal to cover scenes set in the south of France and the Middle East.

I played a character called Simon Nerra, Duke of Burgundy, and American actor Eric Stolz played my 'son,' Robert. Frank Schaffner asked me to play my character with an American accent and because of this sensible decision I became: 'Simon Nair-ra, Dook of Burgundy'. Eric Stolz, both on and off screen insisted on always calling me 'Father,' and I went along with this strange 'method' charade. For instance, with Nana Cecchi and Eric in a Chinese restaurant in Portugal. Eric:

"May I have another glass of wine, Father?"

"No, Robert, you've had sufficient."

I was being naughty, but Eric/Robert obeyed anyway; not another drop did he imbibe that evening.

Apropos the Spiegel/Jewish story, I'm reminded of an event in Zagreb in the mid-'80s. We were filming *Wallenberg*, based on the Second World War exploits of Swedish diplomat Raoul Wallenberg (played by Richard Chamberlain), who saved many Jews' lives by issuing Swedish passports to them. In this film Zagreb became the setting for Budapest, where the actual events had occurred.

We were filming in the old town in Zagreb, and actor Ken Colley and I had broken early for lunch. Declining transportation, we decided to walk to a nearby restaurant together. This was not to work up an appetite, but rather … well, let me explain.

Ken and I walked, intentionally arm-in-arm, across the central square in Zagreb's Old Town. Ken was in the full dress uniform of a German SS officer and I in the garb of a Hassidic rabbi. Yet for the local passers-by we might as well have been invisible for the attention we attracted — none in fact. All eyes were averted. We progressed arm-in-arm across the beautiful old square.

I had been told that during the war Hitler promised that the Croatian people would be given complete autonomy if they offered up to Germany their Jewish population. Croatia went along with this deal and some 30,000 Croatian Jews perished in the death camps. The promise of autonomy was never fulfilled, as Germany lost the war.

A curiously macabre statistic in more recent years. In the Kosovan war, the loss of life mirrored the Jewish loss — about 30,000 — and that too was about autonomy!

But as Ken Colley and I walked across the square that day we were only aware of the local Jewish devastation — Kosovo etc was still a few years off.

As we turned a corner into a street that led off this square we met a bunch of Israeli tourists. They did stare at us.

"What are you filming?" their tour guide asked. We told him.

"Ah, Wallenberg. Wallenberg." Then turning to Ken, in his SS uniform: "And who are you playing?"

"Eichmann," replied Ken. Adolf Eichmann, responsible for the transport of European Jews to the death camps. After the war he was captured in South America and tried and hanged in Israel in 1960 for his heinous crimes.

"Ah … Eichmann. Eichmann," the tour guide sighed.

I piped up: "And you can have one guess what I'm playing." Dressed as I was, as a rabbi, the Israeli tour guide looked me up and down and smiled: "Vot — only vun guess?"

At one point in my book, *How a Film is Made*, I wrote:

> The camera team consists of the lighting cameraman (arguably the second, if not the first, most important person on the set) the camera operator, focus puller, and clapper/loader. The person in charge of sound recording is the sound recordist and his main aide is the boom operator. He is the one who holds the microphone, attached to a long pole, over the actors' heads (but always out of shot). You need strong arms — I know, I tried it once.

Sometimes cameras are put on top of a crane for a wide shot, to get a bird's-eye view of the action below. The cranes are enormous but highly manoeuvrable, and can swing up and down as required.

On *Lionheart*, the camera operator told me this story:

> When we were setting up for a wide shot on the battle scene which you were involved in, Bruce, I was behind camera on the crane when Frank Schaffner wandered over and asked to be shown the angle of the shot. Up went the crane, Schaffner beside me, to the planned POV. But Schaffner asked to go even higher, then higher until finally at maximum height. At that stage of filming I'd barely spoken to Frank and as I was somewhat shy of him, didn't comment that we couldn't surely be shooting the scene at maximum height. Below on the ground dozens of horses, riders and technicians were milling about. Frank asked me for a cigarette. He puffed in silence for a minute or two, then said:
>
> "Nice and quiet up here, isn't it?"
>
> He'd just wanted a break!

The day I left my home in Oxford, I was picked up by a chauffeur-driven car for the drive to Heathrow Airport. Light snow was falling as we took off, but when we landed in Budapest the snow lay thick on the ground. Budapest is the capital of Hungary and has been described as the Paris of the East.

An old mate, Nick Clay, and I flew from London to Budapest on the same flight. We ignored the caviar shop at Heathrow, believing we'd find a constant cheap supply of this delicious stuff in Budapest. But it proved more difficult than we'd imagined. We enquired unsuccessfully for a week (even phoning the Russian Embassy), but finally struck gold at the American-owned Forum Hotel.

After we had collected our daily expense money paid in local currency, we went on for dinner in a nearby restaurant. A violinist and singer serenaded us at table. Once they discovered we were English-speaking, they played and sang 'Daisy, Daisy, give me your answer do' for us … perhaps not appropriate but fun nonetheless.

During our dinner I told Nick I'd been similarly serenaded seven years earlier, that time in a bar in Prague. At the time, Czechoslovakia was still under the heel of Communist rule. I'd been working in that country on an American re-make of *All Quiet on the Western Front*, and at the completion of my small contribution to that movie, a car was designated to take me to the airport to fly back to London. But I told the American first assistant director I wanted to take the opportunity to visit Prague for the first time.

"Where will you stay?"

"I'll find a cheap hotel."

But our first assistant director had a much better suggestion.

"No," he said. "I'll arrange for you to stay in our producer Norman Rosemont's suite at the Intercontinental."

"But I can't afford that."

"No charge, Bruce. The suite's at present paid for, but unoccupied — Norman's in LA. I'll tell the hotel to expect you."

"But what should I do about food and drinks?"

"Just sign for it — it can go on the tab."

I wonder if Rosemont ever heard about that arrangement. By then, it has to be said, I was off the payroll and suites at the Intercontinental were never part of my contract.

In Prague I used my unspent per diem, which was paid in local currency that I couldn't take out of the country, by purchasing a suitcase and then filling it with wonderful, Russian classical recordings, which were so very cheap compared to the UK.

On my first evening in Prague I'd decided to go to Prague Castle to attend a Bedřich Smetana concert.

In the late 1970s there were few foreign tourists in Prague, and some Czechs assumed me to be a Russian soldier in civvies because of my hair, which had been cropped for *All Quiet on the Western Front*. Some folk in the streets muttered under their breath and spat on the pavement, which I found unnerving. On the way to the concert I crossed the river via the beautiful Charles Bridge (deserted in those pre-tourist days) and made my way through the narrow lanes up the hill in the direction of the castle.

With time to spare, I stopped off at a bar called the Napoleon for a beer. The bar was packed, only one chair unoccupied at the corner of a long table. The group at the table obviously knew one another.

I attracted the attention of a guy next to the empty chair. He assumed I was Russian and spoke to me in that language. I looked nonplussed, so he tried German but I still showed ignorance of that language. So he tried English.

"What do you want?" He was not friendly.

"Can I use this chair?" I responded politely.

"For how long?" he said bluntly.

At that moment the beer I'd paid for on my entrance was delivered by the waiter.

"As long as it takes me to consume this beer."

"All right." He reluctantly allowed me to sit.

As I sipped my beer, deliberately very slowly, I got mad. Fuck it, I thought, what a churlish attitude on the part of this Czech. So I ordered another beer from a passing waiter. During this, I didn't make eye contact with any of the group around the table. When my second beer arrived, the waiter placed it on the table along with a very large glass of what turned out to be a strong, locally made spirit. Puzzled, I went to pay — at least for the ordered beer, but the waiter shrugged and indicated the others at the table. I glanced at the group. They were all smiling as they'd decided I was okay. Glasses were raised.

They were all lecturers in the English Department at Charles University in Prague. Once they'd realised I wasn't Russian they became very friendly and when they discovered I was a New Zealander my stock soared even higher. They had a New Zealander working in their midst, the academic Ian Milner.

The other folk in the crowded bar quickly got to hear there was an English speaker in the bar. (I never did get to the Smetana concert at Prague Castle that night) and that was when I got my Prague Serenade. A guy approached the table and sang — well, it sounded like:

"John a Brown a body lie
A mole-drin in the gray-bah.
John a Brown a body lie
A mole-drin in the gray-bah ..."

Naturally I applauded him, though the song would have been more appropriately sung for an American. But by then, Nick, this guy was in full flow. He sang a second number, also in execrable English.

"Yedd-er-day,
Boom, Boom, Boom, Boom, Boom, Boom
Yedd-er-day — etc etc ..."

Apologies to you, Sir Paul McCartney. At the end of a very merry evening two of the lecturers in the group, going in my direction, kindly escorted me back to the Intercontinental, but wouldn't come in when I invited them for a nightcap.

"We'd be stopped before getting halfway across the foyer."

Life under communism.

My dear mate Nick Clay, who I'd known since Nottingham Playhouse days in the early 1970s, died, tragically young, at fifty. I'll always miss him. "But didn't we have such fun, Nick, in Budapest? All that caviar ..."

Cut to the mid-'80s. I'm playing Squire Trelawney in a Disney/ Harlech production of *Return to Treasure Island*, directed by Piers Haggard, who I'd known since the early '60s with the National Theatre at the Old Vic, where he was an assistant director.

Return to Treasure Island was mostly shot in Jamaica, but some scenes were also shot in South Wales, near Cardiff.

My first contribution to filming was atop a Welsh mountain. It was a freezing night and outdoors I had to shout a lot. Unusually for me, I lost my voice. By the next day I could barely summon up a croak, yet was scheduled to do two long scenes with a lot of dialogue, although thankfully indoors, in an inn with a roaring fire.

Piers said: "Have a go — we'll re-voice you at a later date, if need be." The scratchy voice I produced suited Trelawney's character so all I had to do, when my normal voice returned, was to imitate my croaking for the duration of filming.

There were two good chums on that job — Ken Colley (mentioned, as Eichmann) and Peter Copley. A group of us celebrated Peter's 70th birthday on the beach in front of our hotel, the Intercontinental, at Ocho Rios, in Jamaica. Peter and other celebrators at this impromptu gathering witnessed my attempt to jet-ski.

I lay, as instructed, on my tummy at the water's edge, arms outstretched before me, gripping the handlebars of the jet-ski. I bade farewell to my gathered chums and gunned the throttle, taking off immediately at immense speed. Once in the sea, again as instructed, I heaved my legs up out of the water onto the craft, into a kneeling position. The next instructed move was to stand up on the jet-ski but I didn't have the nerve to do that.

After a few helter-skelter moments of bouncing over the azure water I realised I was nearing the exit of the bay, out to the open sea where, I thought with horror, the sharks lived. How do I turn this infernal machine, I shouted to myself. Whatever I did do was wrong, for as I swerved the jet-ski left, I tumbled off. But when a rider loses his mount, the clever jet-ski is programmed to slowly putt-putt in a gentle, tight circle until the rider climbs on again. As I swam towards the craft, I thought: It looks a bit like a shark eyeing up its prey. With difficulty I swung the throttle and clambered aboard as it zoomed forward. My arms were weakening but there I was heading back towards land, at speed. Then more panic, as ahead of me a cruise ship was approaching, heading for the open sea. A quick decision had to be made. I turned left for a second time, and with the same result. In the water once more, my faithful jet-ski putt-putted around. The ship by now was gaining ground but veering slightly away from me.

My arms now weakened, this second attempt to remount my steed was a total disaster. I gunned the throttle but didn't get aboard fast enough. So what happened? Well, the jet stream blew my swimming costume off. That's what happened!

The cruise ship drew level as, with arms and legs flailing in the clear blue water, I struggled to retrieve my bathing costume, down around one ankle. Sixty feet off to my right the ship passed slowly, its decks crowded with passengers all enjoying my predicament.

Jet-skiing nearly turned to tragedy for another cast member in Jamaica. A beautiful South American actress on the shoot tried her hand at it but lost control and hit a mooring rope. They had to film her in profile for the rest of the movie, one side of her face badly bruised, the other side unmarked.

Another bruising happened during the filming of *Lionheart* when in Budapest. The actress who was to play my wife fell in her suite at the hotel on the night of her arrival. At breakfast the next morning her face was badly bruised. She was upbeat, believing the swelling would go down before filming began the next day. What she didn't know was that a decision had been taken shortly after her fall and as we spoke over breakfast, the Australian actress Penny Downie was already *en route* to Hungary to replace her.

Two more stories from my time in Jamaica. Both mention Noel Coward, who lived in Jamaica and is buried there. We'd filmed in a beautiful deserted cove near Ocho Rios, arriving and departing by sea in a flotilla of small boats. On a free day a few of us decided to return to this idyllic spot. Armed with a map we borrowed a film unit vehicle, and after a long bumpy ride down a rough track off the main road we found this magical cove, deserted, though a passing local later offered to knock down a few coconuts for our use before he sauntered off again. Shaded by a palm shelter and with a chilly bin filled with food and drink we enjoyed our day from early morning till dusk, reading, talking, swimming and sunbathing. Bliss.

Around mid-afternoon, however, a jeep appeared down the dusty track and from this vehicle stepped an elderly man, patrician-looking, ramrod straight and very fit. He didn't acknowledge us, entered the water and swam off into the distance with an effortless overarm style — an Aussie crawl like I had been taught as a boy. Half an hour later I saw this same interesting man swimming back to the beach and placed myself at hip height in the water, determined to meet him. As he found his feet in the shallows of the cove he greeted me. His accent seemed frozen in time — an upper-class English accent but from an earlier age. Not unlike Robert Graves when I'd heard him read at the Mermaid Theatre in the early '70s — a classic accent from the past — the delivery of an expatriate, which I assumed this gentleman to be. Phonetically he sounded a bit like this:

"Heh-leow. Are you in Jam-may-ah-ka, on hol-id-daay?" His manner fearfully grand, but not unfriendly. I explained we were filming on the island.

"Oh — end are you the die-rek-torr?"

I told him I was playing Squire Trelawney.

"Oh — en, eck-torr. Did you kneow Nerl?"

I correctly assumed he was referring to Noel Coward, The Master, who'd lived up the coast from Ocho Rios.

"Yes," I replied, "I worked with him at the National Theatre in the mid-'60s."

"Enn did you also kneow Ee-ann?"

I guessed that he was referring to Ian ('James Bond') Fleming, a near neighbour of Noel Coward in Jamaica. Operating within the framework of first-name reference, I replied: "No, I've never met Ian." This strange, elegant man, like a person from another planet continued: "Nerl wuz a free-end [friend] of marn, but in lay-ah-ter years, beck-em a tebbil [terrible] rec-clewse!"

Was Fleming also a friend of his, I enquired 'innocently', keen to know more, as I found this character standing in the water fascinating.

"Oh yarzz. But Ee-an's warff, Enn [Anne] hay-ett-ed Jam-may-ah-ka, sew Ee-an orf-tern spent tarm he-ah al-eow-on. But he did hevv a summah warf" [a summer wife!]. He named her. "She lived up thaar ..." (gesturing in the direction of the hills in the distance behind us) — "she daard [died] own-leh the other dee-ay. In Ey-ens ebsence, she'd plawnt [plant] his gordon [garden], but wee-an Ey-ann [Anne again] kem ee-owt [out] to slum it hee-ah, she'd tarr [tear] the plawnts ee-owt of the garden — and the-row them awehh."

I was by now entranced, or rather enn-trenssed, and asked him: "You live permanently in Jamaica?"

"Oh, yaarz."

"When were you last in Britain?" His answer startled me:

"Whee-en ah wuz en under-gred-you-ett [undergraduate] in the narn-teen twenn-tays."

117

I then walked into the trap. I should have guessed:

"Oh — and how long have you lived in Jamaica?" His answer was a complete surprise:

"'Since — seven-teen-fifteh."

The penny had finally dropped and I realised he was from old colonial gentry. He'd just told me his family had lived in Jamaica since the 18th century — "since — seven-teen-fifteh." 1750!

The other story that involved that marvellous entertainer, playwright, actor, Noel Coward: Peter Copley and I visited his old house on Jamaica, in the company of the German wife of an actor on our shoot who was filming that day.

Noel Coward's old house stands high in the hills with a magnificent view of the coast and sea below. Below, way below, is Ian Fleming's old house, level with the beach and sea. Coward's house, now designated as a museum by the Jamaican government, is as he left it. He died in the house and is buried in a corner where his swimming pool, now filled in, stood. In a garden of about an acre a simple headstone marks his final resting place.

The wardrobe is still filled with his colourful Jamaican shirts, and sheet music is still in place on the grand piano in the small open-sided living area, along with framed photographs of celebrities who visited him. A kitchen is at the back of the house, along with a bathroom and bedroom for his home help. A tiny house. I wonder where his guests laid their heads? One sheet of music prominently on view beside the piano was a copy of his composition, *Don't Let's Be Beastly to the Germans*. Our rather humourless fellow traveller, the German wife, was puzzled and enquired what this title meant. I decided to avoid her question:

"Ah well, that's virtually untranslatable." A version of: "Don't mention the war."

As we departed Coward's simple but beautiful Jamaican home, our guide, who had been Coward's manservant, farewelled us and I said to him: "You must still miss Sir Noel?" His reply was dignified, softly spoken: "Every day," he said.

Back at our hotel, actor Donald Pickering was keen to hear about our visit and Peter Copley described it in detail while I embellished the story: "Yes," I chipped in on Copley, saying to Pickering "...

we did enjoy the experience, but, Donald, I have to admit that I did something you will consider quite dreadful." In saying the word 'dreadful', I gave a passable imitation of Noel Coward's idiosyncratic delivery of that word.

"What did you do, Bruce?" said Pickering.

I told him that prior to our visit I'd soaked an old photograph of myself (circa 1967) in tea "to age it, Donald," and went on to explain I'd placed it in a beautiful silver frame, after writing a message on the photograph: "Thank you Noel for a wonderful visit, Ever, Bruce ..." and had left it on Coward's piano, along with the other photographs, framed, of famous folk, which, as I remember included one from Queen Elizabeth, the Queen Mother.

Pickering was horrified: "You didn't?" he said, in alarm. Donald was so upset at what he clearly deemed a sacrilege, I decided to cut the practical joke.

"No, Donald — I didn't — but I could have done so."

"Oh, Purchase, you are a beast."

"Yes, Donald, just — too, too beast-ly." I told him about the German woman's puzzlement over that word on the sheet music and that amused him.

Practical jokes are often perpetrated in our business, sometimes to alleviate boredom during filming delays. One I carried out on the Jamaican shoot involved director Piers Haggard and a few executives flown in from LA's Disney Productions. I persuaded the wig girls on location to dye one of my powdered 18th-century wigs *pink* and turned up on the set wearing it. The Disney folk and Piers were lunching under an awning out of the sun as I approached. They were deep in conversation. I butted in, saying to Piers, my voice seemingly irate:

"Sorry to interrupt, Piers, but surely, as Trelawney, you don't want me to wear this vivid pink wig on this film?" Piers looked startled, saw me in the dyed monstrosity — vivid, luminescent pink, blindingly so, for the wig girls had done an excellent job.

Piers, a fine director who I'd often worked with, is not noted for having much of a sense of humour, and his reaction was a joy to behold as he looked up at me with complete incomprehension. I ploughed on: "For God's sake, I know this is a Disney production but this coloured wig is nonsense. It makes me look like a Disney cartoon character."

By now the Disney representatives had clocked the wind-up and were chuckling, so the moment was saved. A beat later Piers realised it was a joke, so I whipped off the wig and joined the group for lunch. A few weeks later I'd meet a couple of the Disney group in Los Angeles at the Disney Studios and they enjoyed describing the scene to others.

When any actor had a few days, say a week, free from filming in Jamaica, they would be flown back to the UK — it was cheaper for the company than the price of the hotel and paying per diems. I noted I had a two-week break in the schedule, but with my marriage crumbling, indeed in freefall, I came up with an alternative idea. I decided to travel instead to New York and Los Angeles. Placing the cost the company would spend flying me to and from Heathrow against my proposed American junket, I asked the production office to book my flights and bill me for the difference. It turned out I only owed $US250 to make up the extra.

In New York I stayed with my old RADA friend, Barbara Caruso, and my chums in Manhattan were unemployed at the time. Because I had some money available I was able to be generous to these friends — lunches out, etc and therefore we all had a good time in the 'Apple'. By the time I flew on from there to LA I had blown my cash and so in California I would have to rely on my credit cards. The saying 'give and you shall receive' never proved truer in this case. My friends in LA were all employed and very generous: "No, put your card away, Purchase, we'll pay for this." In fact they were unaware I was strapped for cash. I was also lent a car and an apartment and one day a tour in a limousine provided by Disney Pictures. An LA mate, first assistant director Peter Bogart was working on a Disney film *Down and Out in Beverly Hills*, which starred Nick Nolte and Bette Midler. I was invited on set (Peter's mother was the designer on the film) and that day, because Midler's schedule was heavy, I was lent her limousine with her female driver, for my sole use from sun-up to sun-down.

But my time in LA was cut short. The phone beside my bed rang at about 8a.m. A voice, that of a woman with a Welsh accent, informed me I was needed back in Jamaica earlier than planned — the schedule had changed. With a switch of plane at Denver and again in Miami, I got back with time in hand. The production office in Jamaica had been unable to get through to me, so the Welsh woman was calling from Harlech TV's head office in Cardiff — a circuitous route before the call to return reached me.

Something even more remarkably circuitous happened to me in 1984. I'd been offered a film role in New Zealand and the contract had included a first-class return ticket from the UK.

Before I was due to fly out to New Zealand I'd been working on a BBC TV series, filming first in Birmingham and then, after a two-week break, on the Isle of Man. As my break began I received news that my mother, in Auckland, had had a stroke. I was due to travel to New Zealand in a month but decided to use the fortnight's vacation and head to New Zealand, then return to film on the Isle of Man. The New Zealand film company helped out. I flew out, at their expense, immediately, but tourist class and then back to the UK. This enabled me to be with my ailing mother for ten days. She died the night I flew back to the UK, so on my return to New Zealand after work on the Isle of Man my earlier time with her seemed a dream — a very precious dream.

When I said farewell to her my last words were: "I'll see you in two weeks, Mum." She smiled serenely but a few hours later gently let go of her life, when I by then was in the air over India. Within a month I'd flown 36,000 miles — twelve thousand to get to see her, twelve to get back to the Isle of Man plus another twelve thousand back to New Zealand to commence work on *Other Halves*. Lots of air miles, which even included a side trip to Australia — Sydney, Melbourne and Adelaide then back to the UK again. Within three months a total of 52,000 miles spent on aircraft.

My instinct to fly out to see my mother I have, of course, never regretted. Irreplaceable time spent in her company.

The life of an actor often involves a lot of travel, and in both theatre and film I've been much blessed in this respect. Apart from some of the places already mentioned, film locations have also included Tunisia, Spain, Italy and Morocco, twice.

Some time after the break-up of my marriage I rented a house on the Greek island of Corfu and toyed with the idea of buying an old property to do up. I rented a house high on the hills above the seaside resort of Nissaki, with magnificent views across the expanse of sea to Albania and mainland Greece. It was bliss for a time. I commuted to work on films whilst filling my spare time writing a book on musical theatre, later published by MacMillan. On the terrace of this house I punched away on an old typewriter with a break early a.m. — on my scooter down to the sea for a swim, and again in the late afternoon.

Two stories from this period are worth recounting: the first, amusing, the second, rather dangerous.

On Corfu I'd sometimes take a day off from writing and borrow or rent a boat to speed off up the coast for a bit of fun. The Tourist Office at Nissaki was my contact point for telephone calls and mail and Judy Mackrell, who owned this firm, always knew my whereabouts at any given time. I did not have a phone at my eyrie on the hill. One day I sped up the coast and moored in a pleasant bay to take lunch at the taverna on the edge of the water. I'd barely finished my grilled fish and taken a sip of my retsina when another speedboat entered the bay, slowed, and a voice called out: "Phone your agent, Bruce. You have to be in Madrid the day after tomorrow."

Later that day I flew to London for a costume fitting at Bermans and a day later, with the costume in my luggage, flew to Madrid to commence work on a film called *Casanova*. After a week or so in Spain, the whole unit moved to Venice to complete the filming.

One vivid Venetian scene was a long tracking shot with dialogue between Richard Chamberlain and myself. It was the last day of filming and time only to do two takes before we lost the light. This scene took place on one of the islands and all the motorised boat traffic had been halted for shooting. We completed two takes, the light about to go — the sun sinking rapidly behind the dome of a church on an adjacent island.

"Check the gate," the first assistant director said.

"Clear."

"Okay. It's a wrap."

The first assistant director spoke into his radio and almost immediately the motorised boat traffic started up again. A billionaire could not have bought the peace we enjoyed during that silent hour. We saw Venezia as Canaletto must have experienced it, with just gondolas bobbing about on the blue sea.

The sun went down and next day I flew to London, then back to my sybaritic life on Corfu: tap, tap, tap on the typewriter in between, "Oh, I do believe it's time to have a swim."

The other yarn from Corfu: I was having a drink with John and Mitzi Davies at their villa at Nissaki. We could hear a storm raging on the other side of the island. I thought when I walked down to my motorbike I'd timed my departure perfectly, for I wanted to get to my house in the hills before the storm crossed to our side of the island. But my bike wouldn't start, so I had to push it downhill to fire the engine and by then I'd lost precious minutes. Halfway up the narrow winding road to my village the storm arrived, fork lightning and heavy rain accompanied by gale-force wind. I was frightened but made it to the central square of the village and parked a hundred yards from my house. It was only when I switched off the engine and lights of my bike that I realised that power to the village had been cut by the storm. In between flashes of fork lightning it was pitch black. I waited for another flash, took my bearings and ran for home as everything went to black once more. Seconds later I found myself, like some cartoon character, in mid-air, and falling. Off the square to the left is a terraced cliff and I misjudged direction in the dark and ran over this dangerous drop.

In that split mid-air second, I thought, what a way to die. But, as luck would have it, I landed with a bump on the second terrace down. I recovered myself, clambered up to the road (I'd fallen about sixteen feet) and eventually, shaking with the shock of the experience, made it to the safety of my house, where from a window I watched the rest of the spectacular light show.

*

"What a pity we couldn't have had the Pope visit us during our filming." Herbie Wise was addressing this comment to a Polish priest, advisor on the film Wise was directing on location in Rome. "Why didn't you ask me sooner?" the priest replied.

It was our last day in Rome and we were lunching on a terrace

Being made up as a serial killer in Ruth Rendell's *The Strawberry Tree*, filmed in 1993 in Majorca with Lisa Harrow. Director Herbert Wise is also in the photo.

overlooking the city. Albert Finney and Brian Cox were also present.

The Polish priest left the table briefly and returned to tell us he'd spoken to His Holiness, but as the Pope was to leave for a visit to South America in a few days, he could not spare the time. It was the late 1970s and Albert Finney was playing the Pope in a film about his life, and I played a friend of the Pope — a Polish journalist in Rome. This priest/advisor to the film company told us that the Pope often ate out in restaurants in Rome. He'd wear a suit and dine publicly with friends and colleagues from the Vatican. Although immediately recognisable, he was never bothered by the public — it was after all, a night off for him. He expected no deference and was treated as your average customer by restaurant staff. No fuss made.

Whilst on the subject of filming, one last story — a sobering tale to do with the fragility of fame. Not mine, I hasten to add, for I've always been just a jobbing actor on celluloid.

Once again working under the direction of Herbert Wise (in the 1990s), I was playing a serial killer in a TV production for Granada of a Ruth Rendell story, *The Strawberry Tree*. We were filming on Majorca. Travelling in a mini-bus to our day's location early one morning, I recounted to the others on the bus the following tale, which had been told to me by an English actor, long resident in the USA.

"Richard told me he was waiting to meet with a film director in LA. In a large foyer he was absorbed, reading the script." The mini-bus rattled on towards the bay where we were to shoot. I continued: "A young female PA approached an elderly man on the other side of the room. The young woman, late teens, asked the old man:

"'Are you here to meet with Mr …?'

"'Yes', murmured the old man. Richard said he barely registered this exchange, as he was concentrating on his own script. The girl then asked for the old man's name to check it against her list.

"'Steiger,' the old man replied and Richard looked up.

"My God, it's Rod Steiger, it really is, thought Richard.

"'How do you spell that, sir?' the young girl asked and Steiger politely spelt out his famous surname. 'And your first name, sir?'

"'Rod,' adding helpfully 'R-O-D'."

Those on the mini-bus that morning reacted:

"Oh my God …"

"You mean to say …"

"And she didn't know …"

There was a pause, as the reaction subsided and into that pause, the one person who hadn't reacted to the story turned to me.

"But who is Rod Steiger?" said the seventeen-year-old alongside me (an actress on this job).

*

How a Film is Made (MacMillan Education) — an excerpt from the end of my book:

So here I am at the top of a ladder, the old familiar story: paint-pot balanced, brush poised, out of work and filling in time with some

home decorating whilst waiting for that phone to ring … hold on …
… is it? … yes, it is ringing. Mind the paint pot."

INTERIOR: PAINT POT AND BRUSH PUT DOWN
CAREFULLY. THE ACTOR RUNS TO THE TELEPHONE
TRIPPING OVER THE SLEEPING DOG ON HIS WAY. HE
LIFTS THE RECEIVER. PAINT ALL OVER THE HAND SET.
DOG BARKS.

ACTOR:(TO DOG) Be quiet.

(INTO PHONE): Hello.

HE LISTENS TO THE VOICE ON THE LINE.

Yes … yes … yes, I would be very interested.

PAUSE AS HE LISTENS AGAIN

Did you say Timbuktu?

Yes I'd love to take it.

THE END
ROLL CREDITS

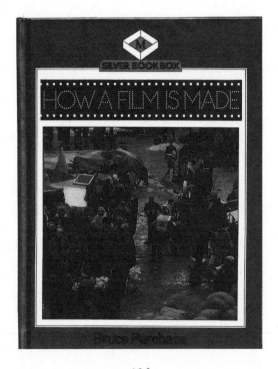

VI

Cut above the rest

WATCHING FROM MY VIEWPOINT IN THE DARKENED WINGS of the Old Vic, I can see, without being seen, the elderly figure of one of the finest acting talents of 20th-century British theatre as he slowly makes his entry, tottering from the offstage area opposite me into the blinding light of the stage.

I'm twenty-four, recently graduated from RADA. I've only ever seen him before on film.

Now, I watch this brilliant actor as he makes a precarious entrance in Michael Elliot's superb 1962 production of Ibsen's *Peer Gynt*. The actor, Wilfred Lawson, is playing the Button Molder.

But first, let me explain my personal interest in Wilfred Lawson.

My mother had known Lawson when she was growing up in North Wales and he played summer seasons at the repertory theatre in her home town, Colwyn Bay. Wilfred always stayed in her family home as my great-grandparents offered good yet reasonably priced lodgings to actors when they came to work for the local theatre. My great-grandfather ran bathing huts on that bit of the Welsh coast.

By 1962 I was working as a dresser at the Old Vic on the Cut at Waterloo. I asked Wilfred about his days at Colwyn Bay. Did he remember his lodgings? Did he recall my mother, then a little girl? Wilfred appeared delighted to have his memory jogged about his early life as an actor in the provinces. He replied in his inimitable fluting voice:

"Madge, oh yes, little Marjorie. A charming bright wee child. Yes," he beamed, "I do remember little Madge. And you say, young man, you are her son?"

The film I first saw Wilfred in was at the Regent in Thames, my home town in New Zealand. I was eleven at the time and learning

127

to call cinemas 'theatres' as is still done in theatrically-deprived New Zealand. My mother took me to see the film version of Shaw's *Pygmalion*, starring Leslie Howard as Professor Higgins, Wendy Hiller as Eliza, and Wilfred as Eliza's dad, Doolittle, the dustman philosopher. I thought at the time the actress Wendy Hiller a dead ringer for my mother and was deeply impressed she had known Lawson: a charismatic figure up there on the silver screen. After all, in Thames we didn't get to bump into film stars in the street!

Forty-six years after that visit to our picture house I got to play Doolittle myself in an enjoyable production of the musical version of the play *My Fair Lady* with Richard Chamberlain as Professor Higgins. But that's a story elsewhere in this book.

Back to 1962 and the Old Vic Theatre.

Now I gazed live at Lawson on the stage in front of me, hypnotized by his performance, trying to comprehend his mesmeric talent — to discern the cogs and wheels of his technique. How did he do it — do so very little — and yet appear so magical?

By the early '60s he was old and frail, yet his candle still burned, flickering by then perhaps, but with a still visible flame.

Prior to his entrance as the Button Molder, Wilfred had been escorted into the wings by a stage manager. Before he went on-stage the attentive ASM handed him his prop (the button mold attached at the end of a short pole) and when his cue came up to enter, he would gently tap the old actor on the shoulder. Then it was up to Wilfred …

Stories about him then were legendary. Some may be apocryphal, but nonetheless capture the essence of a magical talent.

One story involved the temperamental Scots actor, Nicol Williamson. Lawson had returned late to rehearsal after a 'liquid' lunch. The room fell silent as he entered. Actors should never be late, yet for a moment no one spoke. Then, suddenly the talented Williamson took it upon himself to admonish the old man. With his customary verve, Williamson berated Wilfred, tearing a strip off his senior. The sheer vitriol of the attack embarrassed everyone in the room. Finally exhausting his repertoire of abuse, he fell silent.

Into this silence Wilfred calmly replied, as if referring to a section of the play to be rehearsed:

"Hmm. I thought that bit had been cut."

Returning to my point of view in the wings. As Lawson entered the light, Leo McKern, playing the title role of Peer Gynt, would say: "Who are you?" In the text, Wilfred's reply was: "I am the Button Molder." But in one performance I watched him make a mistake.

"Who are you?" said McKern. Wilfred replied, "I am the Mutton Bolder," adding swiftly, seamlessly, as if the addition was part of the actual line, "… oh fuck," even touching perfectly, the final consonant 'k'. But I believe because it was so smoothly delivered as one whole line, in Wilfred's idiosyncratic fluting voice, the audience probably didn't notice the mistake. On the other hand, Leo McKern's face was a study as he resisted the urge to laugh outright.

*

"How's the play going, Wilfred?" the young Richard Burton asked Lawson outside a West End theatre where Lawson was starring in a successful London production. It was an hour before curtain-up. Wilfred replied: "Very well. Very well. Would you like to see it?" With that he took Burton up into the empty circle where they sat and chatted. Time passed. Eventually in dribs and drabs the audience came in and took their seats.

Burton assumed Wilfred would depart for backstage when needed. They talked on but then the house lights dimmed and the curtain rose. Two actors walked on stage and the performance commenced. Burton glanced enquiringly at Wilfred but the old man's concentration was towards the stage below.

Minutes passed as the first scene of the play developed. A door upstage opened to admit another character to the action. Lawson turned to Burton and whispered conspiratorially: "You'll like this bit, for this is where I come on!"

Burton was baffled, until he clicked on that an understudy was filling Wilfred's role that night.

When I witnessed Lawson as the Button Molder I was working by night as a dresser at the Old Vic and by day rehearsing Shakespeare's *Richard III*. That production was destined for what turned out to be an extremely wet outdoors summer season at Ludlow Castle in Shropshire.

After a day at rehearsal and about an hour before *Peer Gynt*'s curtain-up, I was enjoying a pint in the pub next to the stage door on the Waterloo Road side of the Old Vic.

Wilfred entered the bar, accompanied by two disreputable-looking meths drinkers, *habitués* of the park opposite the front entrance. Barely over the threshold, the group were swiftly intercepted by Patrick, the pub's Irish landlord.

"Mr Lawson ..."

"Call me Wilfred, Patrick, for Wilfred surely is my name."

"Wilfred ..."

"Thank you, Pat. Make mine a large ..."

"Mr Lawson ..."

"No, Patrick — Wilfred."

"Sir," said Pat, firmly, "you are always welcome but not, sir, these other gentlemen."

Wilfred fluted mournfully: "But they're my friends!" He knew the game was up though and shepherded his companions out through the saloon door they'd entered seconds before.

After graduating from RADA I'd appeared in a West End production which had but a short run at the Strand Theatre. This was *The New Men*, an adaptation of CP Snow's novel. Then to the old Rep Theatre at Guildford where I played Fluellen in *Henry V*. Then my tenure as a dresser at the Vic, onwards to the season at Ludlow Castle followed by a season of plays at the Ipswich Repertory Theatre, where a fellow company member was the young Ian McKellen, our paths destined to cross time and again professionally.

While at Ipswich I was invited — out of the blue, or so it seemed — to audition for the newly forming National Theatre and after two auditions I was accepted into the company. Going back a year after my tenure as a dresser to what was, and still is, my favourite theatre in Britain. For me the Old Vic always was a cut above in all its activities.

The earlier job at the old Repertory Theatre at Guildford had been fortunate. I later discovered the invitation to audition for the National arose out of my appearance there as Fluellen in *Henry V*.

"Burning our theatres behind us!" I'd said, during a round of golf. I was talking to Corin Redgrave, who had played the title role in

With Ian McKellen *Salad Days*. Ipswich repertory 1962.

Henry V because, as we played golf that day, a few months after our season at Guildford, we'd just heard our old theatre had been burnt to the ground.

During that production, after a matinée which Corin's father Sir Michael had attended (but we'd not met) I'd said to Corin:

"Did your father like the show?"

"Loved you. Hated me," Corin grinned, ruefully.

Yes, that performance served me well. Sir Michael Redgrave recommended me to Olivier, which is how I came to be plucked out of the relative obscurity of Rep at Ipswich. At the same time Ian McKellen too got a break when Tyrone Guthrie cast him as Aufidius in *Coriolanus*, for the première production at the new Nottingham Playhouse — John Neville in the title role. Two years later Ian and I re-met as fellow players in Franco Zeffirelli's stunning production of *Much Ado about Nothing* with the National at the Vic.

Both Corin's father and his sister Lynne were performers in the first season of the National at the Vic. At Lynne's twenty-first birthday bash at her parents' home in Knightsbridge, having discovered Sir Michael had recommended me to Olivier, I thanked him.

"Yes, I was entirely to blame," he replied, with a gentle smile.

At the National, Olivier appointed two associate directors, William Gaskill and the extraordinarily gifted — although occasionally bullying — John Dexter. I'd first met Dexter at an audition for Arnold Wesker's play *Chips with Everything* at the Vaudeville Theatre on the Strand. As an introduction to John Dexter, this audition (where I didn't get the part) could well have bedeviled my theatrical future, but to the contrary it made John think of me with amused affection. He never seemed to forget my strange antics as at one moment I tried to keep my balance.

"I enjoyed your audition, Purchase. Especially your little trip."

That day at the Vaudeville Theatre I'd read on stage from the script of the play, and afterwards Dexter interviewed me from his seat out in the darkness of the auditorium. This was unnerving as I could not see him, only hear faintly his disembodied voice as he fired questions at me. Dazed by the spotlights in my face, which also unnerved me, I walked downstage, both to avoid the blinding lamps and to hear his questions more clearly. As I moved downstage I inadvertently stepped onto the canvas-covered orchestra pit. My left foot alighted on the stretched canvas, sinking under my weight. In that split second, noting my error and realising there was no going back, I threw my right foot forward, hoping to make safe contact with the hard edge of the outer side of the orchestra pit. My right foot did land safely, with my left foot joining the right at speed. There, with both feet on the outer edge I teetered dangerously before I finally recovered my balance, though not my composure. From this highly eccentric position, dignity out the window, I completed the interview. However, now no longer blinded by the lights, I saw Dexter in the half gloom of the auditorium, where he sat a few rows back in the stalls, grinning broadly. "Thank you, Mr Purchase. That will be all," he said, adding, "I think it wiser for you to climb down from your perilous position and exit over there by the pass door to backstage." I lowered myself down into the front row and as I obeyed his instruction he called after me:

"Oh, by the way — I enjoyed the trip." I may not have got the part, but a year later at my National audition he supported my inclusion in the company.

Dexter's general reputation was that of a tyrannical director. This was a self-created directorial style, but it was not the real man, the private John. A personal instance of the kindlier man happened at the end of my first year with the National. It was the summer of 1964 and the company was operating simultaneously out of both the Old Vic and the Chichester Festival Theatre in Sussex. Chichester, in two seasons, 1962 and '63, was where Olivier had assembled a group of actors who were destined to be the nucleus of the National Theatre players at the Vic. I'd joined this group at the tail end of the Chichester season in '63, prior to a visit by the company to the Edinburgh Festival.

Now it was the tail end of the '64 season with annual holidays approaching.

After an absence of four years from New Zealand, my parents had stumped up the fare (a large sum in those early days of air transport) for me to go home for the holidays and, because of the 24,000 mile return trip, I'd applied for and been granted by the National an extra week tacked on to my contractual two-week break. In those days the flights from London to Auckland took thirty-seven hours — with refuelling stops in Canada and Hawaii — or Dubai, Bombay and Perth.

Suddenly, a few days before my holiday was due, with the expensive tickets in my wallet, I was bluntly informed by the National repertory manager that the extra week was to be withdrawn. I was devastated by this sudden alteration to my plans. How to break this news to my parents, who'd saved so carefully to make my journey home possible?

I had an evening free and went to a Chichester tavern, unfrequented by our company, to mull over the problem. I would have to phone my folks on the morrow, at the latest. Oh God.

Shortly after arriving in the out-of-the-way pub, pint in front of me on the bar, Dexter walked in. In his familiar 'tyrannical voice' he said: "Buy me a pint, Purchase." As I ordered my surprise guest his ale, he added: "What are you looking so fucking miserable about?"

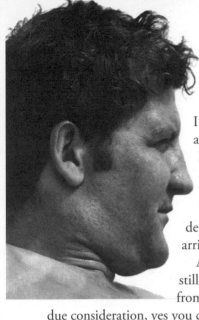

Sailing, Chichester coast. 1964.

I reluctantly explained my predicament and, in between gulps of his free pint, he said unsympathetically, "Serves you right." Then after swiftly dispatching the beer down his gullet, without offering to buy a round in return, he departed as rapidly as he'd so surprisingly arrived minutes earlier.

An hour later I returned to my digs, still despondent. But a message awaited me from the same theatre bureaucrat — "After due consideration, yes you can take the extra week …"

Two days later I flew to New Zealand.

What I learnt later, and this from Laurence Olivier's dresser months after my return from New Zealand, was that Dexter had returned to the theatre that night and put my case to Olivier as he was preparing to go onstage as Othello. Sir Laurence, incensed on my behalf, phoned from his dressing room, reinstating the extra week. As soon as I was told the story I went to Sir Laurence and thanked him and when next I saw Dexter, said:

"Thank you, John."

"Thank me for what?" he snarled.

"For okaying, with Sir Laurence, my extra week in New Zealand."

"Fuck off!" he glared at me and walked off. John never liked being caught out being thoughtful and kind.

He'd heard my news that night from friends in the company and with the energy of an intelligence officer, had trekked around the pubs till he found me, gave me a bollocking, but then went straight off to sort the whole sorry mess out.

John always had a talent for surprise. In 1965 I was switching roles in his production of *The Royal Hunt of the Sun*. At the rehearsal, called entirely for my benefit, in my new role as the Inca chieftain Chalcuchima, I had to lead my Indians in a ritual entrance, which built to a climax, when suddenly surrounded by Spanish soldiers, we all died in a superbly stylized slaughter. This scene was the climax of Act One.

In the scene, before the killing began, I led my followers to a musical accompaniment. I myself was called on to rhythmically beat a cymbal held in my left hand, hitting it with a stick with a pompom attached, with my right hand.

At one point, traversing downstage at a slow march, I struck my cymbal and the pompom dislodged itself from its handle. At speed like a tennis serve it zoomed forward and hit Dexter, in the front row of the stalls, between the eyes with some force. I was horrified, but the scene played itself out to its climax when, after our deaths at the hands of the Spanish, a huge piece of red raw silk enveloped the stage like a sea of blood, settling slow-motion to the floor as the lights slowly dimmed on a spectacle of carnage. Curtain.

As we assembled for notes after the rehearsal all I could think was that now my blood would run — my career was surely over. In the pause as we gathered I wandered miserably upstage like a dunce at school and faced the brick wall at the back.

Suddenly — and yet gently — there came a tap on my shoulder and I turned. It was Dexter, the offending pompom in his hand.

"I think you lost this in the battle, old chum." He smiled before he turned to bark out criticism at the other folk. Hmm, John was full of surprises.

He too, in turn, could be surprised.

The place is a rehearsal on-stage for John Arden's *Armstrong's Last Goodnight*, directed by William Gaskill, John Dexter and Albert Finney. John was in charge of this particular rehearsal which, though not in the cast of this production, I watched from the stalls.

Dexter was loudly tearing a strip off the actors standing about onstage. In the middle of his harangue, a disembodied voice chimed in from the circle above — a musical chant, like some obscure Buddhist contribution —

"Dah Dee Dah Dee Dah Dee Dah — Dahdee/Dahdid/Dee/Dah"

Dexter turned in a flash to face the circle, a smile etching his face, mock fury in his voice. "Did it for the money, didn't I?" grinning and repeating, for good effect, "Did it for the money!"

The altogether familiar voice of Albert Finney, Dexter's co-director, had intoned the theme tune from the long-running radio serial beloved of the Brits — *The Archers*. But what most present that day did not know was that years before Dexter's rise to eminence as a stage director, he'd been an actor — a regular in *The Archers*, playing PC Bryden, the local copper in the fictional town of Ambridge.

Dexter's swift response was indeed witty, as all the performers well knew that the BBC rarely paid big fees for work on radio. "Did it for the money." Finney was reminding him that he too had been a mere actor.

The last time I met John D was twenty-five years later. I was in a production by David Leveaux of Strindberg's *Easter*, at the Leicester Haymarket Theatre. The show starred Jemma Redgrave, my old colleague Corin's daughter, in one of her early professional roles. The start of an illustrious career. Jemma was exceptional in her part. I'd last seen her as a babe in the arms of her mother, Deirdre Hamilton-Hill, who she so closely resembles in both nature and looks.

One night word was out: John Dexter was in the audience. *Easter* had been rarely performed in Britain and this production had attracted considerable attention.

John approached the cast as we stood gathered in the front of house bar after the show. He burst through the group and up to me.

"Buy me a pint, Purchase," an order from the distant past which, like a trained reflex, he knew I would obey.

I ordered his drink and as I did so he praised the rest of the assembled actors, pointedly ignoring any comment about me. But I knew the game and went with it. He received his glass, characteristically without thanks.

But then he turned to me, "Bruce, you old bastard, tell this lot that marvellous story about Robert Atkins — you know the one I mean."

Once again I obeyed this instruction — he was after all the director I so admired and he knew that. After I'd finished the Atkins anecdote he pressed me yet again.

"And that story about …" etc etc. He'd cleverly set me up as raconteur, possibly my favourite role.

When John left that evening he called back over his shoulder, "Remind me to buy you a pint sometime, Purchase." We never met again. A heart bypass operation went wrong and he died in the operating theatre.

After my return from that holiday in New Zealand I commenced my second full season with the National at the Vic.

"Noel," said Diana Boddington, stage manager, "this is Bruce Purchase, who is covering Tony." Noel Coward, the Master, was directing his own play *Hay Fever* for the National. Diana added, "Bruce is just back from a holiday with his family in New Zealand."

"Whereabouts?" Coward said crisply as he shook my hand. He was casually expensively attired, an unlit cigarette in one hand, a gold Dunhill lighter in the other. As I answered him he lit his cigarette, smartly clicking his lighter shut. "Auckland," I said. His eyes brightened. "Ah yes, I remember it well — 'One hunger and tow-heh-rowah soup'. I was there during the Second World War."

He'd answered so swiftly with an unrehearsed quip which needs explanation. Onehunga is an Auckland suburb, and toheroa is a shellfish, the basic ingredient for a soup considered a great delicacy. It used to be sold tinned at Fortnum & Masons.

This Coward comment was my first taste of his ripostes — the speed of his wit. There were many more instances during that memorable rehearsal period, all invariably unexpected. "Wit," he once said, "like marmalade, should be spread thinly."

Hay Fever's stunning cast included Lynne Redgrave, Maggie Smith, Robert Stephens, Robert Lang, Derek Jacobi and that indomitable elder actress, Dame Edith Evans. Tucked in alongside the knights and dames were the equally splendid Barbara Hicks, Anthony Nicholls (who I understudied) and Louise Purnell. Despite the difference in our ages Tony and I were both grandfathers to Oakley Purchase. But that is to digress — that story has a chapter to itself.

Her part was a huge break for the young Louise Purnell (who all the actors in the company adored). Louise had been understudy to Sarah Miles, self-confessed (but only many years later) mistress to our boss, the Great Sir Laurence. Sarah Miles was replaced by Louise shortly after rehearsals began. Noel Coward had insisted on a shorter-than-average rehearsal period, clearly conditional on all the cast knowing their lines by the first day of rehearsal. Sarah was the only one who arrived with lines unlearnt. After a couple of days of making herself unpopular because of this she phoned in to say she'd caught a fish-bone in her throat and could not attend rehearsals for a few days. Coward was incensed — he quite clearly didn't believe the story. Louise Purnell, as understudy, stepped in to rehearse with the others and did know all the lines.

Coward was enchanted. He announced, "Get rid of that other girl, who flounces and doesn't know her lines. I want Louise in the role."

It was the commencement of a charmed career at the National.

Sarah Miles later played Abigail in Arthur Miller's *The Crucible* and also took over a part in *The Recruiting Officer*, already by then in the repertoire and enjoying a huge success. The director of that production, Bill Gaskill, announced to the cast, "All of you be on your toes, for Sarah has brilliant comedy timing." As I stood in the wings with Maggie Smith, hearing Sarah on-stage, Maggie muttered darkly, "Time? She couldn't time an egg!"

Edith Evans, dame extraordinaire, was quite clearly too old to play Judith Bliss in *Hay Fever*, and before the show went on tour after an initial run at the Vic, Edith dropped out and the part was recast, with the wonderful Celia Johnson (remember her in the film *Brief Encounter*?) just perfect as Judith. The rest of the cast remained the same but when Tony Nicholls fell suddenly ill I replaced him as David Bliss. If Dame Edith was too old to be Judith, I was too young for David, but kitted out with a bald wig I did my best.

Nevertheless at the beginning, Edith had a good stab in the part of the eccentric Judith Bliss but she did have problems in rehearsal getting a grip on her lines. Coward and the cast were often frustrated. Yet, in rehearsal, Coward and Edith made a fine comedy duo — director and leading lady!

Dame Edith: Noel, I shall know my lines backwards tomorrow.

Coward: *(wearily)* Edith, you've been saying them backwards today!

Or:

Dame Edith: *(uttering a line incorrectly)* On a clear day you can
see as far as Marlow …

Coward: *(cutting in)* Edith darling, you're saying that line
incorrectly. The line I wrote — and I quote, is:
"on a clear day you can see Marlow …" (then
under his breath) "and of course, on an even
clearer day, you can see not only Marlowe, but
also Beaumont and Fletcher!"

One day in rehearsal Edith accidentally tripped on a footstool
and fell heavily to the floor. Everyone in the room stiffened. Was
Edith okay? But she rolled over, smiling, as her stage-husband Tony
Nicholls stepped forward and gently lifted her to her feet. Once clear
she was uninjured, Coward quipped:

"No, Edith, that will not get a laugh."

The pre-London tryout of *Hay Fever* at the Manchester Opera
House. Dame Edith still in a panic about her continuing inability
to get a grip on her lines. Not acknowledging the real reason, she
pleaded illness, refusing to go on for the first performance, a preview
with a packed house expected. Coward bowed to her wishes and she
departed the building and went to her hotel by taxi, accompanied
by a friend. The disappointed audience, when the show that evening
was cancelled, were given the price of their tickets back.

Coward then called a company meeting.

Coward: We must now do a run of the play with Edith's
understudy. This in case Edith is still not feeling
better for the press night, tomorrow. Who is
covering Dame Edith?

Maggie Smith *(through gritted teeth)*: I am!

At the run-through of the play, Maggie, DLP (dead letter perfect on
lines), was brilliant in the Dame's part and in turn replacing Maggie's
role as Myra, Maggie's understudy turned up trumps too.

Next evening (press night — a full house plus the local critics) I
arrived early at the Opera House. As I walked from the stage door
I overheard this exchange as I passed Dame Edith's open dressing
room door, both protagonists not visible but clear for me to hear:

139

Dame Edith: I'm still not well, Noel, so I'm not going on tonight.

Coward: *(seemingly unperturbed)* Not to worry, Edith. After your departure last night we did a quick run of the play with your understudy. She's rather good so …

Dame Edith *(interjecting swiftly)* Who … is my understudy?

Coward: Maggie. She's actually frightfully good so …

The old diva cut in — her next comment delivered forcefully — like her famous 'handbag' line in the film of *The Importance of Being Earnest.*

Dame Edith: I'm going on.

Noel Coward's ploy had worked, for he knew Edith was mightily jealous of the young Maggie Smith's superlative talent. There was no way she'd not have appeared in her role, once she knew who covered her.

Edith, that night, played erratically — good bits and bad with one early, memorable, 'dry' on her lines. But when she 'dried' she blithely announced, loud enough even for me to clearly hear as I stood at the back of the stalls in the huge Manchester Opera House:

"Well," said the Dame, "it's not my turn!"

Maggie Smith's expression froze. There was no way Maggie would have chosen to utter her next line, which would have made it appear her mistake. Tony Nicholls, gent that he was, saved the day, coming in swiftly with his next line, and thus most of the audience assumed this pause in performance his fault. Yes, during a life-time spent on the boards, Edith had, for personal survival, learnt more than a trick or two.

When a couple of weeks later *Hay Fever* opened at the Vic to a fanfare of publicity, Edith, still too old for the role, was at least in command of her lines and her performance pleased the audience.

Gathered at the Old Vic on that first night were both the glitterati of London society and, from across the Atlantic, well known faces from the theatrical and film world of New York and Hollywood. One such star present was Olivier's ex-wife, the diminutive, still luminous, Vivien Leigh, Scarlet O'Hara herself.

It was an exciting evening and the after-show party was fun, starting in the Circle Bar at the Vic and spilling over into the stalls area.

That production of *Hay Fever* rescued Coward from the doldrums — his plays had for a number of years been sadly neglected. This re-affirmed him as a master of his craft.

A few other memories from the rehearsal period endure, like diamonds in my mind. We rehearsed for a time at the Phoenix Theatre in Charing Cross Road, and one day I was sitting in the stalls beside Maggie Smith as we watched Edith go over and over and over a small scene. Everybody present was feeling frustrated. Maggie, speaking sotto voice, "No wonder she gets to be so good for she gets more rehearsal time than anyone else."

Tension was running high but Dame Edith was the first to crack. She suddenly broke off from rehearsing and headed for the exit.

"What is it now?" Coward, exasperated.

"I'm going away to make myself a glass of Bovril," Edith announced, adding for good measure as she reached the exit, "and I might not come back."

The theatre fell silent after her peremptory exit. Noel placed a Dunhill cigarette between his visibly gritted teeth and with a perceptible tremble to his hand, lit it casually. He took a carefully calculated inhalation, then slowly blew the smoke out before saying crisply and oh so very clearly:

"Edith is a cunt …" pausing for a beat as this shocking revelation was left to sink in, then, "… but what would we do without her?"

Spell broken. Everyone laughed. The master, Coward, had neatly evaporated the tension.

When the old gal reappeared she quite clearly knew the mood had changed, as through the steam rising off her glass of Bovril her baleful eyes swept the space and you could see her thinking, Noel has said something.

Other glittering memories …

Dame Edith: Noel, I'm unable to rise effortlessly, from this sofa. It's too deep. Is this the sofa I'm going to have to use in performance?

Coward: *(fed up by now with Edith's endless carping)* Is it, Diana?

Diana:	*(Stage manager)* I'll ask Roger [Furze, designer].
Coward:	Diana, I'm releasing Edith from rehearsal for the rest of the day. We'll rehearse the first scene with Derek [Jacobi] and Louise [Purnell]. Speak to Roger and if need be rattle up a taxi and take Edith to Maples to choose a sofa more suitable to her needs.
Diana:	But Noel ...
Coward:	No buts, Diana ... Just take Dame Edith ...
Diana:	But Noel ...
Coward	*(frustrated and annoyed)*: Well? What is it?
Diana:	Maples was bombed during the war.

In the end Olivier, Dame Edith and designer Roger Furze chose another, more practical sofa.

One of the stories John Dexter encouraged me to tell in the bar in Leicester involved my only meeting with one of the best actor/director/managers of the early-to-middle part of the twentieth century, Robert Atkins. By the time I met him he was an old man, retired from the hurly-burly of the theatre world he'd so relished. Atkins had first acted at the Old Vic theatre in 1915. In that period between 1915 and 1916 there'd been a gin palace opposite the theatre. Robert said the trade then at that establishment was so very rough on Friday and Saturday nights, no female member of the company of the Old Vic was permitted to leave the theatre without male escort. This edict I imagine suited Robert, as he was always very partial to the ladies.

Perhaps Wilfred Lawson's 'meths drinker' chums had been celebrants at the gin palace as young men — or ghosts from that era.

Robert Atkins directed ninety productions at the Old Vic between 1920 and 1925 — a huge feat. He also later achieved enormous popularity as founder of the Open Air Theatre in Regent's Park, where he directed summer seasons of Shakespeare's comedies. This tradition continues, its recent director an old mate of mine from RSC days at Stratford-Upon-Avon, Ian Talbot, who has bravely battled, as Robert did, to fund these annual summer seasons.

In her book the writer Doris Westwood reports Atkins staging Shakespeare's *Coriolanus* in only a week, at the Old Vic, while he also played in *The Rivals* and *Everyman*: "At one moment he [Atkins] was in the centre of the crowd, disguised in rough serge tunic and hood. At another, he was giving the signal for drum and trumpet, again pushing the soldiers into their places, or raging at rehearsals: 'Carry that coffin straight, for God's sake' and 'Move your bodies, ladies; for God's sake look as though you were enjoying yourselves; take a little stimulant before you come on if you can't do it without'."

In between all this frenzied activity Atkins found time to play several other major roles, among them Caliban and Sir Toby Belch. He'd been an artist with prodigious energy. A monumental talent, with a deliciously 'fruity' vocal delivery — a joy to listen to.

I first set eyes on Robert Atkins at a Vic Wells Association meeting in 1964, this held in the Vic rehearsal room to celebrate Shakespeare's birthday. Other guest speakers sharing the podium in '64 with Atkins were the West End producer, Sir Bronsen Albery, and our aforementioned star, Dame Edith.

"Hail cake," said Edith as she sliced into the birthday offering.

Atkins, in a meandering speech, recollected his own glory days at the Old Vic in the 1920s, liberally dotting his birthday offering with a repetitive phrase: "And when the National Theatre leaves the Old Vic …" Robert, of course, knew the room was at least partly filled with the new incumbents at the Vic — the National Theatre Company. As fellow players in this new company John Stride and I knew this gave us due warning that when the National built its new home on the South Bank, Robert intended to return to his old base, bringing the Glory Days back once more. He'd do the job properly.

Back to the story John Dexter encouraged me to tell at Leicester. After a matinée of *The Royal Hunt of the Sun*, I had an evening free and planned to be out on the town with a girlfriend. We were to meet in the pub next to the Old Vic stage door. Patrick, the Irish landlord from Lawson's meths drinkers period, two years earlier, still in charge.

Dehydrated from the rigours of the matinée performance, I awaited Susie, my Texan belle. I was on a bar stool, my back to the entrance, a welcome pint of Guinness on the bar in front of me.

The door behind me opened and I glanced to see if my date had arrived, but no, Robert Atkins tottered in, accompanied by a woman. I turned back to my Guinness.

Robert Atkins sat himself down at the table behind me and his companion, an American, ordered their drinks. I heard, but did not see, the following conversation as they settled to their drinks.

Atkins: *(leafing through his programme)* Hmm. I enjoyed *The Royal Hunt of the Sun*. Very good. Very good. This Robert Stephens fellah, as the Sun God. How do you say it? Atta … … Atta … …?

Woman: Atawhalpa, Robert.

Atkins: Yes … very good. Is he English?

Woman: Yes, he is. A very fine young actor.

Atkins: Yes, indeed. Very fine. Very fine.

Woman: He's done a lot of very good work at the Court [The Royal Court Theatre in Sloane Square, London]. He also played Germanicus in the film of *Cleopatra*.

Atkins: Did he now? *(pause)* This Colin Blakely. Very good. Is he English?

Woman: Irish.

Atkins: *Irish?*

Woman: Northern Irish.

Atkins: Ah — Northern Irish. Well also very good … as … Piss … Piss …

Woman: Pizzaro, the Spanish General.

Atkins: Yes. *(Pause)* Tell you what though. Came to see Larry's production of *Hamlet* with another Irishman — Peter O'Toole. Bloody awful. They can't play Shakespeare.
(Pause)
Came also to see Larry play Othello. A fucking abortion! No, they can't play Shakespeare.

He continued in this vein and I recalled his line a year earlier at the Vic Wells Association meeting … "And when the National Theatre leaves, the Old Vic."

The door behind me opened again and I glanced to see if it was 'my American', but no, it was their chauffeur. Atkins caught my eye as I glanced back to my now half-consumed pint. I heard them get up to go and the door closed behind them ... or so I assumed ... but no, Atkins had a trick up his sleeve ...

A gentle tap on my shoulder and I turned on my stool. He hadn't left! He stood beside me with a mischievous smile.

"You're in the company, aren't chuh?"

"Yes, Mr Atkins."

"Well, I enjoyed *The Royal Hunt of the Sun*, but ..."

"But we can't play ... ..."

"That's right son! You're right! You can't play Shakespeare."

And with that, the legendary figure from an earlier age sauntered off to rejoin his companion.

The actor John Franklyn Robbins told me he once saw Robert Atkins making a call from the phone at the Old Vic. "You remember the old telephone coin boxes with Button A and Button B?"

"I do remember them."

"Yes," said John, "you first put your penny in, dialed the number you required and when you made connection you pressed Button A and heard the penny drop into the well of the coin box."

"And if you didn't get through — you pressed Button B to get your penny back."

"Exactly," said John. "Well this night as I too waited to use the phone, Robert Atkins inserted a penny and dialed a number. He got through, pressed Button A and the coin dropped with its customary clang into the well of the machine. 'Hello darling, I'm working late. Shan't be back till midnight.' He then hung up."

John said Atkins then put in a second penny and repeated the process — dialed, got through, pressed Button A — the penny dropped. "Hello darlin', see you in fifteen minutes. Oh, by the way my dear, I've got the bread."

Bread? Was that bread as in loaf or as in dosh, cash? We'll never know. But Robert was, as earlier stated, very partial to the ladies.

*

145

In the 1960s I inherited two nicknames and both have endured over the years. The first of these name tags was Bunce, the second, Broochay. The latter was bestowed on me during the run of Franco Zeffirelli's very Italianate production for the National, at the Vic, of *Much Ado About Nothing*. It opened its highly successful run in 1964.

The music for this show was commissioned from Nino Rota, Fellini's screen composer. I played the singer Balthasar and Nino's music for one of my two songs ('Sigh No More') was like a distillation of every Neapolitan romantic tune ever heard. This version became a literal show-stopper.

"Who is the Italian tenor in *Much Ado*?" The question asked by a member of the audience was addressed to William Gaskill, who, with Dexter, was one of the associate directors at the National.

Bill's reply: "There is no Italian tenor in *Much Ado*."

"Oh yes there is."

"Oh no there's not," said Gaskill.

But the persistent questioner then held out his programme and pointed out my name.

"Broochay Purr-kay-zay." Thus he pronounced my name, continuing, "Who is he? I've never heard him sing before. Where in Italy is he from?"

Bill Gaskill enjoyed recounting this conversation to me and I in turn have treasured the story and embraced it as a nickname. Since then when working with Italians, mostly on film projects, though occasionally in theatre, when they've said "Bruce" or "Mr Purchase," I've corrected them — "No it's Broochay Purr-kay-zay," — and explained why!

The other nickname, Bunce, has since the '60s when given me, also endured. This was attributed to me by some wag working for the London *Evening Standard*. The occasion was that newspaper's annual drama award ceremony in 1964. The awards for best actor and best actress that year went to two members of the National troupe — Sir Michael Redgrave and Joan Plowright. The awards ceremony, hosted by the *Evening Standard* editor, Charles Wintour, took place in the upstairs rehearsal room at the Old Vic. When I received my invitation to attend, the envelope was addressed to

Bunce Purchase Esq. Amused, I opened it and on the card inside it read, "Dear Bunce Purchase, you are cordially invited to etc, etc."

On the evening in question Charles Wintour stood at the door to welcome his guests. When my turn came I cued him as he looked enquiringly at me, "Purchase," I said helpfully.

Wintour smiled uncertainly. "Is your name actually Bunce?"

I answered, "No, but I wish it was."

'Bunce' like 'bread', is slang for cash. Cash Purchase. It has a certain ring.

"Hi Buncie," some old chums still greet me.

Franco Zeffirelli's production of *Much Ado* was one of the National's early hits at the Old Vic. Zeffirelli, a mercurial personality, was for the most part fun to work with, although for a time in early rehearsals he did choose me as his whipping boy. He didn't like the way I was interpreting my role and I stubbornly stuck to my guns — to what I instinctively felt was true. Franco continued to vent spleen in my direction, which I as a young actor found very upsetting. I'll always be grateful to Albert Finney (playing Don Pedro) who one day in rehearsal put a sudden stop to all this silliness. Using his rank, his seniority in the cast, he stepped between Franco and myself as I endured yet another tongue lashing from the director.

"Leave Bruce alone, Franco," said Albie, and from that moment on he did. On the first night the 'Sigh No More' scene literally stopped the show, the applause deafening. Afterwards Franco said generously to me: "Congratulations. Your approach was right."

A couple of years later Zeffirelli invited me to re-voice a song on his film of *Taming of the Shrew*, which starred Richard Burton and Elizabeth Taylor, even instructing that I be chauffeured to and from Shepperton Studios in the Burton/Taylor Rolls Royce, which was fun.

During rehearsals for *Much Ado*, Franco took a few days off to re-rehearse Maria Callas back into an opera they'd done earlier in Italy. It was to open in Paris and he flew there, leaving us to continue rehearsals in the capable hands of the assistant director, Piers Haggard. Apparently when Franco was not at early rehearsals in Paris, Callas had asked: "Where is Franco?" She was told he was rehearsing a Shakespeare play in London.

Zeffirelli, on his return from Paris, told this story with relish.

"Maria took solo calls, finally gesturing to me in the wings to come on and share the applause. As we took the first of several bows together, Maria said, out of the corner of her mouth, as the applause continued:

" 'It may not be Shakespeare, but it's *fun*, isn't it?' "

Winston Churchill's funeral took place during rehearsals and we all were given a day off to attend. I secured a place outside St Paul's Cathedral, with a very good view. As soon as the coffin was placed on the gun-carriage I dashed off by underground to take up another position, this time at Waterloo Station. Franco was also on the same platform where I stood and became so excited by the view of the coffin as it was being placed on the train which was to transport the body of this great Englishman to his final resting place, near Woodstock, Franco was moved to try and cross the railway lines from our vantage point but was gently restrained by a policeman.

There was a garden setting in one of the scenes in *Much Ado* with decorative 'statues' played by several of the younger new arrivals to the company. During a moment in this scene these marble figures briefly moved, then froze back into their fixed positions. An effective, light and amusing touch to the scene in the garden. At the technical rehearsal, Franco was placing these young actors in position, instructing them as to what was required.

"What's your name?" he asked one lad. This new arrival gave his name.

"You're a very pretty boy, Michael York," Franco murmured. Like a scene from a Hollywood remake of *A Star is Born*, this presaged Michael York's film career — his first film, directed by Zeffirelli, *Romeo and Juliet*, was the start of a successful film career for Michael.

Much Ado had a cracking cast, which included, as I've mentioned, Albert Finney. Also starring were Maggie Smith, Robert Stephens, Frank Finlay, Derek Jacobi and my earlier Ipswich Repertory Theatre colleague, Ian McKellen, fresh from his success as Aufidius in *Coriolanus*, directed by Sir Tyrone Guthrie at Nottingham Playhouse.

Finney, my protector with Zeffirelli in rehearsal, had just returned before we started the show from a year out from the profession after the release of the phenomenally successful film of the early 1960s, *Tom Jones* in which he played the title role. This sabbatical year he'd spent on the beautiful island of Tahiti, where I too had spent time *en route* to the UK in 1960. In rehearsal we chatted about that place which in those days, before mass tourism, had been paradise.

I told Albert that as the *Ruahine*, the ship I travelled on, pulled into the harbour at Papeete a chap next to me said the place had not changed in the twenty-five years since his first visit as a crew member on Douglas Fairbanks Snr's yacht in the 1930s.

"Did you meet Paul Gauguin's son?" I asked Albie.

"Which one?" Finney laughed.

"The one who thought he could paint like his father, but couldn't."

In chatting about Tahiti I remembered the locally brewed beer, called Hinano. Not made from hops, but fermented onions — fine if consumed immediately — but not if left too long. Also the first time I'd eaten raw marinated fish (delicious) — and delicious too, the charming Paris-educated Tahitian lass who with great patience taught this virgin Kiwi lad a thing or two …

The early days of the National at the Vic have entered the history books. Important, as theatre (unlike film or video and TV, which can return endlessly to haunt or charm) is rather like painting on snow — the snow melts, the memory fades, leaving only yellowing newspaper clippings as reminders of past glories and past failures too.

In 1990 I was working at the Royal National Theatre at its home on the South Bank, only half a mile from the old National Theatre rehearsal rooms in the Nissen huts at Aquinas Street and but a mile from its old haunt, the Vic itself. There in the new building I met a husband-and-wife team who'd made props at the Vic in those early shared days.

"Weren't those days fantastic?" I said.

"The best," they quietly agreed.

"Remember Ivan Alderson?"

"Oh, yes."

"Remember Stephen Skeptason?"

"I do." Our list was endless, those figures from our shared past.

149

The mention of Canadian wig maker, Stephen Skeptason, like a newspaper clipping from the past, reminded me of a story Stephen told me about a fitting he did for the actor Miles Malleson.

Malleson was an erudite man — actor, playwright, director and, like Atkins, also very much a ladies man. He first worked at the Vic in 1945 when he directed Olivier in *The Critic*, one half of a startling double act — the other play *Oedipus*. Again he'd worked at the Vic in 1949 with his own translation from the French, Molière's *The Miser*, in which he also acted. Most folk will remember his screen performances, notably his Canon Chasuble in the film of *The Importance of Being Earnest,* with Edith Evans as Lady Bracknell. In performance he often wobbled his multitude of double chins to marvellous comic effect. In later years he was completely bald and wore, in turn, several toupees of varying length. These wigs were not well made, for you could easily see the join and usually he wore them badly, inadvertently placing them on his head at odd angles, any suspension of disbelief that they be mistaken for real hair dispelled. Miles would announce when wearing his longest-haired wig — "I really must get a haircut," and the next day, announce for all to hear, now wearing his shortest piece, "I've had a haircut. This subterfuge, of course fooled no-one.

When he joined the National at the Vic in 1965 to play in Congreve's *Love for Love*, the designer, Lila de Nobili, decided that as Malleson was actually bald, his character in the production should be played using his natural bald head.

But, as Stephen Skeptason told me with amusement, Miles announced he needed a fitting for a bald cap.

So a bald Miles M would arrive at the theatre wearing one of his terrible wigs and over that fit the bald cap Stephen had to make him. Such is vanity!

Sir Michael Gambon (we were both youngsters together at the Vic) and I spoke recently together about our early days there. We were in the company of two younger actors and described our mix of respect, awe and downright fear in the presence of Laurence Olivier in those halcyon days.

The younger actors were both amazed. Couldn't happen now, was their conclusion. No, it couldn't. Just as Robert Atkins reflected to us when young about his era, Michael's and my early world has also now disappeared into a distant past — an era gone.

One vivid memory we recalled involved John Dexter, Olivier and another young actor from those Vic days.

This young actor (he'd been at RADA with me) came belting on as a messenger in rehearsal for an early scene in *Othello*. His speech — necessarily urgently spoken — informed of Othello's imminent arrival to Cyprus from a storm-tossed sea, and one of the words referring to the sea was 'molestation'. This young bloke pronounced this word as two — 'mole station'.

I noted Dexter looked amused but, in a break, said nothing as Olivier winked at John as he casually crossed the rehearsal space to chat to the hapless young actor.

"Roger," Olivier enquired, "what is your intention in the reading of that line?"

"Well, Sir, the moles are up on the high cliffs," Roger H confidently announced, "in their burrows …"

"Ah — burrows …" murmured Olivier, "Yes?"

Roger continued, walking into the trap laid for him. "Yes, their burrows … their stations, so to speak — looking down on Othello's ship as it's buffeted by the rough sea below."

"I see. I see," Olivier murmured as he wandered off, sipping his tea, leaving John D to go in for the expected 'kill'. Dexter, of course, did so.

"What's this fucking 'mole station', you cunt? The word is molestation. One word. Go and look it up in the dictionary, for fuck's sake."

"And you wonder we were scared?" Gambon and I asked the two young actors we were speaking to as we recollected this event from thirty-six years earlier, that very different era with all the attendant respect for elders, for seniors, that went with it.

In 1970 I worked again at the Old Vic. This time I was in two guest productions brought in by the National Theatre from the Nottingham Playhouse. I was 'back home', once more — Stuart Burge's production of Ben Jonson's *The Alchemist* and Jonathan Miller's staging of *King Lear* with the splendid Michael Hordern in the title role, Frank Middlemass a wonderful old Fool, Penelope

Wilton lively as Cordelia. I played a deadly calm Cornwall, and Surly in *The Alchemist*.

I'd recently married a New Zealand writer, Elspeth Sandys, and Hordern came to the reception in our large mansion flat in Marloes Road, Kensington. My four-year-old step-daughter, Josie, saw Michael Hordern as he came up the stairs to our drawing room and with her little figure suffused with awe, held her arms out wide and bowing ceremoniously, said oh-so-sweetly: "The King. The King." Michael was very moved and brushing a tear or two aside, said softly to this little girl: "No greater compliment have I ever, or will I ever, receive, young lady."

Now fast forward to the 1980s at the Vic, the National Theatre, by now the Royal National Theatre in its new home on the South Bank, described incidentally by Michael Hordern as looking like the KGB's Lubianya Prison in Moscow. I was back at the Old Vic Theatre in a production by Jonathan Miller of George Chapman's impenetrable play, *Bussy D'Amboise*. While we rehearsed our play the very fine Swedish actor Max von Sydow was playing Prospero in *The Tempest* and I chatted to him in the office at the Vic one day. I asked him if he'd ever played Shakespeare in the English language before. His reply: "No, but often Shakespeare translated into Swedish. But what you must understand, Bruce, is that words in Swedish tend to be much longer, so …"

"*Hamlet* — a long evening in English is …"

"Exactly — a very long evening in Swedish!"

During this stint at the Vic, Jonathan Miller complained about his reception at the hands of the critics. Jonathan was at the time artistic director of the company then resident in that famous beautiful Old Vic Theatre, on the Cut. Before *Bussy D'Amboise* had opened I'd rather foolishly told him that my friend John Wain (novelist, professor of poetry at Oxford and the foremost 20th-century biographer of Dr Johnson) would be reviewing the production for the *Sunday Telegraph*. Jonathan looked worried: "I think John likes my work."

"He loves your work," I confidently announced. I would live to be embarrassed by my bold assertion; a case of my mouth in gear and my brain in neutral.

Marrying Elspeth
Sandys in 1969
at the Kensington
Registry Office.
Elspeth's daughter
Josie, momentarily
shy, is in front.

Wain's review for *Bussy D'Amboise* was a slammer. He'd turned up backstage after the show, his face like iron, no visible sign of the bread-breaking, wine-dispensing John I knew over many years. John's first wife Eirean had been a Chapman Scholar and quite clearly John had turned up to defend Eirean's views on this playwright. Critics should never come backstage after a show they will be reviewing on the morrow.

"You didn't like it, did you, John?" I broke the ice.

"No, I bloody didn't," he muttered darkly.

"Oh dear," I responded, trying to lighten the mood, while also being cross he'd dared, as a critic, to come backstage. It had happened only once before in my life and on that occasion it was easier, for the critic had come to praise the show.

"You were good," he offered up.

"John," I said firmly, "don't single me out."

The next Sunday, I read the *Sunday Telegraph*. He had singled me out and I felt terrible.

Why? Well, I'd boldly announced to members of the cast and to Jonathan that he would be reviewing the show. His review (I've not kept a copy) went something like this:

"On my way to see Jonathan Miller's production of George

Chapman's *Bussy D'Amboise*, I should have stopped off at Lincoln's Inn field where Chapman is buried, to see his grave revolving …"

John then set in to criticize everyone involved in the production, with one exception — me. Something like this:

"The only member of the cast who had any knowledge of how to utter Chapman's text was Bruce Purchase as the Duc de Guise, who spoke the lines fluently.

Thank God when I crept into the theatre for the following performance my colleagues found it all very amusing.

"I see your friend John Wain was in."

But Jonathan Miller was not ready to treat criticism lightly and he'd had a lot of negative critical feedback that season.

"They're always having a go at me," he intoned wearily as he drove me back to Hampstead one night after a performance. "No other director has such a hard time of it. Terry Hands makes light work and Trevor Nunn …"

"Makes millions," I interjected — an attempt to cheer him, adding, "surely then Jonathan, there's Nunn the wiser."

Jonathan did not laugh, determined to pursue his paranoid course: "The critics love them!" I tried to cheer him with one final shot.

"Jonathan," I said firmly, "there are lots of folk who'd like to be Jonathan Miller — and you are!"

*

Out of the cornucopia of memories, a couple of final images from the Vic of the early 1960s. It's a 'tech' for Bill Gaskill's production of Farquhar's *The Recruiting Officer*, destined to be a huge hit with both the critics and the public. The technical rehearsal had not run smoothly and the tired cast's morale was at a low ebb as they gathered for notes at the end of the day.

But Gaskill and his production team were otherwise engaged as the cast, which included Olivier, gathered onstage. Bill and his team chatted on in the darkened auditorium as the actors stood disconsolately about, feeling neglected and growing restive.

Olivier, still in his outlandish costume and full make-up as the character of Captain Brazen summed up the acting company's frustration when he walked to the edge of the stage and said acidly in the direction of Gaskill and his team: "Well, Bill, I suppose all we now have to do is to rehearse the curtain-call."

*

Last image culled from many. I'm picking up my mail from the letter rack at the stage door at the Vic. Behind me I hear the door from the street open and hear the reassuring voice of Ernie, the stage doorkeeper say:

"Good afternoon, Miss Dietrich, and who would you like to see?" Her familiar voice replied: "Larry ... Max ... *everyone!*"

Cast of Gogol's *The Government Inspector* at the Crucible, Sheffield, directed by the eminent Russian director Oleg Tabakov. Bruce standing sixth from left.

VII

A village idyll

A FTER A LEISURELY JOURNEY by car from London we neared our destination.

Through an avenue of majestic elms we drove down a gentle incline into the Cotswold village of Ascott-under-Wychwood and with clear instructions to hand easily found the Long House, the property we'd come to view.

Before us stood a fine example of an 18th-century Cotswold stone farmhouse, roofed with slate. With a mature pear tree espaliered on the wall, as well as long-established wisteria and clematis vines, the front of the house was breathtaking. We gazed in wonder. Our months of searching were at an end. The tour of the property confirmed our initial reaction and a trip around the village by pony and trap added magic to the day. Yes, this was where we wished to live. It was 1972.

We'd long wanted to move out of London and buy a place in the countryside, but with little capital it had often seemed an impossible dream. Our first choice had been to search in Kent, but the subsequent discovery of the Cotswolds was a revelation. More rural than the southern county, it was also blessed with villages built of the local honey-gold stone and looked little changed since the 18th century.

In 1973, secured by a generous loan from a cousin and a mortgage, we bought the Long House, Ascott D'Oyley, Ascott-under-Wychwood and moved into the home which remained ours for the next decade.

London friends at first thought we'd taken leave of our senses.

"How will you work from there, Bruce?"

"It's the back of beyond."

"You'll miss living in Hampstead."

"You'll feel totally cut off."

The chorus grew.

But those sceptics, once they'd seen the place, became converts along with us. Our reaction to the initial doubts had been that we had both travelled 12,000 miles from New Zealand to live in Britain, so being only a mere seventy-five miles from London would not be a problem.

We quickly discovered the rail link with London was efficient, easy, swift — and in the early 1970s — relatively cheap too. A short drive from Ascott stands a handsome old wooden building, designed by the celebrated 19th-century railway engineer, Isambard Kingdom Brunel. This is Charlbury Station. Inside the waiting room burnt an efficient coal fire, tended by the Canadian-born stationmaster. But this coal fire, in the mid-'70s suddenly came under threat. The local manager of British Rail announced the coal fire was to be removed. Shock! Horror! Locals decided to fight the diktat and among the signatures gathered was one from Sir Peter Parker, who lived in the area and was chairman of British Rail. The battle was won, the coal fire reprieved.

Over twenty years later, in a film shot in Morocco (*King David*) I played the character of Jesse, father of King David. The role of David was performed by actor Nathaniel Parker, son of Sir Peter, who saved the coal fire at Charlbury Station.

The Long House had been beautifully restored by its previous owner, with no loss of its essential character. With its thick stone walls, slate roof and flagstoned floor it was both cool in summer and,

Lord Buckingham in BBC TV's
The First Churchills, 1972.

157

with central heating and a vast fireplace, cosy in winter. With the interior wooden shutters closed, if a gale was blowing outside, the storm was not audible within.

The refurbishment of the property had included the re-laying of the roof slates and with a host of other repairs, the building was solid enough to last another two hundred years. The slates came from the nearby village of Stonesfield where quarrying first began in 1600. The slate dates from the Jurassic period and was first cut out of the ground through narrow tunnels. After being brought to the surface the blocks of slate were kept wet until the winter frosts split them into shards, which were then manually shaped into twenty different sizes for use as roof tiles — the twelve-inch square slate is called a 'bachelor'. During the 17th century, as a result of quarrying in Stonesfield, the first dinosaur remains in Britain were discovered.

At the rear of the Long House lay a vast courtyard paved with large slabs of York stone. Into the gaps I planted succulents and sweet-smelling herbs. To one side of the courtyard stood a greenhouse where I grew tomatoes and beyond a barn, which included a stable, was a large garden and a separate kitchen garden and all of this surrounded by beautifully constructed dry stone walls. In the garden a Bramley apple tree and damson trees and under a netted frame in the kitchen garden, gooseberry and raspberry bushes — oh — and stinging nettles, in profusion, uncontrollable profusion.

Aaron Hill's poem from the 18th century springs to mind:

Tender-handed touch a nettle, and it stings you for your pains,
Grasp it like a man of mettle, and it soft as silk remains.

Carefully picked and gently steamed, nettles are delicious, like spinach. Food for free!

Later the barn (that intersected the courtyard and gardens) was converted and became the private domain of Elspeth's teenage daughter Josie. With a wood and peat-burning stove it was snug in winter. The date of the conversion is easily remembered because when I was staining the interior roof beams the music blaring from a portable radio was interrupted by a news-flash — John Lennon shot dead outside the Dakota Building on Central Park West, NYC.

When we moved into the Long House in 1973 it was my instinct, having grown up in a small New Zealand community, to keep a low profile in the village, to allow the locals time to make up their minds about us. As is often the case, it was the children who broke the ice. Out walking with the kids one day we saw a village couple approaching. Josie, aged eight and Reuben, then three, greeted them. "Hello, Uncle Roly, Hello, Aunty Heather," the children chorused confidently.

Josie, a warm-hearted, friendly lass, a person who had the talent to light up a room on entering it, had been at Christchurch Primary School in Hampstead but easily settled into the village school, where two years later she was joined by her brother Reuben.

John Stanyon, headmaster of this Church of England-sponsored primary school, was a fine character and popular with the children. Watching John leading the pupils off on a country ramble and encouraging them to dance with verve around the maypole are just two of many images I remember from those distant halcyon days.

Denys Jackson, publican at The Swan in the village was the first local to break the ice of this newcomer's diffidence.

Early on I'd taken to having a pint in the little-used snug, whereas the regulars favoured the larger public bar on the other side of the half wall dividing the pub.

But slowly, Denys, a quiet, and charming man, began to engage me in conversation. At first he just offered me useful local information — where best to buy logs and coal for the huge fireplace in the living room at the Long House — "You can phone your shopping list to the Co-op supermarket at nearby Milton-under-Wychwood and they'll deliver to your door." And yet even after complete acceptance into the village life one bit of information was never divulged — where the local large field mushrooms grew! Given them, yes, most generously, without charge, piles of those delicious fungi, but not where they could be found, in season. You had perhaps to have been born in the village to be privy to that knowledge.

After a month or so of low-key visits to the local, a villager on the other side caught my eye, lifted his pint of Morrell's bitter like a salute and said, "Evenin". A nod being as good as wink, I twigged that assimilation into village life, acceptance, had begun. From then on I enjoyed my pint or two in the public bar in the company of the locals, many of whom became mates.

One early glitch, however. Elspeth, a writer, when the children left for school in the morning, wished to maximise her available working time, so she advertised in both the local village shop and post office for help in the house and secured the services of Mrs Stowe, a widow, who lived at the other (Ascott Earl) end of the village, but her tenure was to be all too brief. When Elspeth asked Mrs Stowe her hourly rate the amount quoted was shockingly low, yet when Elspeth suggested an increase, Mrs Stowe would take not a penny more. In that still near-feudal society, Mrs Stowe's other employers ran a sort of cartel, keeping wages low. Mrs Stowe's belief was that to accept an increase from our household would upset the village applecart.

This attitude disturbed Elspeth's egalitarian sensibilities and she told me she was going to increase Mrs Stowe's wages the next week.

"If you present that to Mrs Stowe as a *fait accompli*," I said, "you will lose her."

"Nonsense," replied Elspeth. Next week the extra was added to the envelope and sure enough, Mrs Stowe, without a word, never showed up again.

Yet Elspeth's instincts were correct and she finally bucked the system. She advertised a second time and Mrs Bertha Carpenter from the village accepted the job and at the higher rate. After that the silly cartel was broken and individuals negotiated more realistic wages.

When the children of the Long House were young, Bertha Carpenter's daughter often baby-sat, as did another villager with a wonderful name — Mrs Rainbow.

As we settled into village life our home became a magnet for friends and family from near and far. Some came for a day, some for a weekend and others for longer. Next-door neighbours Robin and Jessica, architects both, were weekenders (their main base in London) generously lent their house as extra habitation when we were inundated with guests. It was like having a West Wing.

The appeal of the Long House took many forms. One friend, Fiona Wise, said to me years later: "I so loved your compost heaps."

And Rachel Dean, about the same age as Reuben:

"Em [her sister] and I so envied Josie and Reuben's life in Ascott. It was paradise. Your garden too — all those broad beans."

I became an avid gardener, branching out from the existing kitchen garden into extra space, a double-sized allotment, rent for this payable to the Parish Council — 50p a year!

On the allotment I planted both main crop spuds, new potatoes, and, as Rachel observed, row upon row of broad beans, a favourite crop.

On the adjoining allotment was an old chap who'd been born further west in the Cotswolds. His Gloucestershire accent was impenetrable to this Kiwi and, combined with loose-fitting dentures, his oft-proffered gardening advice was difficult to fathom. One day the old man said to me what sounded a bit like this:

'Toopwentshluggeepotaytossheusshe — sholt."

It took some acute listening to understand my neighbour was advising the spreading of block salt to prevent slugs from gnawing his potato crop. The solution worked.

I had help on my small-holding, in the form of a real local yokel who lived a mile or two down the Evenlode valley and walked to work across the fields. Summer, winter, spring or autumn, Bill Hyde always wore the same woollen suit with waistcoat, woollen overcoat, flat cap and heavy boots or black rubber Wellingtons. He rarely removed any article of clothing, even in midsummer, even in the heat-wave and drought of 1976. His face and hands were ingrained with earth and it was wise to stand upwind of Bill, as — apart from rain when caught in the open — water (and soap) were of no interest to him. I soon discovered if you employed Bill Hyde you had to keep a close eye on him, as Bill and hard work were not close cousins.

Denys, from The Swan, once saw Bill leaning on a hoe in the centre of a garden and an hour later, passing again, Bill still stationary in the same part of the garden.

"Shouldn't you be weeding, Bill?" But Bill Hyde, not at all put out, replied, without moving a muscle. "Ahm lissenin' to em grow." Both weeds and plants, perhaps.

Most locals thought Bill somewhat simple but we didn't share that view — sly, yes, but simple — no. Bill Hyde was smart, yes — dead smart and a real child of the soil. He'd stand very still in the landscape, like a scarecrow, which in shape, form and dress he so resembled. The merest flicker of an eyebrow scared the crows!

When Bill died I saw his brother, Cyril, in nearby Charlbury.

"My condolences, Cyril."

"Ah well," replied Cyril, calmly, "just one of those things."

Being of an obsessive nature, when not called away to earn a crust as an actor, with the aid of a battered old edition of a Women's Institute recipe handbook I turned my mind to other tasks …

Chutneys made from tomatoes grown in the greenhouse and from the plentiful supply of Bramley apples — row upon row of bottles filled with my own preserves. And from blackberries collected by the family in lanes and fields, blackberry jam and jelly — more rows of bottles — gooseberries, raspberries and damson too, plus exploding bottles of home-made ginger beer in the barn at the back and butter made in the kitchen with the aid of a glass churn with wooden paddle. Another interest, if not so English rural — home-made pasta — rare then in the Oxfordshire. It was made with a machine bought in Italy and presented by a friend — spaghetti drying on every available surface in our large farmhouse kitchen. Lasagne too with a delicious sauce cleverly made by Elspeth, a favourite when friends arrived from London.

Then the M40 opened, linking London and Oxford, and country life began to change. New settlers moved into the area, as did burglars too. London criminals quickly realised the Cotswolds was largely 'unlocked', so with the quick access by the new motorway, rich pickings were to be had from houses and churches.

A gifted actor, John Hurt, when he and I were working together on the BBC TV's *I, Claudius* (Hurt brilliant as Caligula and me, his assassin, Sabinus) indicated his desire to move to the Cotswolds. Swiftly he found a beautiful house in Ascott-under-Wychwood which he and his partner, Marie-Lise, bought. We'd been fellow students at RADA. Jenny Hesslewood, who'd been at the National Theatre with me in the mid-'60s and her actor husband, the talented Freddie Jones, bought an elegant home in nearby Charlbury and as Elspeth's writing career blossomed, links and friendship developed with writers in the district, most notably with Peter Buckman and his beautiful Swiss-born wife Rosemarie and their family. The

Buckmans' generosity and hospitality provided connections with other authors, notably Charles Wood, Iris Murdoch, John Bayley and Peter Grose (who became Elspeth's literary agent) and, at Secker & Warburg, Elspeth's publisher, Tom Rosenthal.

Assimilation into community life encouraged commitment. I became chairman of the Parent Teacher Association of the village school; chairman also of a newly formed committee, the too grandly titled Ascott-under-Wychwood Society. This group was formed because of an ecological blight on the landscape. Dutch Elm disease was killing off all those majestic elms which had so impressed us on our first visit to Ascott.

The society advocated re-planting of trees but not everyone was in favour — John Badger of Crown Farm was one dissident. I asked John, a mild-mannered, reasonable man, why he was against re-planting, even on the public verges.

"Well, what would happen," replied John "if someone had a blow-out of a tyre on their vehicle? They might crash into one of those new trees."

I laughed outright, as bizarre images sprang from an imagined past: wheels coming off horse-drawn coaches, postillions thrown against trees, traces broken, dozens of fatalities caused by the elm trees of the past. "For goodness sake," I said to Badger, "if such accidents were common, why were trees ever planted?" The planting went ahead.

From early on Josie had started riding lessons and during the decade in the Cotswolds became the proud and dedicated owner of two ponies, the second as she outgrew the first. To feed the livestock Bertha's husband Roy and I mowed the grass verges, later harvesting the hay and storing it in a barn for winter fodder.

In winter months Josie kept her pony in the stable to the rear of the house but rather than reaching the road, via the fields, she smartly chose a shorter route, across the courtyard and through the Long House — it had a flagstone-paved hallway from back door to front. To prevent her pony from slipping on those glass-smooth, 18th-century flags, Josie would roll out, the full length of the hall, a carpet — literally a red carpet. We had long got used to this ploy, but then an American friend came from New York to stay.

Barbara Caruso, who'd also been at drama school with me, lives in Manhattan. Shortly after her arrival Ba, in the farmhouse kitchen, saw the pony appear in the hallway.

"Oh my God," cried out Ms Caruso in alarm, 'there's a horse in the house!" Not your average Manhattan experience.

Shortly after we moved into the Long House, the 18th-century bell-pull of the front door sounded its mellifluous note and Elspeth answered it. From the kitchen I heard the following conversation:

Woman:	*(very upper class accent)* You must be Mrs Purchase. Welcome to the village. Have you settled in?
Elspeth:	Thank you. Yes we have. I'm Elspeth.
Woman:	Let me introduce myself. I'm Mrs W … from …
Elspeth:	How do you do, Mrs W.
Mrs W:	As you know we have an election coming up, so I thought I'd take this opportunity to drop off some Conservative Party pamphlets.
Elspeth:	We don't vote Conservative, Mrs …
Mrs W:	Oh dear, we're losing so many these days to the Liberals.
Elspeth:	We don't vote Liberal, Mrs …
Mrs W:	Oh, well … I was only saying to my husband the other day — there's a lot to be said … for the Communists!

She'd leapfrogged the possibility the household might support Labour, which we did. Or perhaps she'd just called on neighbour Phoebe de Syllas, also new to the village, who had been a communist in her youth. Mrs W must have concluded the Reds had moved in to the Tory Blue Cotswolds. When, prior to the election, the Long House displayed a Labour sticker in the front window, the locals, in this Tory bastion, thought it was a deliberate joke, which infuriated Elspeth, although their reaction amused me.

One other exchange with our 'Lady of the Manor' was when she phoned me in my role as chairman of the school PTA, during the long hot drought of 1976.

Mrs W:	The children of the village are trespassing on our land.
Bruce:	Oh! Where, Mrs W?
Mrs W:	At the big pool, near the Mill House.
Bruce:	I think you'll find the children of the village use the public footpath across your land to reach that pool. No trespass involved.
Mrs W:	Well, in any case they have no right to swim in our river.
Bruce:	The Evonlode river does not belong to you, Mrs W.
Mrs W:	It passes through our land. In any case the village children have no right to …
Bruce:	Our children, Josie and Reuben …
Mrs W:	Oh, I don't mind your children swimming in the pool. It's the village children …
Bruce:	I must point out to you, Mrs W, that our children, Josie and Reuben, are also children of the village.

No further complaints about swimming in the big pool — Elspeth and I during that long hot summer joined the village children.

Josie and Reuben, living in Ascott-under-Wychwood, swiftly took up speaking with the attractive local Oxfordshire accent of their peer group, a natural affinity, a wish to identify with their friends, not to be seen as outsiders to their group.

As a New Zealander having lived in the UK for thirteen years I was only too aware of how in Britain — well, certainly in England — individuals are judged by their accents, as to class, education, origin, where they hail from, etc. By one person upon another, this is often a cruel assessment. I said to Josie and Reuben as a way of highlighting this social fact:

"You kids live in a home where our guests are a mixed bunch from all over the world, so listen, be aware of different accents," adding, "Be bi-lingual, even tri-lingual." At the time the children didn't know what the hell I meant, but Reuben, who was beginning to follow in his father's profession, later remembered what I'd said to him: "It was years later, when I was about ten I suddenly realised what you'd been on about us having a go at being bi-lingual. It was the year the village was snowed in and the valley road to Shipton was blocked so we tried to get through via the top road. Halfway up the hill, a van approached us and windows were lowered as we drew level. The stranger driving the van asked where were we headed. 'Shipton,' you said, mimicking the stranger's Cotswold accent. He told us we'd get through and you said: 'Thank you very merch,' still using broad Oxfordshire. At the top of the hill we turned left in the direction of Shipton and a Range Rover approached and slowed to a stop alongside. A similar exchange, like that with the van driver, took place, but the driver of the Range Rover spoke 'posh' and you mimicked him with your reply."

"Did I?"

"You did, Dad."

"And did we get through to Shipton?"

"Yes," my sixteen-year-old son smiled, "and back."

One final memory of Mrs W. The scene — a parish council meeting in the village hall, chaired by Ascott's milkman, the ruddy-cheeked, cheerful Harry Cooke. Someone in that audience said something about being a member of the working class and Mrs W chipped in with her cut-glass accent:

"We are all working class, for we all work," she said imperiously.

166

Moving teacups in her drawing room perhaps, but I never did see her tilling the fields. Now that's what I'd call work!

Incidentally the village hall in those days, then called the Tiddy Hall, had been a bequest from one Reginald Tiddy, an influential figure in the field of country music prior to the First World War. The bequest was made after he died from his war wounds. The Tiddy Hall of those days has now been replaced by a modern structure but I remember the old wooden building with affection. It was a place of much communal celebration and where one Christmas I appeared, heavily disguised as Santa Claus, with our own children sworn to secrecy.

The clearest indication of acceptance into the heart of village life was when I was invited onto the Amenities Committee. Unlike the middle-class do-good behaviour of the Ascott Society (of which I still remained chairman!) the 'Amenities' as it was referred to, was made up entirely of members of the local trades and went about its work in a discreet, almost invisible, unheralded way doing useful work. Any villager who was ill or in need was aided by this band of brothers (no sisters) and at Christmas every pensioner received a small personal gift.

At every committee meeting the others would mock what the posh Ascott Society was up to and as chairman of 'that lot' I always sat silent, good-naturedly accepting the joshing until the moment passed and we moved on to other business.

While village affairs were always important to me, the movement of so many actors into the Cotswolds affected my social life. Freddie Jones' fiftieth birthday was a splendid occasion at the Jones'

As Sir Peter Teazle in *School for Scandal* Theatre Clwyd, mid-1970s.

house in Charlbury, near Ascott, where he and his wife Jenny lived on until 2007. I did get somewhat carried away with the likes of Denholm Elliot and Jimmy Villiers and was driven home by my dear wife, definitely in disgrace. My own 40th was also a splendid affair, organised with flair by Elspeth, wine bought at low cost via an American ally from the PX store on the American base at Upper Heyford. I remained sober-ish at my own party and a good time was had by all.

When Richard Eyre directed the film *Iris* about Iris Murdoch, I was reminded of Cotswold conversations with her in which she always stood *mano-a-mano*. I would sometimes feel like a startled rabbit in the headlights of her steady, unwavering gaze as she offered up one penetrating question, followed close on the heels of my answer, by another — all the while seemingly fascinated by the information she was receiving. The process sometimes unnerving, but flattering too.

Another memory was of Iris and her husband John Bayley dancing barefoot with complete abandonment in a world of their own, oblivious of the others on the dance floor, accompanied by loud music. This was at a birthday party for Rosemarie Buckman in an impressive house owned by a wealthy friend of the Buckmans.

Joseph Hone, travel writer, broadcaster and novelist, also lived in the area. He told us a story which involved the much-admired writer, James Cameron. Both Cameron and Hone had worked in Cairo at the time of the 1956 Anglo/French invasion of the Suez Canal. They'd both frequented the same bar in Cairo. Years later Joe Hone revisited Egypt and called in for a drink at their old haunt in Cairo. The barman who'd served them years before was still in place and spoke to Joe as if he were still a regular: "The usual, Mr Hone?" Later, as Joe paid up and made to leave, the barman said: "Do tell Mr Cameron that his bar bill is still open."

Joe immediately offered to pay off the outstanding amount but the barman was adamant. "No — just tell Mr Cameron his bar tab is still open."

Joe, back in England, told Cameron and a few years later Cameron found himself back in Cairo on business. He walked into his old local.

"The usual, Mr Cameron?" The barman, Egyptian imperturbable.

I later checked this when Elspeth and I met James Cameron and his wife. "Ah yes," said James, "after several drinks I suggested that I settle my bar bill. My twenty-year-old bar bill and payment was accepted, without fuss."

Incidentally James Cameron once described the American writer, war correspondent, Martha Gellhorn: "She has a cold eye, but a warm heart." Takes one to know one. Both great writers.

Elspeth had continued to work at her writing. Her first novel, *Catch a Falling Star,* about the early life of poet and churchman John Donne, was published by Blond & Briggs. One day in London to rehearse a television play at the BBC I dropped off several chapters hot off Elspeth's typewriter at Blond & Briggs' office in Blooms bury. Anthony Blond I'd not met, but on the day I called he was the only person present in the office. I recognised him from photographs in the press. As I entered he was hunched over work at a desk. "Yes?" he said abruptly, as he looked up crossly from his work. "What do you want?"

I explained why I was there but because of his abrasive manner didn't bother to introduce myself. He told me to place the material from his author on a desk at the other end of the room. I did so but as I made to leave, he said, curtly: "And who are you?"

Elspeth's surname is Sandys so I chose to reply, because of his offhand manner:

"I'm Mr Sandys."

"No you're not," he answered crisply, glancing briefly to a noticeboard on his left, then turning back to face me. "You're Bruce Purchase, actor." With the flicker of a frozen smile, he returned to his work and I departed.

So much for you being a Kiwi-born smart arse, Purchase, I reflected as I sloped off down the stairs to the street.

At the launch of Elspeth's novel a year later, to avoid conversing with Blond and more importantly to let Elspeth bask in the glow of her special evening without her actor husband pulling focus, I kept in the background, witnessing her pleasure, as folk buzzed around the star of the occasion.

But a woman approached me as I stood in a corner quietly sipping a glass of wine. "Are you with the publishing house?" she enquired pleasantly. I heard myself say a line which was completely impromptu: "No, I'm with Penguin."

Oops, I thought.

"You're a writer?"

"Uh huh."

"What's your subject?"

By now warming to my fictional theme, I murmured: "Middle-East politics," adding for good measure, "Iran in particular." It had the desired effect, her eyes glazed over and she swiftly made her departure.

As the evening progressed I honed my little tale to what I thought, perfection, repelling all boarders. Other pairs of eyes also soon glazed over and their owners drifted away from me. But then later I saw the first woman crossing the room to me, in company with a lean man. She said upon arrival: "I'm sure you'd like to meet Ian Grimble," and left us on our own.

Grimble asked me — etc, etc — when I got to, "… Iran in particular," his eyes, in marked contrast to my earlier interrogators, lit up with evident interest and he interrupted my flow, bursting in with, "Good Lord. I'm professor of history at Tehran University."

I was stunned, but in a split second hissed at him, my voice a croaky whisper.

"It's a lie, it's a lie, it's a lie," I said in panic.

Grimble's turn now to be startled by this madman in front of him. "What do you mean. I am professor of …"

"No, no, no, I mean me. I'm Elspeth Sandys' husband and want it to be her night. I'm actually an actor and …"

"Are you?" said the professor. "I write plays in my spare time."

We then had a grand evening together, sipping wine with me listening to him tell me all about his unpublished, unperformed plays, and as I had in fact visited Iran in 1969 we talked about that country too.

That evening Ian Grimble told a fascinating story. As an eminent historian he'd once been given access to letters and other documents kept at Windsor Castle. He'd discovered in papers stored in the vaults the fact that Victoria's Prince Albert was illegitimate. His real father was the music master to the Saxe-Coburg family, a Jew by the name of Messel. So Albert was half-Jewish and this information was known to the House of Windsor when he married Victoria.

The journalist and biographer, AN Wilson raises this very issue in *The Victorians* (2002), where he asserts Prince Albert was actually the son of one Baron von Mayern, a Jewish chamberlain at the court of Saxe-Coburg — not the son of his supposed father Duke Ernst I, who was syphilitic. Wilson also says he believes Queen Victoria (daughter of Princess Victoire of Leiningen, Duchess of Kent) was fathered by her mother's long-time secretary, Irish-born, Sir John Conroy. This putative parent was not liked by Victoria, who eased him out of the court after she became queen. He died in 1854.

Professor Grimble gave me this version of Albert's real father in 1978. He believed the direct line of descent from Messel, the music master, was to Lt-Col Messel, father of designer Oliver Messel and father too of a daughter, who became Countess of Rosse, mother of photographer, Anthony Armstrong-Jones, who, when he married Princess Margaret, was ennobled as Lord Snowdon.

Cousins?

Soon after this conversation at Elspeth's launch party I asked Robert Hardy, who was playing Prince Albert in *Edward VII,* a series for ATV (in which I played Tsar Alexander III), if he had heard this story.

"Yes, I've heard the rumour."

"Rumour? But Professor Grimble said ..."

"But he may be mistaken."

"Perhaps."

Shortly after our move to the Cotswolds the TV director Alan Cooke offered me a fine role in the BBC TV series, *A Portrait of Katherine Mansfield,* based on the life and short stories of fellow New Zealander, the splendid writer Katherine Mansfield. Vanessa Redgrave played Mansfield and Jeremy Brett, Mansfield's husband John Middleton Murry. This was the beginning of a fruitful working relationship with Alan Cooke which only ceased when Alan and his family moved to Los Angeles.

Alan always cast me in challenging roles. A favourite was as Denholm Elliot's elder brother in a series based on stories by Graham Greene, *Shades of Greene.* This production for Thames TV had Graham Greene's brother, Sir Hugh Carleton Greene, as script editor.

After the read-through of *Under the Garden* Hugh came over to me and said:

"During the summer holiday we'd stay at an uncle's large property in the country, as Mother couldn't afford to take us to the seaside. So we felt the lack of beach holidays. Years later when Graham and I were in our fifties, we made a return journey to our uncle's estate and while standing in the orchard together, as we recalled our childhood memories of the place, the gardener we'd known in those distant days appeared through the trees, wheeling a barrow. We'd remembered him from childhood as then an old man, yet forty years later, here he was again still at work. As he passed us, without pause, he addressed us. 'Hello, Master Hugh. Hello, Master Graham.' As he disappeared into the trees he called back over his shoulder, 'Better than the seaside, innit?' Graham and I, as if in the re-play of a dream, stood startled, rooted to the spot."

His comments made me realise that Ascott was proving better than any seaside resort I knew: a new perspective for a New Zealander who'd lived amidst the most glorious beaches.

At the same time I went on meeting more and more theatrical people with whom I'd worked.

John Davies had directed me in the serialisation of Arnold Bennett's *Clayhanger*, a long contract as we completed 26 episodes.

Two brothers in *Shades of Greene*: Thames TV, late 1970s.

A good friendship developed between our family and his. Along with his wife Mitzi and the children, he lived in a vast house about twenty miles from ours. It became a tradition for us to gather there on Boxing Day and this happy arrangement lasted many years until their marriage ended and Mitzi went to live on Corfu.

As an alternative to the annual village fête in Ascott, I suggested a craft fair, which proved very successful. The talents of the community came to the fore, while outside folk came to enjoy a perfect summer's day.

At its end we had a party in our garden and our guests, standing around the barbeque as dusk fell, thought we'd also planned and arranged the old steam train that chugged by on the railway line in the distance, 200 yards from our celebration.

"Did you arrange that, Elpie?" said John Davies. "Of course," laughed Elspeth as happily triumphant as I'd ever seen her.

Also present was our neighbour, Phoebe de Syllas, who'd sold us our house and who'd become almost a part of our family. Phoebe had moved to Ascott-under-Wychwood from Highgate, but took some time to learn country ways.

At the end of our road was a milking shed where sometimes I'd get cream to make butter in the churn I still possess, but alas no longer use. The farmer, John Townsend, had fields nearby. One day Phoebe complained to him that the mooing of his cows kept her awake at night, so would he be a good chap and move them elsewhere.

"'Fraid not," said gentle farmer.

"Why?" said Phoebe, in her most imperious manner. "I can't sleep at night, their moos keep me awake."

"I can't move them for that's where the available grass is at present. They do have to eat," smiled John T. But by then Phoebe had the bit between her teeth, determined, as she often was, to get her own way. But John won out, his manner, firm, yet gentle.

"Phoebe, you're no longer living in London. You've come to live in the country, where cows live and yes, sometime, moo at night."

Another neighbour, directly opposite us, was Celia Cooke, an elderly woman crippled by arthritis who eked out a small living cleaning and plucking pheasants in season and who kept chickens. Because of her infirmity, we fed them and collected their eggs. One of her cousins ran the village corner shop and another was Harry Cooke, village milkman and chairman of the parish council. Celia had been born in the village and had never travelled outside the district, but was well informed and a veritable fount of local history.

"During the Reformation the village divided itself up. Protestants at the Ascott D'Oyley end of the village and Catholics at the other Ascott Earl end would each arm themselves with staves and have a pitched battle every Saturday. Whoever won got the use of the church in the centre of the village on the following Sunday."

"A very democratic arrangement, Celia, but who refereed these fights?"

"I can't remember," said Celia. "Somebody, I imagine."

I was always pleased to share Celia's company and although largely immobile, with her walking stick she'd hook and pull towards her anything she needed. Although untravelled, she had a worldly wisdom, wide knowledge of events and was a major source of gossip in the village. We drove Celia to London one day to show her the sights but she appeared unimpressed. She'd seen pictures in books after all and on the dozens of jigsaw puzzles she possessed.

Next to Celia lived a fine joiner/craftsman, Frank Tucker, who worked for Cornbury Park Estate, the fiefdom of the not-much-liked local landowner, Lord Rotherwick. Frank's wife Joyce, a helper at the village school, made beautiful corn-dollys. Frank was from the West while Joyce hailed from Northumberland. When Frank got in a new supply of West Country scrumpy (cider),

Big James Yarlett in the ATV production of *Clayhanger*, a 26-part production of Arnold Bennett's trilogy of novels.

Big James leads a group singing at the Dragon.

he'd invite me over for a glass or two. It was a drink, I'd not the heart to tell him, I didn't like, but I so enjoyed his quiet company and that of his gentle Joyce. To my design, Frank built a reading platform high up in our hallway. Reached by a stepladder you pulled up behind, it was a getaway spot for me and beautifully crafted with its balustrade, neat little gate and bookshelves — with armchair and lamp. An escape from the hurly-burly of family life below.

Phoebe, as I've mentioned, was one side, and Robin and Jessica Sutcliffe on the other, our 'west wing'. Our house was called the Long House; the Sutcliffes', Long House Cottage; and Phoebe's referred to as Long House Barn. The three had once been one large single property. When the Sutcliffes moved north their property was bought by the Brainin family, Liesel and Yussi, grandson Tom and daughter Carole Angier, an author like Elspeth. She recently

175

As Big James Yarlett in *Clayhanger*, and opposite, a still from that series.

published an authoritative book about the life of Primo Levi.

Apart from Josie's two ponies, our other livestock were a dog and cat who arrived as kitten and puppy and over the next twelve years became an integral, much-loved part of our lives. Reuben, aged three, was given the task of naming the animals on their arrival at the Long House. Without hesitation he pointed to the puppy and pronounced him 'Meego' and then at the kitten, a ball of black fluff and christened him 'Oddball Beety' — and thus, without fuss, they were named. Meego and Oddy became very definable personalities. The dog never needed a bath as the cat kept him spotless and, returning the compliment, Meego cleaned the cat's ears. Always a well turned out pair.

Elspeth briefly came out of her retirement as an actress when invited to appear in pantomime at the newly opened theatre in nearby Chipping Norton. Out of this we developed a friendship with Nicky Asquith, who owned a riding stable near Stowe-on-the-Wold. Years before her marriage Nicky had been a stage manager, most notably at the Chichester Festival Theatre. When we met her she was divorced with a young family. When Elspeth sold her first novel, Nicky said her mother was a writer too — Elizabeth Jane Howard, who was then married to Kingsley Amis, her stepfather. Several years passed before we discovered who her real father was in the long summer of 1976.

"Let's go to my father's place and have a swim in his pool," said Nicky.

"Where does he live?" It was a very hot day and we didn't fancy a long drive.

"At Slimbridge."

"Oh, not so far — that's where Peter Scott, the son of the Antarctic Scott, has his bird sanctuary, isn't it?"

"Yes. Peter Scott is my father."

We met her dad that day, busy painting — not his well known bird paintings but lots of watercolours of the fabled Loch Ness monster. My favourite was from the point of view under the belly of the monster with the surface of the water above, illuminated by the reflection of the sun. Beautifully conceived.

On another occasion Nicky invited us for dinner, to meet her mother and Kingsley Amis. But long after we'd completed our meal they phoned Nicky to explain that on their journey from London they'd stopped for a quick drink at the Bear Hotel in Woodstock.

It became a long drink after they met friends in the bar, and they decided to book into the Bear for the night and return to London in the morning. Nicky's disappointment was palpable and I got the impression this was not the first time her mother had treated her in this way.

Nicky told us a story about her godfather, the conductor Sir Malcolm Sargent. When she was a youngster he'd taken her to a concert and they'd occupied a private box.

"In the interval," said Sir Malcolm, "a very, very good friend will join us in the box for the second half of the concert."

Sure enough, in the break, a tall, elegantly dressed man entered the box and Sir Malcolm greeted this man effusively, then turned to his small god-daughter, Nicky. 'This is my very, very good friend, Olav, Nicky," adding in a conspiratorial but loud whisper, "… King of Norway."

Olav politely corrected Sir Malcolm. "Sweden," he said.

I've always enjoyed the wit, at times somewhat biting, often distinctly cruel, of writer Gore Vidal. I was told by Nicky that he entered a party in London given by Elizabeth Jane Howard and Kingsley Amis and threaded his way through the crowd until he stood in front of Elizabeth Jane Howard. She had been considered quite a beauty in her early years, but that evening Gore Vidal looked at her, by then a woman of mature years and said: "Oh my God, what happened?" Remembering Nicky's sadness the night of her dinner party, I thought, Well put, Gore Vidal.

Years later I was in a disastrous stage version of his novel *Live from Golgotha*. I played St Paul and am so grateful Gore Vidal did not come to see it.

It was said that when Truman Capote died and Gore Vidal was told of this, his reply was: "A very good career move." They had not cared for one another.

A kinder tale about another writer, also considered a beauty in her youth. Elspeth in the '70s made a stage adaptation of a novel by Rosamond Lehmann, *The Weather in the Streets*. In a secondhand bookshop in London I found a first edition of this novel and paid a handsome price as a gift to Elspeth. I asked Rosamond if she would inscribe it. By then in her eighties but still considering herself a

On location at Elstree for *Clayhanger*. Harry Andrews centre, myself at right.

femme fatale, she held this precious first edition in her hands and batted her eyelids at me.

"I don't have a first edition of my novel," she said, challenging me, I guess, to give it to her instead. I held my ground and after a few seconds she added:

"Do you have a pen?" She then inscribed it for Elspeth and handed the book back to me.

As a family we often rented a cottage at Talland Bay in Cornwall, but other holidays were taken with a New Zealand couple who owned a house on Menorca in the Balearics. Once when Josie holidayed with her father in the States, Elspeth, Reuben and I stayed in a cave house on the Greek island of Santorini. Inside this comfortable cave, away from the blazing Mediterranean sun, we would draw cool water from a well in the centre of the main room, using a bucket and a length of rope. A long walk down a precipitous path to the sea, but a magnificent view of the crescent-shaped bay from the terrace in front of the cave house, and spectacular sunsets. A unique holiday.

On our return to the UK we met Josie off her return flight from the States. Josie, assuming an American accent (bi-lingual had got through as an option at last).

"My God," said Josie, pointing, "what a goddam small truck." "That, Josie," I said looking at the large vehicle ahead of us at Gatwick, "is a British articulated lorry."

Josie grinned. "Still looks like a goddam small truck to me."

Elspeth and I shared a research trip to Greece and Egypt, as preparation for her novel *Love and War*. We visited Crete, Athens, Cairo and Luxor. On Crete in a village high up in the White

Mountains, where Patrick Leigh Fermor held the German Commandant Kreipe prisoner after capturing him in an audacious roadblock, I espied in a taverna a huge mural of Colonel Gaddafi, depicted as a heroic figure on horseback amidst a field of grain. When I asked an old man in the taverna why they had this unusual image — it was huge — on the wall, he winked and pointed south.

"Colonel Gaddafi lives just over the sea in that direction." Hedging their bets, Elspeth and I concluded, as only a few days earlier at nearby Maleme Airport

As the very wicked pirate captain in BBC TV's *Dr Who* series written by Douglas Adams (author of *Hitchhiker's Guide to the Galaxy*), late 1970s.

(where the Germans invaded in the Second World War) a defecting Libyan pilot had crash-landed his fighter plane and then asked for political asylum from the Greek government.

The next day in a village inland from Maleme we spoke to an old Cretan, the mayor of the place, who described how a group of Maori soldiers retook his village from the Germans without using bullets, but with the loss of many lives, as the memorial in the central square bleakly made clear.

"You see that ridge over there," the mayor pointed. "The Maori lads appeared on it and ceremoniously emptied the bullets from their rifles, then drew and fixed their bayonets to their rifles and attacked the Germans with cold steel."

Another fascinating, though sad meeting was with the Cretan who wrote *The Cretan Runner* which described his experience with the Greek Resistance under the command of Patrick Leigh Fermor and Xian Fielding. Both were British officers who'd been parachuted in to fight behind the German lines. This brave Cretan suffered greatly during the Greek civil war that followed the Second World War and ended up tending, not the allied war grave at Suda Bay, but the German war cemetery on Crete.

Onwards, via a stopover in Athens, to Cairo. In that bustling city we stayed in a wonderful old colonial hotel called the Windsor, before finally holidaying at Luxor in Upper Egypt, where we visited both the huge-pillared Temple of Karnak and the tombs on the other side of the Nile, at the Valley of the Kings, which includes that of Tutankhamun.

On our return journey by train from Luxor to Cairo, I fell ill and Elspeth nursed me through an unnerving experience before we flew directly back to the UK. In Cairo we were befriended by a young medical student who referred to himself as Godot, echoing Samuel Beckett. At the time our Egyptian Godot dreamed of getting to the USA but on a later trip I re-met him, by then a doctor. In the run-up to the Gulf War he'd found work in Saddam's Iraq. This time I found him more sinister. Sharing a taxi with me he pointed out some Kuwaiti exiles and said contemptuously: "Our guests."

In the Cotswolds Elspeth wrote *Riding to Jerusalem,* an excellent radio play for the BBC based on a factual 19th-century village event.

Later she developed the story into a novel. It dealt with a local farmer who sacked his workers because they'd joined the newly-formed farm workers' union, then replaced them with non-union workers (scabs) from nearby Leafield. The wives of the sacked workers responded by burning the farmer's wooden gates and hayricks and were arrested and jailed. But Queen Victoria took an interest in their plight and personally pardoned them, giving each £5 and a silk petticoat. They rode back on a cart, in triumph, from Oxford gaol and the whole scene was re-enacted on the centenary of the event. The women are known as the Ascott Martyrs and a memorial was erected on the village green. As we were living there Elspeth was prompted to write her radio play in which I was cast as the wicked farm owner, a part written specifically for me.

Near Ascott is ancient Wychwood Forest, which was King John's hunting domain. Now part of an estate called Cornbury Park, it was owned by Lord Rotherwick. Then, in the '70s, it was and still is, a hunting forest hired out to clients as a killing field for deer and pheasant. But on Palm Sunday every year it is open to the public as a historic right. On this one day some locals from the nearby village of Leafield have the rights to collect firewood and from an old well, draw water to which magical healing qualities are attributed. The water is called Spanish Liquor.

Along with friends we often took advantage of the Palm Sunday walk through King John's old forest. One year I unleashed our dog Meego and out of the forest appeared one of Lord Rotherwick's staff, who admonished me. Fair enough, but the man was deeply unpleasant, though I kept silent and put the dog back on his lead. I'd been earlier talking to other walkers about just how unpopular Lord Rotherwick was and in the presence of the hireling, my friends' young son Nick said innocently:

"Is that the bad man, Dad?"

"No," my friend Richard said. "That I think is the bad man's bad man."

Incidentally, this employee who put me in my place was a few years later jailed for stealing from Cornbury Park Estate, while my own career was taking a new turn.

"Where do you live, Bruce?"

"A forty minute drive from Stratford-Upon-Avon."

"How long have you lived in the area?"

"Seven years."

"Why then have you not worked with us before?"

"Until now, Terry, you'd not invited me."

'Invited' — now there's a word no longer in current usage. Actors then, were 'invited' to accept a job. Now we just get asked, offered, or not, as the case may be.

That exchange just recounted was with Terry Hands, then the artistic director of the Royal Shakespeare Company and I'd just joined that company. It was 1980. I would remain with the RSC for the following two and a half years. They were good years — enjoyable years, but destined — out of a mixture of my hubris and a contract agreed but not honoured to the letter by the company — to end discordantly. But that tale is not part of this idyll.

An uncomfortable moment in the film of Christopher Fry's *A Phoenix Too Frequent*, mid-1970s.

Our life in the Cotswolds came to an end in 1982. Josie changed schools, leaving Burford Comprehensive for Oxford Girls High School. Reuben left the village school to take up a place at Magdalen College School, also in Oxford.

"I hear you're selling your house?"

It was my accountant from London on the phone.

"Yes."

"I'll buy it. What are you asking for it?"

I told him, adding: "But Michael, you've never seen the Long House."

183

"That's correct, but I know an awful lot of folk who have."

Penny, his wife, viewed it the next day — and, good as his word, they went ahead and bought it for the asking price. He didn't see the place himself until after the sale had gone through.

Just before we moved from the Long House, I said to Elspeth: "Leaving this house will break my heart."

"But you'll always carry the memory of it."

She was right.

Another scene from the film *A Phoenix Too Frequent.*

VIII

Painting up a storm

A DECADE BEFORE HIS APPEARANCE AS GANDALF in *Lord of the Rings*, Ian McKellen played the title role in Shakespeare's *Richard III*. This production along with *King Lear* (Brian Cox as the Old King) played twenty cities in eleven countries. Later the tour of *Richard III* was extended — five more cities were played, over a four month period in the United States. This National Theatre tour was arguably the most ambitious theatrical tour to come out of Britain in the 20th century. The journey began in Tokyo in September 1990 and with the extension to the United States, was completed two years later, September 1992. Throughout I was cast as Edward IV in *Richard III* and the doctor in *King Lear*.

An event five months prior to rehearsals for the two productions became inextricably linked to the world tour. On 10 October 1989 I started painting, first with oils, later gouache (poster paint) pastels, watercolour and acrylic. One major reason I accepted the world tour was the realisation that I'd get to see major paintings in galleries, worldwide.

"Why on earth, Jo, do you think I'd be any good at painting?" My stepdaughter had just presented me with a starter oil painting set. Josie smiled: "I just have an instinct you'll be good." Josie was herself a promising painter.

But I was dubious and placed the gift high on a shelf in my Oxford, bachelor-pad kitchen.

Josie however, was a determined young woman of twenty-four, and she would not let me off the hook. First, over a period of weeks, she gently cajoled her stepfather, but as weeks became months, issued an ultimatum: "If you don't start I'll claim the paints back." So, I began and was hooked immediately. It was as if I'd been painting all

Cartoon by Robert Hewison of Bruce Purchase with John Bowe and Jenny Agutter in *Arden of Faversham*, Royal Shakespeare Company, Stratford-Upon-Avon, 1982.

my life. Images, no shortage, appeared, as if of their own volition. There they were: seascapes, landscapes, portraits, animals, the lot.

I remember one of Josie's own paintings when she was about eight. It was a triangular shape with a vividly painted single 'tulip', growing out of the point of a triangle at the top of the paper.

"What's this, Josie?"

"It's you," she replied.

No other portrait could move or flatter me more. Later, in sixth form at Oxford Girls High School, Josie won the art prize at A level.

After a week or two of continuous painting I was very committed to the task. I phoned an artist friend: "Tony, will you pay me a call, for I think I'm painting." He came and viewed my daubs, oils

186

executed on the backs of television scripts, drying all over the place, on any available surface and the floor too.

"Should I book in for art classes?" I breathlessly questioned.

"No, Bruco," Tony smiled, "just carry on, but change from oils to gouache, paint on larger sheets of paper and [looking at my tiny brush] treat yourself to a longer brush."

Tony and I had first met in New Zealand in 1968 when I played the king in a New Zealand Ballet television production of *Sleeping Beauty*, which he designed.

Anthony Stones was for a number of years president of the Society of Portrait Sculptors in Britain and in recent years has become a visiting professor of sculpture in several Chinese universities. With his Chinese wife, Lily Feng (an accomplished paleontologist), he splits his time between the UK and China, with a busy creative life in both countries. In 2007 he was occupied with a larger-than-life-size running warrior commissioned for the Beijing Olympics and several commissions in the United Kingdom.

Now, many years after those early painterly tips, when I ask for advice from Tony his reply is more sophisticated, as I've come on a bit: "Try paraphrase and metamorphosis, Bruco," one such recent note. But in 1989 his first helpful hints brought my next bundle of works into new focus. With the change from oil to gouache the paintings dried instantly so output increased dramatically. I was like a playful puppy paddling in a colourful lake. By December I was painting so fast, another Oxford friend, journalist Chris Gray, was heard saying: "Yes, Brucie had a blue period — it lasted a morning!"

I developed a new, idiosyncratic approach. I'd chuck a sheet of pre-soaked paper on the floor by my kitchen sink and with the cold tap gently running, apply the colour from my set that my eye first lit upon. Standing and leaning forward over my work, I splashed away with enthusiasm, using my longer brush. Good exercise for the back too! Out of the watery colour on the paper at my feet, images, some impressionist, some expressionist, never abstract, appeared, as if by magic, my brush a sort of wand. This completely instinctive period produced some paintings that were very bad but many more that were interesting. One 'face' that just appeared, was, to put it mildly, scary, a portrait that looked half-man/half-animal, with piercing

Playing the king (third from right) in a 1969 TVNZ production
of the *Sleeping Beauty* ballet; set design by Tony Stones.

eyes. But it was a powerful image which I set aside not believing it
would ever sell, for from the start I knew I wanted to sell. No artist
in the garret for me. A year later, however, that very image did sell
— to an Iranian theatre director.

"Why do you want that one?"

His answer has haunted me ever since: "It reminds me of my
torturer and me," he said, "and I find it very healing." He'd been
tortured in Iran during the Shah's rule. He had it beautifully framed
and it hangs in his study where he can look at it every day.

188

The sheer mystery associated with the processes of painting still fascinates me.

From the beginning I decided to keep a photographic record of my paintings, in chronological order, to study my progress. Knowing neither shame nor shyness in those early days, I showed the albums of my photographs to anyone who was even half-interested and to others who weren't remotely interested! These albums, more easy to transport than the actual paintings, soon became a sales ploy.

"Get yourself an early Purchase," I shamelessly trumpeted.

My daubs began to sell, at first for modest sums that didn't remotely cover my costs.

During a spell out of work as an actor, John Wain — novelist, poet and one of the original Angry Young Men — said to me: "Brucie — I think you are the only person I've ever met who has painted his way *out* of a corner."

At times I did get above myself: hubris would set in. I said in a Camden town bistro: "I'd happily give up acting if I could earn a living as a painter."

My companion at dinner was not impressed. Tom Wilkinson, a fine actor, nominated for an Oscar for his performance in *In the Bedroom*, responded to my brashness with innate North Country common sense: "Tell the truth, Bruce," he said, affectionate but firm.

"Why do you so often paint Kapiti Island?" My interrogator was Peggy Garland, sculptor, painter and mother of cartoonist, Nicholas Garland. Peggy, then aged about ninety, was a formidable person and I'd dreaded showing her my work. After looking without comment, she'd finally said: "Yes, you are a real artist, but why do you so often paint Kapiti?" A spell was broken by her observation. I remembered myself as an eight year old, standing on a beach looking out at Kapiti and thinking it was the most mysterious island I'd ever see. Forty-four years later Peggy had broken that spell — I'd been unconsciously painting and repainting a distant memory of a strangely shaped island off the western coast near Wellington. Kapiti Island, now a conservation sanctuary, was the 19th-century fiefdom of a powerful Maori chief, Te Rauparaha, a military genius.

*

189

"What world tour?" It was March 1990. Having just returned from a holiday in New Zealand, I was a little out of touch with events in my profession. I'd been summoned that day to meet director, Tim Albery, for consideration for a role in a play written by Racine. I was talking to a member of the National Theatre casting department. She had just told me that the National's artistic director, Richard Eyre wanted to talk to me after my interview with Albery — "about the world tour." In that instant I knew my destiny lay not with the Racine, but with the tour. Sure enough, after my meeting with Albery I found Richard Eyre waiting for me in the corridor.

"Come this way, Bruce." He led me to his office and told me about the ambitious world tour and offered me, on the spot, the two roles of Edward IV and the Doctor. Though neither role is particularly arduous I agreed immediately, quickly realising I was not only being offered a long period of prestigious employment, but also exciting world travel and, the great bonus — a kind of art scholarship.

On 19 March 1990 rehearsals began for the tour. Bucks Fizz (champagne and orange juice) was served to us at 11a.m. and Richard Eyre, without notes, introduced everyone present, some forty in all. Then with models of the *mise en scène* in place for us to see, the two designers, Cork-born Bob Crowley (*Richard III*) and the beautiful Hildegard Bechtler (*King Lear*) described both sets and costumes. Then we sat down at a long table to read both plays.

It's always fascinating to witness how actors handle this first commitment — the read-through. Some mumble their lines while others are more forthcoming. For instance I remember Laurence Olivier usually 'gave' at the read-through, his performance. But it's early days …

On day one I met an actor I'd not known. Over the following two years a splendid friendship developed. Sam Beazley, then aged seventy-six, had been a child actor along with Alec Guinness. But he gave up the profession and became one of London's most successful antique dealers, with Portmeirion Antiques in Pont Street. At seventy-four he retired as an antique dealer (and talented, also successful, interior decorator) and returned to acting. Since then Sam Beazley has not stopped. I saw him recently, still fit, lithe with marbles all intact, this Edwardian gent, getting all his laughs, in a delightful production at the National of *His Girl Friday*. Seventeen years after our first meeting we are still close friends. In 2007, at age 91, Sam was still acting, dancing and singing. He is also a fine watercolourist and this cemented our friendship. On the world tour with painting in both our minds, we visited art galleries from Cairo to Cork, Paris to Prague, Milan to Minnesota and more. It became our day job.

From his antique-dealer days, along the route of the tour, Sam met startled ex-customers, notably Lauren Bacall in New York and Gregory Peck, to name-drop just two. One member of our troupe, actor Richard Simpson, commented dryly in New York:

"I suppose even the Duchess of Windsor was one of your customers?"

"Yes," Sam replied briskly, "and a good one too. She'd choose something and the next day, her Commendatore would come in to pay for it."

Both productions were rehearsed simultaneously, between the two rehearsal rooms, a logistical nightmare — actors dashing this way and that — a real production line. Both shows opened, after a thirteen-week rehearsal, within days of each other. Forty performances of each play then followed over ten weeks at the National Theatre in London. Then — the start of the world tour — Tokyo.

During the rehearsal period I continued to paint, even mounting an exhibition in a garden in Oxfordshire. It sold well. As I continued I started to focus more and more on images from the two productions. Then I had a brainwave.

I asked our tour manager, Roger Chapman, if the National intended to tour a shop selling company memorabilia. He said no, so I presented an idea to him. I would produce signed limited edition prints of both productions, for sale on the tour. Roger was enthusiastic and gave me the go-ahead. He also went one better, introducing me to Mr Tamura, who was on a visit to the UK and was the manager of the Globe Theatre, where we were to perform in Tokyo. Tamura San was equally enthusiastic. As well as extending my brief, he'd supply an outlet not just for the sale of the prints but also a space for my original paintings.

For my images I decided to focus on the heart of the plays, suggesting character is all, but star quality helps. So there were two portraits each of Ian McKellen and Brian Cox. In Oxford at a cost of £3000, I had 1200 prints made, 300 of each image, signed, numbered and dated. A bold venture!

One morning on the Cotswold-line train on my way to rehearsals, I met my ex-wife, Elspeth Sandys. She was on a visit to the UK, having moved to New Zealand. Novelist Sandys had married another New Zealand writer, Maurice Shadbolt. It was her third marriage and Shadbolt's fourth. Didn't seem to bode well and after a short marriage the inevitable happened. They both seemed to share a similar quality, a yearning for elsewhere. Perhaps they felt that it is never too late to marry, nor too soon to divorce!

But on that train journey, that sunny spring day, Elspeth enquired about my painting. I handed over two volumes of photographs of my work, and as she leafed through the images, I in turn looked at Elspeth, the woman I'd loved and lived with for fifteen years. Maybe "too soon" is a bit tough. And she was mother, too, of our son Reuben.

Elspeth finally looked up from the photographs.

"There's an element missing."

"Oh, what's that?"

"Your wit."

Perhaps Elspeth had heard I'd occasionally raised a cheap laugh by describing myself as "the second husband of Mrs Shadbolt the fourth," but it is true that, at that stage, I found it hard to bring laughter into my painting. The whole business seemed too 'serious'. Now I hope that I can call up a touch of playfulness, even wit.

One reason I took my unexpected gift so seriously was the result of a mysterious experience just before our departure for Japan. I was painting in my dressing room (more a cubbyhole) at the National. I'd run out of paper, yet felt the urge to paint. I searched and found some crumpled brown wrapping paper, so sellotaped it to the wall: "That'll do." With no idea what I would paint, I started with horizontal strokes, to apply a 'ground' to the brown paper, the colour a slightly darker gouache brown than the paper itself. I was giving myself time to decide what I might do. Fellow actor Kae Kazim appeared in the doorway, "What are you about to paint, Bruce?" I turned and flickered him a glance before replying:

Painting, 1990. *Oxford Mail and Times* photo.

"I've no idea — yet."

I continued my horizontal strokes but then, with Kae still watching, something very strange began to happen. As I applied the paint, Kae Kazim's features began to appear — much like the way there is an inexplicable image on the Turin shroud! A shiver went down my spine. Kae said softly: "My God, you're painting me?"

"It would appear so," my voice a whisper as I did not wish to break the spell ... "but how?"

I never altered the horizontal sweeps of the brush yet by the time I reached the bottom of the paper, Kae's features, a sketch, were clearly visible. No one has ever given me a satisfactory explanation of how this happened and it has never happened again.

*

Ian McKellen also came to watch me paint. As an actor Ian is very much a technician, so his question was typical:

"When you first started, for instance, how did you decide to hold the paintbrush?"

"I tried it this way, then that, then this — I just experimented, for when I started, I knew nothing."

Ian and I first worked together at Ipswich Repertory Theatre in 1963. Over time we've built an enjoyably easy and bantering relationship. I was glad he visited New Zealand when he was filming *Lord of the Rings*. I phoned him in Wellington.

"Have you enjoyed your time here in my homeland?" His reply was serious, thoughtful, "Yes, it has been a blessèd year."

We had an amusing exchange during early rehearsals of *Richard III*. We'd just completed a run-through of a scene. For those who didn't see either the stage version or Richard Loncraine's film, the production was set in the 1930s, with *Richard III* and his coterie depicted as Oswald Mosley-like, black-shirt fascists. All the Royals in the play spoke with the cut-glass accents of the '30s. We had dialect lessons to that effect.

As we finished this scene and assembled for notes from our director, Richard Eyre, Ian amusingly tried to bait me — a Kiwi from the colonies.

"Brucie," Ian drawled in his characteristic way.

"Yes, Ian?" I replied warily.

"Shouldn't you pronounce Marquis, as mar-kwess?" Ian said teasingly. I'd just pronounced it as mar-kwiss.

"No, Ian."

But McKellen, having by then secured the attention of everyone present, pressed his case.

"Oh, no," he said — "it's mar-kwess, not mar-kwiss."

As our actor-king smiled triumphantly I fired back my answer:

"It might be pronounced that way ... in Bolton" (where Ian came from).

Richard Eyre, interceded — "Bruce is right Ian, *kwiss* not *kwess*. Okay let's do the scene again ..."

Ian smiled, I grinned back. Game over, now back to the hard slog.

We arrived in Tokyo, exhausted after our flight. A few days before we left for Tokyo, veteran actor Basil Henson said to me:

"Tell the young men in your company that the Japanese girl dressers at the Globe Theatre in Tokyo don't look as if they do it, but, they do!"

I passed on Henson's practical advice to the lads in our troupe. The girls did, so our lads did. I on the other hand, didn't, being somewhat long in the tooth for such dalliance. I do remember a bit of helpful advice on the rubbish bins in the dressing rooms — *All Cigarettes Should Be Distinguished.*

At the Gala Night performance all was more serious as Anne, the Princess Royal, and the Crown Prince of Japan were our honoured guests. We were presented to them after the show. McKellen, throughout the tour, was a supporter of my prints and suggested I present a set of the prints to Princess Anne. Once her lady-in-waiting had correctly established this was a gift not from me, the artist, but an official gift from the National Theatre, the prints were graciously accepted. At the party that followed, Peter Hall was intrigued by my exhibition of prints and paintings. "I didn't know you painted, Bruce." He and his new bride, Nicky Frei, were in Tokyo on honeymoon.

Tamura San was as good as his word, given a month earlier in London. He allocated an area in the foyer for the display and sale

Punting on the Cherwell, Oxford 1962: friends Barbara Caruso from New York & Vincent O'Sullivan, New Zealand. At right: the punter.

of my work. After each performance I went front-of-house to check how much had been sold. One evening I approached the display area and the three pretty sales girls applauded me. Their manager explained:

"They have sold many of your prints tonight." She smiled approvingly and the shining faces of the sales girls sparkled like water.

"Have you played much Shakespeare?" the Crown Prince of Japan asked me, his English accent impeccable, very 'Oxford', where he'd studied.

"Yes, I have," my reply.

"Ah-so-yaar," said the Crown Prince — an amalgam of the clichéd Japanese 'ah so' and very Oxford 'yaar'.

When it was announced, years before, that the Crown Prince of Japan was to study at Oxford, the vice-chancellor Sir Patrick Neill was asked what the Crown Prince would study. His reply was brilliant, remembering the unpopular Japanese whale fishing policy: "I think marine biology will be appropriate."

We had one free weekend whilst in Japan. Most of the company took the bullet train to see the temples at Kyoto. I, on the other hand,

accepted an invitation to stay with an old mate, the Australian-born journalist Murray Sayle and his family, long resident in Japan. They lived in a town near Tokyo. I'd first met Murray at the American bookshop in Paris in the early '60s when he was working for Reuters. He now lives in Australia.

Apropos of the Japanese royal family, in 1988 Murray and I, along with my American friend, the actress Barbara Caruso, spent a few days cruising the English canal systems on a narrow boat. Bliss. But in those pre-mobile phone days, Murray had to make inconveniently regular landline calls because Emperor Hirohito of Japan was on his deathbed and when the old man died Murray had to file his copy.

My house gift to the Sayles came as a result of my friendship with Finnish-born designer, Paivii Makarinne Crofts. At the same time as we were performing in Tokyo, Paivii was also in town, staying with a Japanese friend. Paivii was a remarkable woman. Her decision to travel to Japan at that time was exceptionally brave, as only two months earlier she had endured a ten-hour operation when surgeons in Oxford attempted to remove a brain tumour. After the operation she'd been told by her medics that they'd not managed to remove the tumour entirely, which was malignant. Therefore her life was

197

still in danger and seven years later, at 50, dear brave Paivii died, after a long courageous battle. My last meeting with her was shortly before her death. As always, she was looking sensational. She was lying elegantly on a *chaise longue*, beautifully dressed and with a cheerfully coloured silk scarf around her head. As I was about to leave I stood and looked down at beautiful Paivii and said: "You're a bit of a miracle, aren't you?" She smiled her gentle smile and replied softly with her characteristic, slow, Finnish accent: "Yes — people have often said this about me."

In Tokyo, seven years earlier, she came up with perfect gift for me to take to the Sayles. Paivii's Japanese woman friend (they'd been fellow design students in Britain) was making a commercial for television — its subject, a traditional English Christmas. At the end of the shoot the Japanese still had two frozen turkeys, which had been flown out from the UK, surplus to requirements. Paivii, God bless her, secured one for me. The gift was a great success.

I sold so many prints in Tokyo I was laden with yen, but left my bag of loot and wallet at a roof-top restaurant. But I got it back, credit cards, yen and all. "Yeah," said Sayle when I told him, "the Japanese tend not to steal personal property." Amazing.

Next step, Nottingham, after a long flight back to the UK on Virgin Airways, with its owner Richard Branson on board. I observed he flew tourist class. Clever.

Everywhere (Nottingham, Cardiff and Leeds) we went, reviews of the two plays were full of praise, and I had good sales of the prints as well. In Belfast sales were down — we played the Opera House, beautifully restored after having been blown apart by an IRA bomb.

On to Germany where in Hamburg at the Kunsthalle I saw work by artists I'd not known before — Lovis Corinth, for one. Expressionist painters like Dix, Grosz and Kirchner. In Britain, German art is disgracefully under-represented. In Germany I feasted my eyes on paintings by Marc, Klee, Kandinsky, Schiele, Schmidt-Rottluf. The experience was richly rewarding.

In Milan, at the Lirico Theatre where we played, I turned not one but two dressing rooms into studios for my work. I visited La Scala and also the famous Georgio Strehler's Piccolo Theatre, where we saw a delightful production of Goldoni's *The Servant of Two Masters*. Ian McKellen christened Strehler, an exceptionally vain man, with his blue-rinsed hair, 'Betty Blue Rinse'.

Madrid followed Milan, but our performances were cancelled because of a technician's strike. Instead we had a week's holiday and every day I enjoyed the glorious Prado Museum. The Goyas are wonderful, including also the powerful, brooding dark works executed at the end of his life. And, just up the road from the Prado, Picasso's 'Guernica,' with all his preparatory sketches.

In spite of the cancelled performances, a planned gala party took place — an odd occasion for we had nothing to celebrate. But VIPs had flown in …

An hour into the party a Japanese-American member of our publicity department interrupted the very agreeable conversation I was having with a bunch of Madrileños. She instructed me to go to the other end of the ballroom and be presented to our guest, Princess Alexandra. But when I got to the meeting point there was a long line of folk and, assuming I'd not be missed, I returned to my agreeable group of locals. Our conversation continued and attentive waiters kept my glass of champagne topped up!

But my absence had been noted. An hour later, someone gently touched my elbow and I turned round. It was Ian McKellen and, standing beside him, the lady herself. They had come to me. Ian introduced me to Princess Alexandra and she said:

"Who do you play in *Richard III*?"

"Edward IV, Ma'am."

"And how are you costumed?"

So far, so good, but my reply, champagne infused, edged me off the rails: I answered her second question thus:

"I'm dressed in this production most royally, Ma'am." McKellen swooped in on this rhetorically fulsome reply. He quickly described how *Richard III* was staged. This attempt to smooth over my comment amused me and as Ian completed his description I interjected:

"Do you know, Ma'am, I've always adored you?"

Ian's face was a study. He was aghast. But if Princess Alexandra was flabbergasted she did not show it, though she momentarily rocked slightly back on her heels, before calmly asking me a third question.

199

Her demeanour appeared serene.

"Have we met before?"

Dancing on the champagne bubbles in my bloodstream, I ploughed on:

"No, Ma'am, we have not met before — but — I have always adored you." It was, after all, the truth! By now Ian had given up!

Princess Alexandra stayed with me for several minutes and we had a pleasant conversation, no doubt to the puzzlement of the line of VIPs behind her, which included the chairman of Guinness, the British Ambassador and Alexandra's husband, Angus Ogilvy. Of course, by the end of the evening, Ian McKellen had embellished the story — "I think you're a beaut sheila, Alex."

Greatly refreshed after our free week in Madrid, our next port-of-call was the Odeon theatre, in Paris. Walking one day with Sam Beazley on the Left Bank's St Germain, he suggested a detour. Sam wanted to check if an antique shop, remembered from his past, still existed. It was still there, a shop on a corner, with no sign, no name. He explained it'd been owned by a Madame Caistang: "She'd be a hundred, if she is still alive." Two days later he passed that shop again, this time on his own, and lo and behold there was Mme Caistang greeting her customers, as of old. 100 years old!

Twenty months later in a museum, I think it was in San Francisco, I was looking at a fine oil painting of a young woman. The artist was Soutine and his subject, the title, 'Madame Caistang'. I called Beazley over: "Yes, she was Soutine's mistress," Sam said.

"I'm pleased to be here on this day of liberation," the voice was that of our director, Richard Eyre. He'd just flown in from London. Richard was referring to Mrs Thatcher's resignation as prime minister that day.

We were invited for lunch at the British embassy. Before lunch the ambassador, Euan Fergusson (he'd played rugby for Scotland), encouraged the lads who played the young princes in *Richard III* to clamber up a huge bronze by Henry Moore which stood at the end of the embassy's garden — even joining them and clambering up himself. Then, after an excellent lunch, he showed a group of us his private quarters. In a drawing room he described Mrs Thatcher's visit, shortly before her resignation. He said he and his wife were with Thatcher, watching television. On the screen was TV political journalist, John Sergeant. It was a live appearance, as Sergeant was actually standing outside on the embassy steps. When Sergeant commented he thought Mrs Thatcher would not stand for re-selection in the next round of voting, Thatcher fumed and rose to her feet. She then left the room, followed by the Fergussons. She charged down the stairs, across the foyer, through the front door and up to Sergeant who was still speaking live to camera.

"Of course I will be standing," said Mrs Thatcher, on prime-time telly. Euan Fergusson then said to us, with relish.

"So I watched Mrs Thatcher commit political suicide on the steps of my embassy."

In his autobiography, *Give Me a Few Seconds*, Sergeant claims Mrs Thatcher had not been watching him on TV, but that's not what Ambassador Fergusson said.

In Paris, Beazley and I revisited favourite old haunts — the Musée D'Orsay, the Pompidou, the Picasso galleries etc.

Next stop, Cork city in Eire, where for the first time I discovered the talent of painter, Jack Yeats, brother of poet WB. In Cork we played only a few days but nevertheless I moved some of my stock. I did a self-portrait, using gouache, then with dampened paper took a print from this painting which I'd executed on my dressing room mirror! My dresser wanted to buy it and she got it in exchange for a bottle of illegal poteen — a strong Irish potato-brewed spirit.

It was a split week — within a short period we'd closed in Paris, played briefly in Cork and then opened in Cairo! Culture shock! The British Council in Cairo were endlessly generous to us. Because of the build-up to war in the Gulf there were very few tourists in Egypt so Saqqara, the Sphinx, Pyramids etc we enjoyed virtually on our own. On the tour the exceptional, if volatile actress, Clare Higgins, had a habit of always changing her hotel room. It became a good-humoured 'family' running joke — as one exited the lift to find one's room, Clare would enter the lift, heading for the hotel desk to remonstrate with staff — in yet another city. When Clare was exiting the Great Pyramid, actor David Bradley (superb as the Fool in *King Lear*) was waiting to enter that magnificent edifice: "Oh, changing your room, Clare?" he quipped.

Seeing the sun come up on the Pyramids while mounted on horseback; sharing a camel ride with veteran actress, Joyce Redman; and, on horseback again, galloping an Arab stallion across the desert — some rich memories from the Egyptian portfolio of my mind. In Cairo we played the Opera House but because that place was managed by a Muslim Fundamentalist group it was inappropriate for me to sell my wares.

We finished our performances in Cairo on 16 December. We were to be free over the Christmas and New Year. Most of the company flew home immediately but a few of us stayed on until Christmas Eve. First I visited Alexandria. In 'Alex' I stayed at the Cecil Hotel, overlooking the bay. That hotel features in Olivia Manning's novels — *The Balkan Trilogy*. Sightseeing included visiting the stylish tomb where the Roman emperors and senators buried their favourite horses — no doubt those steeds included Caligula's, the one he made a senator! Then I flew to Aswan and stayed in the fabulous Old Cataract Hotel. Tea on the terrace, as the sun goes down on the Nile, is one of my favourite views in the world. The Nile at that point, near the Aswan Dam, is very wide with several islands, including one that Earl Kitchener turned into a private garden. I said to one of the younger actors who'd also stayed on: "Do you see that building half way up the hill on the other side of the Nile?"

"Yes, what is it?"

"It's the tomb of Rita Hayworth's father-in-law."

He was too young to grasp my reference. The building is the last resting place of the old Aga Khan, whose son, Aly Khan, was married to — yes, film star Rita Hayworth.

On Christmas Eve I arrived back in Oxford. A personal storm-cloud was gathering that would shortly devastate my life. Just after Christmas my son Reuben was involved in a fracas and was charged with causing grievous bodily harm. The events that followed will be dealt with more fully in a later chapter.

Next stop abroad, Prague. McKellen knighted in the New Year's Honours List. First night at the Prague Opera House more flowers were thrown on the stage than I'd ever seen, and the applause seemed to go on forever. Our new knight lifted up a bouquet and threw it in the direction of the box of Václav Havel, the president and playwright. An arm appeared as the flowers were caught. A spontaneous and joyous moment.

We were invited to the British embassy. Another guest expected that night was the American ambassador, Shirley Temple Black, but with the troubles in the Gulf, her security advisors persuaded her not to venture out. I prefer to think she was more a-feared that the collective persuasion of the National Theatre Company would coerce her into one more rendition of, 'On the Good Ship *Lollipop*'. Upstairs at the British embassy is a large guest bedroom that was once Mozart's apartment. The view from the window to the narrow street below is virtually unchanged from his time.

Lady Soames DBE, daughter of Winston Churchill, chaired the board of the National Theatre. Mary Soames is good company, and gave us an impromptu party in her hotel suite in Prague. We arrived after a snowball fight on the way back from the theatre. Mary there at the door of her suite, smoking a cheroot, greeted her band of distinctly damp thespians with laughter and good cheer.

In a privately hired jet we flew from Prague, bound for Bucharest in Romania, but were informed *en route* that the plane was being diverted to land at Sofia in Bulgaria because Bucharest Airport was snowbound. Two Bulgarian air force fighter jets escorted us within Bulgarian airspace as we were an unscheduled flight. We were off-loaded into the dismal transit lounge at Sofia and saw our jet take off, leaving us stranded. After a few hours, however, we were rescued by the British ambassador's staff and bussed to a bleak hotel on the outskirts of town. We were the only guests, which did not surprise us at all. We endured a mediocre evening meal, saved only by excellent Bulgarian red wine at knock-down prices. One of the waiters did a floor show for us — he dressed up as Adolf Hitler and stomped about. Very odd.

Next morning two coaches turned up to take us on the all-day drive to Bucharest. We had one stop-over in a polluted city called Pleven. For the bemused locals it must have looked as if Hollywood had hit town, as on the pavement we sang:

We're in Pleven,
We're in Pleven

As a result of our appearance, the price of coffee from a street vendor escalated dramatically — all this against the background of huge statues of Lenin *et al* in the city square. At dusk we crossed the Friendship Bridge into Romania and by mid-evening reached Bucharest where I fell exhausted into my depressing, single-bulb lit, hotel room. Clare Higgins probably went ballistic.

From the moment I walked on-stage to view the theatre and a stage weight fell from above, missing me by inches, I started to dislike Bucharest. Our stage technicians were mightily pissed off when the crates of beer they'd brought to Romania, as a gift for the local stage staff, were stolen by the very technicians they were intended for. Everything had to be locked up or it was stolen.

Heavy snow on the ground and the only colour in that grim city, the brightly-costumed gipsy women employed to shovel the city streets clear. It was bitterly cold so I wore a fur hat I'd bought cheaply in Budapest years before.

"Nice hat, Bruce," commented Joyce Redman, who played my mum in *Richard III*. I attempted what I thought was a joke: "Yes, Joyce — I think it's ocelot because it didn't cost-a-lot," but this feeble rhyme fell flat: "Don't be ridiculous, it's mink!" I would never dare wear it in Britain.

Back in the UK for a few days I was able to lend support to my twenty-year-old son at one of the many court appearances he had to make over the months that led up to his trial. Considering the strain on him, his spirits seemed to be holding up.

In both Leipzig and Dresden I was faced with a challenge. Actor Peter Jeffrey was rushed off to hospital before we left Germany so I had to take over his two roles.

In *Richard III* I was to play both his role as Clarence and my own role as his brother, Edward IV. This necessitated an incredibly swift costume and make-up change, as one scene followed the other. First I was dragged off-stage as Clarence, to be "drowned in a butt of malmsey", then I miraculously reappeared a minute later, as Edward IV. This in front of stunned German audiences, who probably thought "Clarence and Edward, we know, are brothers but they appear also to be — identical twins."

With thanks to Brian Cox for his great support, I quote from his book, *The Lear Diaries* (published by Methuen) where he generously recalled my 'baptism' as Gloucester: "Bruce was, needless to say, very nervous. He'd been in the company for a year, a wonderful actor, very distinguished. Ironically he played my father in a television series about Henry II." (Brian had played Henry with me as his dad, Philip Plantagenet).

"I told Bruce to use his largeness as a sensualist; that was what was important, that sensual drive. He used it, I think to advantage and certainly in the Dover scene his wailing was incredibly moving."

An excellent review. Thanks Brian. Both Cox with Gloucester and Ian McKellen with Clarence, in the absence of our directors Deborah Warner and Richard Eyre, lent me staunch support for which I will always be grateful.

Next stop Edinburgh. Peter Jeffrey, by then recovered though still very weak, to my relief reclaimed his roles. In Edinburgh *King Lear*, because Brian had other commitments, finished its tour of duty. Cox celebrated, before the party that followed, by cutting off his long white hair and beard.

Another break from the world tour and Elspeth arrived in the UK from New Zealand to lend support to our son in his hour of need.

With some changes of cast, *Richard III* then played Aberdeen, Bradford and my home base, Oxford. Then in 1992 with a new cast, except for Beazley, Richard Simpson, Phil McKee, myself and McKellen, we re-rehearsed for the extension of the world tour — the four-month journey around the United States. In spite of events that occurred in my son's life and the stress and sadness this afforded me, the United States leg of the tour was wonderful, though the lid I'd put on my pain was to explode — the crisis for me happened in San Francisco.

But another glitch occurs, one, I hasten to add, not remotely painful, just annoying. On day one at the National, for rehearsals with the new cast, our splendid tour manager the unflappable Roger Chapman made a surprise announcement. He made a pointed reference to such sales, as mine, of prints on tour: "The US authorities will not allow it." Several pairs of eyes in the room looked sideways at me to see what my reaction was, but, though inwardly furious, like a good 'gun-fighter,' I didn't blink.

Sales of my prints had been generally good in most cities prior to this, though in places like Bucharest, Prague, Leipzig and Dresden, for economic reasons — zilch. So I still had product left and had expected to sell in the States.

The diktat did not in itself upset me, but the way it was presented did. I think that Richard Eyre didn't like my salesmanship so closely associated with his production and cooked up an excuse to stop me in my tracks. I decided to be diplomatic and not complain. Equally I decided not to change my ways. When we left for New York a few months later my remaining prints were in my luggage and I'd not said a word to my original source of encouragement, our tour manager Roger.

My form of diplomacy in the States was always to wait until Roger and Richard Eyre left town, then set up shop as I had done before. This ploy worked in New York, Washington DC and St Paul, Minnesota, but in Denver I got my timing wrong — maybe in that mile-high town not enough oxygen was reaching my brain …

"Fuck it! Purchase is still at it!" a fellow company member overheard Roger say, when he saw my prints adorning the foyer at the Buell Opera House where we were performing. But Roger said nothing directly to me. I've always assumed this was because Sir Ian interceded on my behalf. For McKellen was completely aware I'd disregarded the diktat and as both co-producer and leading man had both supported what I was doing and going one better, even countersigned the prints, which increased both the price of each print and the volume of sales.

Another supporter was the chair of the National Theatre board, Lady Mary Soames, who had framed a set of my prints and hung them in the boardroom and also presented me with a book she'd written about her father's paintings. This book, which I treasure, included beautiful coloured plates of her dad's work. She gave it me shortly after her party in Prague.

Mary also hosted a memorable party for the company in a downtown New York restaurant after one performance. Superb food and wine was served and the evening included a floor show, a pair of talented tap-dancers she hired in. It was very stylish and Richard Eyre, near the end of the evening, made a gracious speech of thanks to Mary. Standing atop a chair, alongside me, as the applause that followed died away, Lady Soames called out to all assembled: "There's still pudding!"

In an interview with the *Daily Telegraph* in 2002, Lady Soames said: "Six happy years as chair of the board at the National Theatre — the rummest appointment that was ever made." Oh no, Mary, oh no, we would all have chorused if still together — you were fantastic.

We played at the Brooklyn Opera House (where Enrico Caruso sang) opening to a blaze of Big Apple attention. Several other parties also happened — one hosted by British-born journalist and editor Tina Brown, another (a tea party in Sting's duplex on Central Park West) hosted by McKellen, and a third I gave in an apartment owned by a friend Joan Copeland, in the same building as Sting's, overlooking Central Park, a magnificent view.

Also in New York City, Beazley and I took in the art at MOMA and the egg-shaped Guggenheim, saw the Frick collection and a bonus, Sam gave me a master-class on American furniture after we'd taken in the glorious collection of paintings in the same building, the wonderful Metropolitan. Next stop was the Kennedy Centre in Washington DC, Beazley and I again on the day job at the National Galleries, and my personal favourite — the Phillips Gallery — plus the only gallery in the world specialising in women painters, where I discovered Tamara de Lempicka. As a company we also enjoyed a private tour of the White House.

The only place in the States where I didn't sell was the Curran Theatre in San Francisco, but that for two very different reasons. The main reason was I had a personal crisis, a health scare. For almost a year I'd kept the lid on the pain caused by allegations made against me by Reuben at the time of his trial in Oxford. With medication I was able to at least perform effectively, not missing any performances. As is always said — the show must go on. And the other reason — well the Curran has a tiny foyer and no shop, so there was no space for display. One bonus in San Francisco though, I discovered the San Francisco Bay painters, and looking at their work helped steady me.

But prior to that we played St Paul (Minnesota) and Denver. Not much in the way of art in St Paul, but nearby Minneapolis with the Walker Gallery was rewarding and I also saw Tyrone Guthrie's theatre in that city. He'd always been a hero of mine. We'd worked together at the Bristol Old Vic in 1966.

Enjoyable car journeys also, in the US of A. The first on Skyline Drive near Washington, staying overnight in a mountain cabin and hearing the hauntingly familiar, but there for real, blast of a railway horn far down in the valley, near the Shenandoah. Visiting the battlefield of Manassas and learning, on site, about that awful first battle heralding the gruesome American Civil War. Yet another trip, with Barbara Caruso, first to see George Washington's house and a day later, via Richmond, Virginia, to visit Jefferson's fascinating house at Monticello. Then a drive, over a two-day period, between Denver and Las Vegas, a staggering visual feast — two cars in tandem, one driven by me and the other by Olivia Williams who since then has developed into a fine screen actor. Also in the group my Paris-based artist friend, Laura Buxton, and actors Phil McKee, Tristram Wymark and last, but definitely not least, the illustrious Anastasia Hille. From Las Vegas, after handing back our hire cars we then flew to San Francisco. And a final drive down the Pacific Coast Highway, taking in Carmel, Big Sur and, memorably, Randolph Hearst's opulent castle/folly, San Simeon, high in the Californian hills overlooking the Pacific. That last drive accompanied by National Theatre musician Martin Allan who, like me, saw out the whole world tour.

In LA we stayed in Westwood and played nearby at Royce Hall on UCLA's campus. One day in Los Angeles, Sam Beazley, Richard Simpson and I went to Paramount Studios. We'd been invited by an old colleague, actor Patrick Stewart, to watch an episode of *Star Trek* being filmed. Trekkies will recall the scene in a bar with all the clichés of the Wild West, piano player and poker game, but added to this, a gun-toting kid dressed up as a cowboy.

Pat Stewart was directing the episode and as he was working through lunch, Sam, Richard and I adjourned to Paramount's commissary where Pat had booked us a prime table in the conservatory. As we entered the building I was leading the way … and about to miss out on a 'golden' opportunity. In the foyer I was surprised to see a film star I recognised immediately. What startled me was that she was about ten feet in front of me, beaming her delicious, infectious smile at me. It was Goldie Hawn. As she warmly greeted me it felt as if we had known one another all our lives:

"Hi — how are you?" Goldie Hawn beamed at me.

But I blew it. Lacking entirely the chutzpah I'd displayed so confidently with Princess Alexandra in Madrid, I responded stiffly to her easy, warm-hearted greeting: "I'm very well, thank you," sounding and behaving like some uptight Brit as I peeled off to our right to where I'd been told by Pat Stewart our reserved table was.

Blast! I said to myself, as I took my seat, you've just missed out on a delightful chance encounter by behaving like a twerp.

By then joined at the table by Sam and Richard, who were completely unaware of what had just occurred, I knew it was too late to save the day. I told them what had happened, adding as a too late afterthought:

"She might have seen us in our production at the Royce Hall, so knew exactly who we were."

The awful thing about this tale is that I've always wanted to meet Goldie Hawn. What must she have thought. Sorry, Goldie. Goldie Hawn — now there is a princess too, a Jewish princess. Why on that sunny hot Californian day didn't I say to Goldie: "Do you know I've always adored you?" It was after all a line I'd practised with that other princess, Alexandra! Maybe I needed the champagne.

In LA my print sales reached a record level, but after a two-week stint it was time to fly back to the UK. The amazing world tour, which had begun two years before, was over. It was September 1992.

On the flight to London, memories from the tour crowded in: … whitewater rafting with 76-year-old Beazley on the Shenandoah River … our whole company in rubber rings, floating slowly down Minnesota's Apple River … boating and bathing, again in Minnesota, at Lake Minnetonka … driving through frightening pelting rain in the Colorado Rockies … and in fine weather, the glorious desert with its ever-changing landscape — Bryce Canyon and Zion National Park, *en route* from Denver to Las Vegas … watching dear Laura playing blackjack in a casino … the huge redwoods of northern California … veteran film star and idol, Cesar Romero, smiling up at me from his seat in the front row at UCLA's Royce

Hall ... drinking coffee with flavoured vodkas in the Russian Café in Denver and, also in that city, viewing vibrant early Western art ... eating delicious Cajun food in the beautiful, dark wood-panelled Gage & Tolner restaurant in Brooklyn ... conducting American cocktail research after performance in the amazing bar at the Hotel St Paul ... and, more sobering, the loss of my lucky New Zealand greenstone in Los Angeles — further back in time in Bucharest — espying in the decrepit, but attractive, old French quarter a man with a wooden leg trudging through thick snow, his prosthetic leg under one arm ... 'The Last Supper' being restored in Milan ... buying cheap Beluga caviar surreptitiously from a waiter in a Prague restaurant ... anguish after visiting the Jewish museum and cemetery in Prague ... devouring oysters and delicious cassoulet in Paris ... witnessing in the darkness of the Egyptian desert while waiting for the sun to come up on the Pyramids, director Deborah Warner's horse falling to the ground asleep from under her and her insouciant reaction ... encountering the wretched devastation of Dresden by allied Second World War bombing and the pointless destruction of that once beautiful city ... all of these memories and dozens more, flooding back, as we flew from LAX to Heathrow.

Later on this flight I read in *Time* of a major retrospective of Matisse at MOMA. The largest-ever assemblage of his work would only be seen in New York, although later part of the exhibition would travel to Paris.

Four months earlier, a New York wine merchant had seen a photograph of a painting I'd done in Provence and had expressed interest in buying it, so a week after my return to the UK I was on a flight again to New York, the painting in my luggage. I did sell it and saw the Matisse every day for a week.

Six months later I was bankrupted by the Inland Revenue in London's High Court, for a sum that once would have been a modest overdraft. I'd always been careless with tax and expenses. As I came out of the High Court on that sunny March day, a beggar near the steps politely asked for some change. I explained, with as much wit as I could muster, that I'd just been made bankrupt. His reply was brilliant: "Yes, it's happening to so many these days." My response was to reach into my pocket and gave him all I had, six pound coins.

With a travel card I then took a bus to meet a friend on the fifth floor at Harvey Nichols department store in Knightsbridge. As I walked into the smart bar my old friend enquired as to the outcome in the High Court. I told her.

"You could do with a large gin and tonic," Patricia said … "and then we'll have a late lunch here. Oh, by the way, lunch is on me."

I was facing an uncertain future, and I had large problems surrounding me, but regardless, I have learnt that there is life after debt.

Antony Andrews,
Gerald James,
Arthur Lowe and
Bruce rehearsing
for a Shakespeare
production for BBC TV.

With Reuben, a few days old,
December 1970.

IX

All the king's horses

IF THE ALLEGATIONS MADE AGAINST ME sixteen years ago were
intended to hurt and harm me, it can be said the protagonists
succeeded. This is a tale told reluctantly.

In 1991 my son Reuben brutally attacked a young man of
his own age. He was charged by the Oxfordshire police with the
offence of causing grievous bodily harm. One of the consequences
of this encounter with the law was that Reuben was 'counselled'
by a woman with no professional qualifications — an actress, Kate
Nicholls, who had been both a colleague and a friend. As a result
of Kate's ministrations, Reuben 'discovered', from what is called
'retrieved memories', that I had sexually abused him when he was
two years old. This type of discovery is usually known by both
specialists and the public as 'false memory syndrome'. I was not told
of my supposed sin until after Reuben was sentenced.

It took ten months to bring Reuben's case to court. It was a stressful time for him, but he had loving support from his mother (my former wife Elspeth) and myself, and from his sister Josie and his many friends. Elspeth made two expensive journeys from her new home in New Zealand to be with Reuben, although I felt she tended then and now to underplay the gravity of his offence. She recently referred to it in a New Zealand magazine, as: "the kind of trouble young men get themselves into."

The solicitor I hired to protect Reuben's interests told me before the trial that he thought Reuben would be given a lengthy period of probation rather than a custodial sentence if he was found guilty. He was right. Reuben was sentenced to eighteen months probation. Prior to this, in the time leading up to the trial, his stress was exacerbated by numerous appearances in the Magistrate's Court, where he was repeatedly told no date had been set for the hearing.

In spite of my commitment to the National Theatre's world tour, I was able to attend the early court proceedings. Elspeth, on the first of her visits from New Zealand, came with me, and there we sat, anxiously holding hands. Both of us were impressed by Reuben's dignified demeanour. However I was made anxious by the fact that

Josie & Reuben on Hampstead Heath.

he didn't show any signs of remorse for his actions and the serious injuries the boy he had attacked had suffered.

You can't repent when you don't feel remorse.

During this time Reuben was living principally in my Oxford flat. He told me he was keen to visit the Nicholls' family, who lived out in the country in the Cotswolds. I was opposed to the idea, for no very good reason, and said so, but he ignored my advice and sought solace with a new family. Over the weeks that followed he became inaccessible to me, "He's out for a walk", my calls not returned. When I attended his next court appearance, his manner was strange, uncommunicative, as if in a trance and the ever present Kate, acting as his minder, drew me aside and told me my son found my presence in the courtroom "awkward". I felt she was driving a deliberate wedge between Reuben and me, but he was, after all, not a child, so I reluctantly left my twenty-year-old son in her care. She promised to keep me informed. Three days later his solicitor wrote to me to say his client did not want me to attend any of the court appearances or the eventual trial. Though upset, I felt Reuben's feelings had to be paramount. I should have smelt a rat, but one is so often wise after the event. So, with me out of the picture, the plot to blame me for Reuben's actions by turning him into a victim proceeded apace. His mother meantime was back in New Zealand.

After the trial, Kate phoned me with news of the probationary sentence. I expressed my heartfelt relief and asked if I might speak with him, but as always, he was unavailable.

Shortly afterwards, a week as I remember it, on the day of a close friend's funeral, I learned more about the 'counselling' Kate had given Reuben and the 'discovery' my son had made. The plan had been to use the abuse information as a defence, but as I could have told them, it would have been/was, in fact, inadmissible, except possibly as part of a confidential psychological report in mitigation. I think I was probably never to have been told of the way I had been used. All they wanted was to poison my reputation without my knowledge. But as soon as I was told of the allegations, I confronted the whole ridiculous story head-on. The plot may have been pathetic and pointless, but the cat was now out of the bag, and the intended victim knew it all. Panic in their camp and my ex-wife, who'd flown in for the trial returned to New Zealand without confronting me. Both Reuben and his mother then made a fearful error. They put their accusation in writing — a brief note from each of them, which I still have.

Reuben's note was very explicit as to the crimes he said I'd committed. If there is any vestige of comfort in this bleak tale, it is that his letter seems to have been dictated to him; it is his hand, yes, but not his voice. It felt as if Reuben had been manipulated, but by then the damage was done. He might as well have been abducted by some mad religious cult. On the other hand his mother's note professed liberal concern at my predilection as she wrote of "the treatment you so desperately need ..."

Both letters caused me sadness and acute pain.

I was, however, given the 'opportunity' by both Kate and Reuben to go (alone) to the Nicholls' home, to be arraigned by the two of them. I imagined a sort of Kangaroo Court. I declined, suggesting instead that Reuben and I (without Kate) meet either with a mutual friend we both trusted, or with his lawyer and/or a trained counsellor. This suggestion was not taken up.

To Elspeth I wrote a reply to her note, asking: "Where were you when our son was a child? Would you not have known ...?" Josie, my step-daughter, was more sensible, assuring me both on the phone and in a letter that those 'memories' were Reuben's — not hers.

By then her mother was back in the safety of her Auckland home, in her new husband's house in the Titirangi hills west of Auckland, leaving our son to see out his probationary period in what, she must have assumed, were the capable hands of Kate. Kate Nicholls, the untrained amateur counsellor, was the mother of four children and lived with her partner Ian, father of three of the children.

Dealing, as best I could, with the effect of these false child abuse allegations on me, I half-joked to a friend:

"I'll make a prophecy. Kate will have a child by Reuben."

"That's ridiculous. I know you've been hurt, but ..."

"She will not want to lose him, so she'll have a child by him. She'll announce she's pregnant near the end of Reuben's probation."

My prophecy was spot-on and when Kate told Ian, her partner, the child was Reuben's, Ian departed. There is roughly a seventeen-year age gap between Kate and Reuben.

"It will not last," I commented.

Kate and Reuben's child was born and they named him Oakley.

"Why Oakley?" I was asked.

"Possibly he was conceived in Oakley Woods." This, a wood near Oxford. I added:

"Perhaps it might be said that from a little acorn, Oakleys grow!"

Reuben and Kate then reinvented themselves. After some four gap years in a row, Reuben returned to his studies and Kate to hers. I was told that at A level he passed everything with straight A's and then went on to University College, London where he gained a First in anthropology. Kate, evidently putting aside her interest in counselling, returned to her lone studies in biology at Oxford's Bodleian Library. When I heard of my son's achievement, I was proud and said to my agent on the phone:

"Reuben got a First at UCL."

"Really — and any O levels in commonsense yet?"

" 'Fraid not."

Kate Nicholls is a remarkable woman. As anyone who has met her would probably agree, she has a feisty personality. I first came across her when she was about ten, when I stopped in the street to chat to her mother, Faith, in Hans Crescent, Knightsbridge. Kate's father Anthony Nicholls was a fellow National Theatre player at the Old Vic in the mid-1960s. Laurence Olivier was our boss. Tony died many years ago. That sunny day in the street I remember very well. As Faith and I chatted, I was aware that Kate was huffing and puffing, brassed off at the delay. Out of the corner of my eye I observed her spoilt-child carry on, and thought to myself: she's trouble. How right I was, for twenty-seven years later the trouble in my life was caused by Kate, by then in her late thirties.

As I predicted, in spite of their child, Kate and Reuben's relationship didn't last. A couple of years after my grandson's birth, with Reuben by then out of Kate's life, she upped sticks and with her five children, moved to Botswana, her intention to further her studies as the self-trained biologist she'd become — a sort of latter-day Jane Goodall. Goodall, chimps and Nicholls, lions! Exchanging her comfortable life in the Cotswolds, she went to live with her children and a new partner, geneticist Dr Pieter Kat, in a tented encampment a long way from the nearest town. There in the Botswanan bush Pieter Kat and Kate studied, for a number of years (but now no longer) big cats — lions.

At the time of the allegations I decided to keep silent, for the most part — to let people make up their own minds. I lost no real friends, although I will always wonder how many professional contacts became reluctant to use my skills on the 'no smoke without fire' basis.

In 2003, Elspeth said to a mutual friend, Fiona Walker: "It's important Reuben now seeks a healing with his father." Fiona told me she replied:

"Then why don't you yourself start with an apology?" This because his mother had herself been culpable as she had rushed to support, endorse and believe her son.

Some acquaintances wavered. Caroline Lewis, a friend in Oxford, phoned me several months after the trial, suggesting we have a meal together. Over lunch she announced:

"I owe you an apology."

"Oh? Why?"

"I was so confused."

"And what has changed?"

She explained that recently she'd gone to visit her boyfriend in New York and told him of the allegations against me. "Bullshit," her boyfriend commented, adding that he didn't know "this Bruce Purchase guy," but didn't believe the allegations. He asked her to read Arthur Miller's play *The Crucible* about the Salem witch-hunts.

Reuben Purchase.

217

She concluded:

"So I owe you an apology."

"Accepted, of course. But before we leave the subject, may I ask you just one question?"

"By all means." She was relieved to have got it off her chest. But she was not yet off the hook.

"What happens if you change your boyfriend?"

Before Reuben and Kate called it a day as a couple, I met him by chance in Oxford. It was our first meeting since I learnt of his accusations. Oakley by then had been born.

"Hello, Reuben. Did you have a good Christmas?"

He mumbled a reply.

"And how is your son Oakley?"

Another mumble, but then, suddenly, he found his voice. He turned and boomed at the passers-by in that busy Oxford Street:

"You see this man? He is my father and …"

He expressed his obscene tale as the puzzled passers-by continued on their way. I started to stumble away in shock and pain the like of which I'd wish on no one. But Reuben had not finished with me yet.

"I see you are shaking with guilt," he taunted.

"I'm shaking, yes, Reuben, but not with guilt."

But my unhappy son continued his attack and I finally rounded on him, speaking to him with as much calm as I could muster.

"Reuben, you did it for the trial."

This brought him up with a start.

"You thought it would be admissible, as part of your defence. It wasn't! You made a terrible mistake. Go. I love you, but I won't listen to lies about your childhood."

Before that meeting with Reuben, having kept a lid on my feelings for more than a year after the trial, I'd had a health scare while performing at the Curran Theatre in San Francisco.

"You've not had a heart attack," Dr Howard Thornton explained, "but may I ask you — have you, for a long time, been suffering a great emotional strain?"

From my supine position on a mattress on the dressing room floor, relieved to be free to answer the good doctor's question,

218

Ink drawing of Bruce Purchase as Edward IV by Laura Buxton,
in the Curran Theatre, San Francisco, 1992.

"Oh — ye … ss," I bemusedly replied.

He gave me medication which calmed me — said I could continue
to act but to rest up for a couple of weeks and take my medicine.
In the comfort of my splendid 17th-floor apartment on Post Street,
I began to recuperate, only going out to play in *Richard III* each
evening, not missing a single show at the Curran. In my apartment
with its magnificent views I not only rested, but allowed myself to
give full rein to my hurt — I raged and wept and because of this, a
process of self-healing began.

Laura Buxton, a young artist friend, broke off from her work
on a huge mural in Charlotte, North Carolina and joined me in
San Francisco for a week. Laura and I had driven between Denver
and Las Vegas shortly before my collapse. With her practical and
emotional support, I began to recover. Now years after those bleak
days I still see Laura in Paris, where she lives with her partner,
musician/composer John Greaves and their two children. Laura has
been like a daughter to me.

After that meeting with Reuben in Oxford I returned home

shaken, to find a grotesque message from him on my answerphone. I have, as with his explicit letter, kept the tape. But I wrote Reuben a short note telling him not to do it again, explaining what I was going to do. He didn't repeat his action. Then I phoned the False Memory Syndrome group and told them my story. Until then I'd thought I was the only person in the world who'd been thus wronged.

After completion of the National Theatre world tour in Los Angeles in 1992, my spirits were still very low. As a result, I didn't put up much of a fight to avoid the bankruptcy action against me, and the fear, the loss perhaps, of my flat which was deep into negative equity. My necessary outgoings had spiralled up, as my income had spiralled down. Suddenly I was both homeless and bankrupt.

But life moved on … the old familiar mix of moving between theatre, film and television continued and that, plus my work as an artist kept the wolf away from my rented door. I had exhibitions of my paintings regularly in the '90s in Oxford and London, and, on trips to New Zealand, showings and sale of my work in both Christchurch and Auckland.

In the theatre a favourite role was as Pozzo in a fine production of Beckett's *Waiting for Godot*. The production was set in the desert with Vladimir and Estragon played as Arabs and Pozzo like a demented British ambassador (white suit and Panama) who'd got lost in the desert along with a crazed American — Lucky. This introduced me to its director, the beautiful American-born Lisa Forrell. She and her partner, legal broadcaster and writer Marcel Berlins, have become good friends.

Another unique friendship developed around that time, with the late and much-lamented John Wain: poet, scholar, novelist and author of an authoritative biography of the eminent 18th-century man of letters, Dr Samuel Johnson. Among his many literary achievements, Johnson created the first comprehensive English dictionary

Shortly before his death John wrote a one-man show for me, *Johnson is Leaving*, which deals with a day near the end of Sam Johnson's life. It's a superlative piece and a joy to perform, as I found when I first presented it in 1995 at St John's College, Oxford. I then took it on tour to the Lichfield Festival.

A few years later Lisa and I re-mounted this bold venture, and in 2003 it had showings at the Royal Shakespeare Company's Swan Theatre at Stratford-Upon-Avon as well as in private houses and public spaces around Britain and also in France, New Zealand and the USA. At the Johnson House in London's Gough Square I have often performed in the room where the renowned lexicographer spent nine years writing his famous dictionary. A good experience.

The play runs one hour and twenty minutes and I perform it sans interval. The production has been critically well received by many, including novelist Dame Beryl Bainbridge, critic Irving Wardle and the Shakespearean scholar, Katherine Duncan-Jones.

Two moments in the play have a powerful resonance in my own life. The first when Johnson reasons:

> Is there some primal curse on the human race when it comes to the dealings of sons with fathers? The Bible tells us that Adam and his wife Eve had two sons, Cain and Abel. Cain murdered Abel. The Bible doesn't tell us anything about how Adam tried to bring up his sons, but he must have told them murder was wrong. And yet, in spite of that, one of them killed the other. So the first upbringing that ever happened was a failure ...

And another quote, with similar reverberations:

> ... so I tried to let my mind go back to the days when I knew him [Sam Johnson's father] and gather together all my memories of him and call him back to life in my mind. Tell him I was old myself now and I understood what it would mean to have the love and support of a son ...

When Reuben got his First at UCL, I wrote to his mother:
"I'm very proud."

No reply to that, nor to the following from a further letter I wrote to her.

"A couple of years ago, at an *I, Claudius* reunion at BAFTA, Johnny H[urt] told me of his meeting with you all, and, with dismay, of the allegations against me ..."

At the BAFTA day, actor, friend John Hurt explained to me the events he had witnessed in New Zealand where he was filming. He had visited Elspeth because we had all once lived as neighbours in Ascott-under-Wychwood. John said that although Reuben was present, he let his mother Elspeth voice the accusations against me.

At the end of this 'presentation' John told them he didn't believe the allegations and turned to Reuben:

"What's the matter with you? I knew you as a child — your father adored you."

John Hurt and I were fellow students at drama school. We've known one another since 1960.

On tour and in the West End I played the Archbishop of Rheims in Shaw's *Saint Joan,* with Imogen Stubbs in the title role. My confidence was fully restored that same year when I had the opportunity of playing Doolittle in a handsome production of the musical *My Fair Lady.*

In other words, both friends and my love of acting helped Humpty Dumpty to put himself together again. Neither the King's men nor their horses with their vain endeavours were needed.

Part of the long-term self-repair included an appearance, albeit brief, in a film of *Richard III*, based on Richard Eyre's stage production for the world tour. The film was directed by Richard Loncraine, and I believe it was his direction of Ian McKellen, in the title role, that transformed Ian from the fine stage actor he has always been into the equally fine film star he has become. Apart from McKellen, I was the only other actor from the stage version to appear in Loncraine's excellent film, but not in my original role. As Loncraine explained to my agent:

"Bruce, on screen, looks younger than McKellen so he can't play his elder brother!"

John Wood, who does look older (and more like Ian's 'brother') besides being a star, played Edward IV and I appeared (blink and you'll miss me) as the Lord Mayor of London. My spirits, however, from the battering by both 'counsellor' Nicholls and my much-loved son Reuben still went up and down. In a TV series called *Law and Order* I was, frankly awful, but better in a TV commercial made in Paris (a chance to see Laura cheered me), better again in Lynda La Plante's *Killer Net* as a pathologist, and Ruth Rendell's *The Strawberry Tree* as a serial killer. In another TV series called *Bob Martin* I appeared as a millionaire North Country fruit and veg man. But the cherry on the cake was touring as Doolittle in Europe in *My Fair Lady*. More about that later.

As the Archbishop of Rheims, with Imogen Stubbs in the
title role in Shaw's *Saint Joan*.

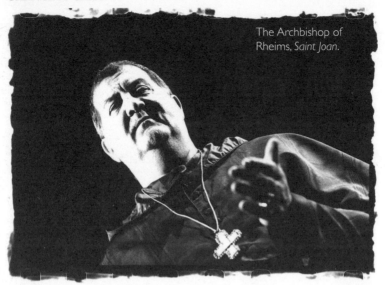

The Archbishop of Rheims, *Saint Joan*.

Support in my years of need came from one surprising quarter — from my ex-wife Elspeth Sandys' third husband, New Zealand writer Maurice Shadbolt. In 1997 he sent me a very supportive verbal message but, because he was still then married to Reuben's mother, I thought it inappropriate to reply. However, in 1999 I did reply just after Maurice had published a volume of autobiography:

"I very much enjoyed reading your latest memoir. In this letter I'd also like to thank you for a 'message' received from you a few years ago, 'delivered', via a mutual friend. At the time I received [it] I was standing on a terrace, overlooking Menton! The communication related specifically to your views on my son Reuben's allegations against me. My reaction at the time: 'Thank you Maurice, I'm touched by your generous message.' At the time it did not seem appropriate to respond, but now, with such a deluge of water under so many peculiarly constructed bridges, it is time to transmit the above thought, thank you Maurice, it was a 'message' gratefully received.

"I note on page 228 of *From the Edge of the Sky*, your reference to a panicked unnamed partner, sailing off into the security of Auckland suburbia. I, too, remember a partner of many years, also to remain nameless, who, when the going ever got tough, did a runner! As for my reaction to my son Reuben's allegations, it's best summed up by quoting Ezra Pound's last reported words: 'I live on a street named Tough. The further you go, the tougher it gets — and I live at the end of the street'."

I didn't expect a reply, but I got one. Maurice's handwritten letter is dated 22 August 1999. I'll only quote his last few lines. The whole letter was highly critical of both Reuben and our joint-ex-wife.

"— and I wish I could have helped you more. I have written this letter a hundred times in my head over the last years, but have never put it down on paper. My guilt is great. If I can help you — even at this late stage — let me know."

When Shadbolt wrote this letter to me his marriage to Sandys was over. He died after separating from Elspeth and a long illness in a nursing home in New Zealand.

I imagine one day my letter to Maurice might end up with his papers at Wellington's Turnbull Library, where his reply to me may join it. The *Turnbull Library Record* tells me Elspeth has already sold 22cm of his letters, 'restricted access', to the library. In the meantime his letter to me lives in the safe-keeping of my lawyer, for in its entirety it's an explosive document.

Life is often stranger than fiction. I learnt only recently that Maurice began his courtship of Elspeth years before we divorced. Secret meetings happened in Oxfordshire. In our home in Oxfordshire, Maurice, then visiting us with his third wife, whispered to my wife: "You could do better than this." Elspeth recently mentioned this verbal billet-doux in a New Zealand magazine; in an earlier article she had said I had introduced them to each other. Now it is public knowledge that in trysts years earlier he'd confessed his love for her.

After *Saint Joan* finished its West End season I flew to Berlin to rehearse for *My Fair Lady*. I was secretly petrified at the prospect of having to dance. On the other hand I was joyful at the thought I'd be singing two delightful numbers 'Get Me to the Church on Time' and 'With a Little Bit of Luck,' both potential show-stoppers.

On the seven-month *My Fair Lady* tour, which travelled widely in Germany and also France, Austria and Switzerland, I painted and visited a lot of galleries and exhibitions — "painting my way out of a corner" as John Wain had said to me a few months earlier. John died on the day I commenced rehearsals for his monodrama *Johnson is Leaving*. Two days before his sudden death he'd added the following lines to the completed manuscript:

"It's impossible to mistake the onset of death when it really comes — when it really comes, I mean, as mine is coming now."

Did he know …?

The offer to play Doolittle originated out of Los Angeles. Eleanor Cooke is a casting director in LA and also an old family friend.

"Would you like to play Doolittle in *My Fair Lady*? (Would I!) You'll have to audition for both the director, Joe Hardy and the musical director, Jack Lee. The audition will be in London. I know you will be marvellous in the role and Richard thinks so too …"

"Richard …?"

"Chamberlain — he's booked to play Professor Higgins."

Eleanor told me later, as soon as I'd departed the audition the music supremo Jack Lee leapt to his feet: "Book him!" He was a big help to me in the rehearsal process. When the full orchestra flew in from New York and sat down to play at the Schiller Theatre in Berlin, the sudden transition from piano accompaniment to the big band was exciting. Over the following seven months we played seasons, twice in Berlin, twice in Munich, twice in Frankfurt, twice in Zurich and other dates included venues in Hamburg, Cologne, Vienna, Stuttgart and the Mogador Theatre in Paris. We were meant also to play London but a suitable big theatre could not be found. It was a hugely successful tour and fun to play. Every performance was like having a great time on holiday.

The acute feelings of the loss of my son from my life slowly became slightly less painful and my confidence and authority as a performer came back into focus. Of course, short of a healing between father and son, there will be no real cure — it is a life sentence, perhaps. Not being a convert to the Manichean Heresy, where God and the Devil are seen at unending war with one another, I prefer to believe that there is no such thing as evil, merely (merely?) a lack of good. But all family schisms have powerful repercussions — for instance, the loss of Josie Harbutt, my step-daughter out of my life is hard to bear. They may not have been her 'memories', but understandably she supports her mother and half-brother. Josie now has two children, Eve Marie and Carlo and recently spent a year working for the OECD in Paris.

Josie is a fine human being — very much her own person.

But family schisms are family schisms and because of my son's alleged memories I am still, and I remain in 2008, the 'fall guy' in a stupid and unnecessary scenario.

But life moves on. That fear of not being any good as a dancer in *My Fair Lady* was totally unfounded. If Josie had still been closely in my life, she would most likely have good-naturedly mocked my doubts. She would probably have said:

"Of course you can dance. Do it!"

Well, Jo, if you're out there In the ether, let me tell you — I did. Within a week I was kicking as high as any of those young Americans in the show.

I painted like a demon too, selling *en route*, most of what I produced. Being able to re-visit the Kunsthalle Gallery in Hamburg and to see once again paintings I'd first seen on my earlier 1990 visit was very satisfying, as was a formidable exhibition of Kandinsky in Munich, a Renoir exhibition near Stuttgart and, in Stuttgart itself, a hugely enjoyable Picasso exhibition. The theme of the Picasso

exhibition was 'children'. Many of these I'd not seen before. They included paintings of his own kinder and of other children, as well as Picasso painting 'like a child'. In Cologne when I saw a painting by Francis Bacon, the scales came off my eyes and I saw, for the first time just what a fine painter he is. In Munich, there was an exhibition of works by famous artists, with the theme of clown

Bruce as a tramp in *Another Day*, a video production by Josie Harbutt.

My Fair Lady cast in Berlin, 1996, at the start of a splendid 8-month European tour. Bruce as Doolittle and Richard Chamberlain, front right, Professor Higgins.

paintings. This prompted me to do a clutch of clown paintings of my own, which proved to be popular, as I sold the lot. All this, plus new galleries discovered along the way, meant the tour provided me with an extra bonus, and extra cash too.

With a few exceptions the *My Fair Lady* company was a great bunch and one or two new friendships were made, Guido Frackers, our Dutch/Indonesian production manager, notably at the top of the list — brilliant at his job and good fun too:

"What we need, Bruce, is wine in the glass and food on the table," as he ordered up yet another memorable banquet. Guido and I share a similar sense of humour. One of our practical jokes was when we persuaded the company we'd long been both friends and also business partners. Our fictional firm was Frackers Purchase, supposedly with offices in London, Paris and New York. We even had our own headed notepaper. We chatted publicly about our, often bizarre, business deals — massive transfers of different currencies between countries — we dealt in anything from whole forests in South America which were turned into billions of toothpicks — to rockets we planned to 'sell' to North Korea. Post-September 11 we'd probably be arrested.

One joke we kept running and running, was how we planned to offload hundreds of thousands of pairs of poorly made, phoney-labelled, designer women's shoes. Anyway we finally 'sold' them to either Brazil or the Argentine — or both!

The company were mainly American. Richard Chamberlain was excellent as Professor Higgins and he was a pleasure, as always, to work with. Meg Tolin, who played Eliza has an excellent singing voice and both her Cockney and 'refined' accents were very good. Two British performers, Bernard Horsfall and Helen Ryan, played Colonel Pickering and Mrs Higgins, and both were on good form. I'd worked before with Helen when she played Queen Alexandra in ATV's TV series *Edward VII*. Timothy West played the title role and I played Tsar Alexander III.

Other recollections from the *My Fair Lady* experience — friendships made with clown/actress Desirée Angersbach, a wonderful young woman who I met in Berlin; Guido, of course, and a handful of other Americans from the cast. Group outings with the company, one to Mount Titlis, when we were playing in Zurich; the other, a meal of glutinous Swiss fodder, this in Zurich, our hostess a middle-aged Swiss 'groupie' who followed us on the tour. The whole company seated like her nephews and nieces and all of us trying to behave well! Mozart's house and a production of Britten's *Peter Grimes*, both in Vienna, and on a more serious note — a sobering visit to the former Gestapo headquarters in Köln, now a museum.

But like all good fun and all theatrical companies, after seven months, the tour finished and at Stuttgart airport we embraced and flew off in our separate directions.

An actor's life.

The '90s had me involved in two films that sadly never saw the light of day — or should I say, the patterning of light in darkened cinemas. Both films just didn't capture the commercial interest of the distributors, though *Sea Change* was okay and *Another Life* really rather good. Television work, theatre work and exhibitions of my paintings continued to take up the slack. Another tour, too, in 1997, *Coriolanus*, in which I played Menenius Agrippa, with its director, Steven Berkoff, also playing the title role.

Coriolanus played in Edinburgh, Jerusalem and Tokyo. I was looking forward to revisiting the Globe Theatre in Tokyo where I'd appeared on the world tour in 1990 and seeing my old friend Murray Sayle and family, but it didn't work out that way. I'll explain.

Steven Berkoff, writer, actor/manager and director, is a highly original creator and a sort of idiosyncratic force of nature. Not everyone in the profession likes him, but it's difficult to ignore his prodigious talent. I enjoyed his direction in *Coriolanus* and playing the role of Menenius with him. The reasons I didn't play Tokyo were twofold — two misunderstandings over the interpretation of the contract (but in essence about payments), agreed on my behalf by my agent, Joyce Edwards. The first misunderstanding was sorted out about an hour before the first performance in Edinburgh, but the second problem, which manifested itself at the end of our tour of duty, in Jerusalem, was never resolved and Steven refused to honour my contract. His behaviour endorsed Sam Goldwyn's belief that 'a verbal contract ain't worth the paper it's written on.' I departed the company. Steve and the rest went to Tokyo and played a version of *Coriolanus* that lacked one central character, Menenius, a sizeable gap, as there wasn't an understudy to replace me. My name did appear alongside Menenius in the Tokyo Globe Theatre programme, which probably puzzled the Japanese as Menenius's lines were shared among the other actors.

The trip to Jerusalem was enjoyable. We were guests at that city's arts festival. The audiences were very good and we played to full houses. I saw all the religious sights, which included the Great Dome of the Rock, the Garden of Gethsemane, Bethlehem and the Wailing Wall. At the Holocaust Museum I was sobered by what I saw and learnt. There is in that museum a huge book that lists the names of victims of the Holocaust/Shoah. My Jewish great-grandparents, Zander by name, emigrated to New Zealand in the 19th century — settling in Whangarei, north of Auckland where my father's mother, my grandmother, was born. Nell Zander was her maiden name. My much-loved Nana was born about 1885 in New Zealand. My great-grandfather became a successful builder in Northland, New Zealand. One building on Kawau Island I've always loved was one I discovered years later which he had, in part, designed and built for New Zealand's Governor Grey.

I opened that huge book at the museum and turned to the listings of names under the letter Z. There is one Zander in the list of victims, first name Julius. He'd been born about the same time as my Nana — she in New Zealand and Julius in Germany. Were they cousins? This discovery haunted me and a couple of hours later, in the Church of the Holy Sepulchre I lit a candle for Julius, then walked swiftly to the nearby Wailing Wall.

At the Wailing Wall, which is cordoned off, there is a small entrance. Beside this point of entry, on a chair, was a box of keppels (skull caps). I took one and placed it on my head. An elderly rabbi standing by the gate said to me:

"Money for the temple?"

"How much?" I knew there was no official charge to the Wailing Wall.

"Twenty shekels," the old rabbi told me.

I gave him ten shekels, then walked down to the wall. As I reached the wall, a young rabbi asked me why I was there and I told him about Julius Zander, a victim of the Shoah and perhaps a distant cousin. He asked me if I could speak Hebrew.

"If you give me the Hebrew, line by line, I will be able to repeat it."

He agreed and with one of his hands touching me and his other, touching the Wailing Wall, we remembered the existence of Julius Zander and his death in the Shoah. When we'd completed this solemn task, I thanked him and of course was not surprised when he said: "Money for the temple?"

"Ah — ha! How much?"

"Fifty shekels."

I gave him twenty. As I turned to leave, a half-smile on my face. But the game was not yet over. Another voice:

"As you are here, why don't you pray for your whole family?"

This query addressed to me by a middle-aged rabbi with a Canadian accent. I immediately agreed to this helpful suggestion, and line by line, repeating the Hebrew, remembered my whole family — beginning with my Zander great-grandparents and concluding with my son, Reuben. I thanked this pleasant Canadian and...

"Money for the temple?"

"Ah — yes. How much?"

"Fifty shekels." I gave him twenty.

As I walked away, by then I was smiling broadly at the sheer temerity of the scene that'd been played out since my entrance at the gate. As I approached the exit, the old rabbi looked at me shrewdly, but did not ask me again. I removed my skull cap and replaced it back in the box. I thought to myself:

"I've just saved myself a hundred shekels!"

"We've just taken him for fifty!" the old, the young, the Canadian middle-aged — the three generations of rabbis probably thought.

Jerusalem is a city where it is hard to go unnoticed. A few months earlier, in London, I'd been introduced to a Palestinian who was resident in Israel. Bassam Eid edits a publication called *Human Monitoring Rights*. It reports on cases of torture carried out by elements of the Palestinian Authority against its own citizens. Bassam is a member of Amnesty International and his office is in Jerusalem. I made contact and, on an evening free from performance at the Jerusalem Festival, Bassam took me out for dinner. We drove to Bethlehem. I noted, as we left Israel and entered 'Palestine' there was no border control. Later that evening on our return journey as we re-entered Israel there was a border control post manned by Israeli soldiers. You can leave Israel freely, but not re-enter without the required papers. Bassam had told me to bring my passport. Over dinner in a Bethlehem restaurant he asked me if I liked the food:

"Yes, it's delicious."

"This restaurant is where the Palestinian secret police eat."

I was startled and glanced about me at the packed restaurant before replying:

"So you're showing your head above the parapet?"

Bassam smiled. "Correct," he said.

"And who the hell will they think I am?"

As we left the restaurant, the patron came up and spoke in Arabic to Bassam Eid. As we walked to the car I asked what the restaurateur had said:

"He asked me if I was Bassam Eid and I said I was."

Next stop Border Control and our papers were examined, which included my passport. I was asked what I was doing in Israel and

Bassam Eid explained I was a guest of the Israeli state, performing at the Jerusalem Festival. Our papers were in order.

A week later I left Israel. At the Jerusalem airport, a beautiful uniformed young woman asked me at check-in to unpack my hand luggage in front of her. As she examined the contents she questioned me:

"Have you had a good visit?"

"Yes, I have enjoyed my time here."

"And who have you met?" she enquired, pleasantly.

I thought it an odd question but described to her a list of folk at the Jerusalem Festival and adding for good measure,

"... plus of course a lot of taxi drivers, staff at my hotel ..."

"And Bassam Eid?" she smiled.

"Yes — and Bassam Eid." I smiled too.

By then she'd finished the search through my belongings.

"All right, Sir, you may go through."

*

In 2002, a book was published by Orion called *The Lion Children*, written by Kate Nicholls' children, including my grandson Oakley. It's a beautifully produced book with lots of excellent photographs of Oakley Purchase. Until I saw the book I'd never seen pictures of my grandson. In 2002 he was seven. He's a handsome boy with an intelligent look and a charming smile. He looks both like his beautiful mother and his good-looking Dad, a gentle mix of both parents.

His mother was interviewed for an article printed on 22 June 2003 in the *Sunday Times* magazine. The heading of this piece neatly mirrors her children's book, for it's entitled *The Lion Queen*. It deals with her life in the Botswanan bush where, with her former professional geneticist partner, Pieter Kat, she spent several years studying lions in their natural habitat. By 2007 this partnership had ended.

Apparently these lions have, among them, a very high percentage of the feline equivalent of HIV. Most scientists, the article explains, do not believe this will kill off the lion population, but Kate Nicholls thought differently, for the numbers had fallen by two-thirds. This may be explained by the widespread hunting of lions and it's said that Kate's research did not make her popular among the hunting fraternity. One hunter is quoted in the article as commenting that there's no credible data to substantiate her research and that Kate was an actress not a scientist.

Kate Nicholls also talked of a horrendous attack made upon her in 2002. She says she was raped at knife-point by three men. She goes on to say that although they (the three men) should have only taken half an hour of her life, they've in fact taken a year, but that now she wakes up smiling.

When I was accused of sexual abuse by my son, my step-daughter Josie said:

"Even if it was true I'd still love you."

I said to her then: "But it's not true!"

My experience took me a long time to learn to live with — certainly more than a year before I woke up smiling.

If, as I believe, my ex-wife Elspeth had contested the vile allegations, it would have helped.

In mid-2005 a brief typed letter arrived from my son ... a sort of apology ... but no address for reply. I contacted Missing Persons and asked them to find him and deliver my brief acknowledgement to his missive. This they did, but since then further silence.

I believe that he lives in Wales with his partner, a psychiatric nurse and her children ...

It is now, in 2007, seventeen years since his foolish accusations were offered up to me. His attempt at apology may have assuaged his guilt. As I write my health has suddenly seriously failed me and my sadness has intensified ... but with his letter Reuben has at least taken a step in the right direction and perhaps there will be further such steps.

We are all in a sense victims, not of evil, but just a lack of good.

X

Dialogues and monologues

A version of this chapter was first published in *Intimate Strangers*, published in 2000. Editor Janet Wilson's introduction said: "Bruce Purchase's recollections, presented as voices in interrelated sequences, reveal the terms of affectionate intimacy he developed with both Dan and Winnie Davin. As Purchase maintained a vigil at both their final hours, they have the force of a goodbye."

*

Gossip, talking behind people's backs, is a necessary ingredient of our social culture, indispensable to it, and at its best one of the finest instruments of our civilised living. ...

But gossip about the dead? ...

But these people ... are not dead; not wholly dead, at least while their work is alive and they themselves are remembered.

— from *Closing Times*, Dan Davin's book of literary anecdotes

CLUTCHING A PEWTER TANKARD filled with college ale, I am in the company of an older man — Daniel Marcus Davin.

Dan, a New Zealand Rhodes Scholar in the 1930s, was for many years academic editor at the Clarendon Press, the academic wing of Oxford University Press (OUP) and was a highly influential publisher, much respected. Later Davin became Secretary to the Delegates ... a cumbersome title to outsiders but the role is, in effect, CEO of the entire Oxford University Press.

I'd joined him at Balliol College in Oxford at the appointed time, having learnt long before from my host, a railwayman's son, that punctuality was the keynote. He didn't just expect it, he demanded it from himself and others.

But of course an actor's life demands it too, so for me it's also second nature.

DMD had an effortless talent for putting folk at ease.

"Any trouble finding your way?"

"No," I replied. "In fact the porter approached me as I entered College. His directions to the buttery here were perfect."

Dan, hiding his humour, spoke gloomily. "Told the Head Porter I had a guest coming for lunch, gave him your name but he stopped me in mid-sentence. 'Oh you mean Mr P ... from the Royal Shakespeare Company at Stratford? Don't worry, Sir, I'll recognise him!' DMD continued,

"Cheeky blighter, after all my years here as a Fellow of the College, he barely recognises me!"

In one practised fell swoop, my host had achieved his first objective, flattering his guest and putting me instantly at ease.

In his later years DMD often suffered from Churchill-like 'black dog' depression, but now retired from his eminent position as Secretary to the Delegates this gifted publisher and writer could still, in congenial company, be drawn out, becoming once again the Dan of old, the charismatic friend loved by so many.

To talk of him is also to remember his equally gifted wife, Winnie, and in later years when Dan found it difficult to write she proposed to me and others, to take turns recording Dan's reminiscences, hoping it might encourage her husband to take up his pen again. I took note of this and would place a microphone in front of this grand old man, who thus encouraged would speak, editing the material as he talked. Rarely requiring a prompt, I became the audience. The stories would roll forth.

At one session: "When Paddy Costello (another New Zealand-born academic, who joined the Consular Service) died in February 1964 of a massive heart attack he was able, as a former army intelligence officer, to describe to his wife Bil all the symptoms. He assessed the situation, estimated the enemy's frontal attack would prove successful ... As indeed it did. He died soon afterwards."

"Do you have wheels today?"

"Yes."

"I wonder if you'd mind driving Winnie ...?"

Dan didn't drive, nor did Winnie. Having free time, as actors often do, I was often called into service, always happy to oblige.

"You turn left here," Winnie, tail gunner in the back, would say. Then when I ignored her note, "You should have turned left back there."

"No, Winnie, it's next on the right."

If Dan was on board: "Leave Bruce to do the driving, Winnie. He knows the way." Adding *sotto voce*, "Winnie has no sense of direction."

You're right, darling Bruce," Winnie again. "I was confused. There used to be an elm tree on that corner." Followed by another staccato burst of fire. "Left now!"

I waited for the oncoming traffic to clear and turned right. Winnie agreed.

"That's just perfect, darling, you were right all the time." This tail gunner laughed at her joke. "Now just along here …"

Dan from his postilion position alongside me, a dangerous growl: "Winnie!"

I made many trips to and from their beautiful thatched country cottage at Dorchester and, much later, shared journeys with other conscripts between Oxford and St Andrews Hospital in Northampton. One day I found Dan in truculent mood. How to draw him out?

"What do they charge you for these visits, Dan?" I knew the answer, for Winnie had told me medical insurance mostly covered them. An ominous growl from the postilion seat. Oops!

"One thousand and eight pounds a week," he muttered darkly.

"My God, how do they justify the extra eight pounds?"

It'd done the trick. Dan was smiling — that open and generous smile, his head slightly rolling back, eyes to the heavens, his wonderful 'silent' laugh. It was on this journey he told me the following story about his most important mentor, Kenneth Sisam. A distinguished medievalist, Sisam was, like Dan, a former New Zealand Rhodes Scholar and had been Davin's predecessor at Oxford University Press.

"As a young boy he was walking with his father in the New Zealand bush. They paced rapidly along the rough track eager to be home before nightfall. Both were famished. A Maori on horseback came down the track towards them, accompanied by another on foot. Sisam Senior knew the rider and fell into conversation in spite of the dying light. After a few minutes the Maori astride the horse turned and looked down at Sisam Jnr:

"That boy looks as if he could do with a good feed."

The attendant swiftly removed a big fruit cake from the saddle pack and, producing a long and dangerous-looking dagger from his belt, expertly sliced a huge wedge of cake, handing it to young Kenneth, who gratefully munched it. Later, nearing their homestead, the light now gone, Sisam Snr said from the blackness, as they stumbled on home: "Do you know who the man on the horse is, Son?"

"No, Father."

Dan paused in the telling to give the punchline added weight, then softly quoted Sisam Senior again.

"The great Te Kooti."

The story told in Dan's fine baritone, timed to perfection. Dan had perhaps learnt a trick or two from the travelling Irish storytellers of his Southland childhood. At the time a shiver went down my spine, for Te Kooti Arikirangi Te Turuki had been a formidable foe against the British forces at the end of the land wars in the 19th century. He used guerilla warfare most effectively against 'the enemy'. He was a prophet, faith healer and founder of the Ringatu Church.

On a personal note, a hundred years after Te Kooti's death, in September 1998, a son was born to my nephew Anthony. The child's name is Noah Te Kooti Purchase, his mother Lana a direct descendant of that charismatic and famous figure.

Dan and I had much in common. As expatriates we were both still absorbed in our separate childhood Edens — Davin's in the South Island and mine in Thames on the Coromandel Peninsula. I'd once remonstrated with an English-born friend long settled in New Zealand for describing me as an ex-New Zealander, an expatriate.

"Converts are always the worst," said the ex-Catholic Davin. I told Dan of the response of another New Zealand friend when I'd complained of this slur against my birthright: "Well, what I say, Brucie, is that you can take the boy out of Thames, but you can't take Thames out of the boy."

"Nor Southland," mused Davin, adding: *Caelum non animum mutant qui trans mare currunt.*

With Tony Stones and Dan Davin outside the Gardeners Arms, Oxford, late 1980s. *Marti Friedlander photo.*

"You've lost me, Dan," my hapless response.

"Horace."

"Still lost, only third-form Latin."

The measured delivery from the fine baritone: "They change their skies, not their souls, who run across the seas."

The Southland of Dan's youth in the 1920s not unlike the Coromandel of mine in the '40s.

"We made our own entertainment."

"Yes, I needed a canoe for the Kauaeranga river, built a wooden frame, tacked a sheet of corrugated iron around it, sealed the joints with tar."

"You needed a sledge, then build it yourself. Sand the runners, add soap, smooth as silk …"

239

"Shanghais [catapults] and shotguns, blasting away at anything that moved." We'd both finally rejected guns: Dan after being wounded in the Second World War Cretan battlefield and me after I nearly shot a mate when hunting wild goats on the family farm in the King Country area of the north island of New Zealand.

"… hit the water-filled tyre on the tractor instead, should have unloaded, faulty safety catch, missed him by inches, water spurting everywhere. Better than blood, I guess."

"Yes, certainly better than blood," Dan's sombre reply.

We'd both supplemented our scholarships to the UK, salting money away, Dan working as a docker and me in the freezing works.

We had something else in common. Both Davin and my father were friends of Bernard Freyberg, their commander and they had shared a few battles together, Dan in Intelligence and my father in the Tank Corps. Both were wounded, Dan lightly, my father severely on two occasions. Both were decorated, DMD with his military MBE and Bill Purchase, his MC gained at Cassino.

I needed to talk to Dan about the war. I'd attributed my father's death in his fifties to his wartime wounds.

"He left more than just his blood at Cassino."

"He did at least come home from the war," the old soldier, Davin said.

"I'd hide behind the sofa when his comrades came to call … to hear the tales of wartime he'd never otherwise discuss. Wish I'd told him that."

"Told him what?" Dan, quietly.

"That I was behind the sofa."

"He knew you were there," Dan, well acquainted with this childhood trait.

General Freyberg, in command of the New Zealand forces during the war, was also a hero of mine. I'd seen him at a distance when I was eight, when he'd pinned the Military Cross on my dad at a ceremony in Hamilton just after the war.

Years later I'd stood a few feet from the distinguished soldier at a reception at the Connaught Rooms in London, just after my arrival to study at the Royal Academy of Dramatic Art.

"I was too damned shy to speak," I told DMD.

"What would you have said?"

"Excuse me, Sir, I'm Bill Purchase's son."

"You should have spoken. Tiny [Freyberg's nickname] would have appreciated that."

Dan loved to talk about Freyberg and, as official historian of the battle on Crete, he also wrote of him. On one occasion Dan told me the now well known story: "Montgomery paid us a visit in the desert and said to Tiny: 'Your chaps don't seem too keen on saluting.' To which Freyberg replied, 'No, but if you wave, they'll wave back'."

Dan and Winnie's grandchildren and great-grandchildren called them both 'DanWinnie' as one. After Daniel Marcus Davin went (for old soldiers never die), the new, younger crop, embracing early words, referred to their great-grandmother as 'GreatWinnie', again one word. How right they were to call her great.

One memory of Winnie is when Dan instructed me to buy, as his birthday gift for her, a cashmere cardigan. When I entered the snug bar at the 'Vicky' (the Victoria Arms, a favourite haunt of theirs in Oxford, near their home) the next night and proffered to Dan the brown paper parcel, DMD gruffly instructed, "Give it to Winnie." I handed over the unromantic looking parcel. Winnie immediately made excited noises (she'd played the game before) as she briskly opened the package. At the sight of the cashmere she gasped with surprise. "Is this for me?" looking in Dan's direction.

"Happy birthday," he mumbled self-consciously. Trilling with delight, she slipped the cardigan on, flicking the buttons expertly into place as if she'd done it a thousand times. Like a Chekhovian actress her mood altered in a flash. Exasperation infused her as she looked at the mirror hung high above the fireplace.

"The trouble with you men," she glared at us all, now switching to fury, "is that you hang mirrors up too high for us girls."

With that she plonked a stool down in front of the fireplace and in a split second leapt, like a gazelle, atop the stool. I was entranced. In her mid-seventies Winnie K Davin had made a leap worthy of Pavlova or Fonteyn. From her balcony, 'Juliet' enthusiastically admired the cashmere in the mirror, then turning, looked down at her Romeo below.

"Oh, thank you darling, it's beautiful."

Looking more like Buddha than Shakespeare's young hero, Dan tried without success to hide his evident pride in her performance. Our heroine then slipped lightly, effortlessly, to the floor and executed a fluent, coquettish pirouette for the rest of the audience — me still transfixed.

"Isn't it wonderful?" she trilled again. Then sat down swiftly, picked up her pint of bitter, sipped and carried on from where she'd left off …

"Godfrey, you were saying …"

At the pub like a sentry coming on duty, Dan would invariably be at the appointed place bang on opening time. If alone he'd drink his pint and read. Winnie would mosey in half an hour later and, if the place was still quiet, pick up her pint and head for the fruit machine and woe betide any interruption! She'd bang away at the slot machine until it coughed up its rightful dues to her. One evening she carefully placed her substantial winnings in a fine silk purse and, when her grandson Ben came in, as expected, presented him with it. Ben, then an undergraduate at Balliol, Dan's college, smilingly accepted the gift of hard currency.

"More useful than a sow's ear," Dan murmured.

Winnie Davin, as a memory bank, was phenomenal. Long before the Gates and Windows opened to us all she operated her own internet.

"Anna," I asked Dan and Winnie's eldest, "do you know anything about ancient Japanese sword-making?"

"No, but Winnie will." And she did.

Her thirst for knowledge was insatiable, her transmission of information prodigious. Her press clipping agency, on behalf of family and friends at their house by the canal on the edge of Oxford's Port Meadow, made Reuters and Oxford's famous Bodleian Library look like small corner shops. A voracious reader, she'd assemble neat piles of cuttings from magazines and newspapers, relevant information awaiting distribution. If she didn't have the answer to a question at her fingertips (rare!), it wasn't long before she found it, either in a book from their vast library or from a quick phone call to "someone who will know". Her excitement when she gleaned another fact was infectious.

My portrait of
Dan Davin
(collection of
Reginald Hunt).

"What do they call your language?" This to her grand-daughter Kate's Kurdish-born husband-to-be, when Winnie first met him.

"Medish," his reply.

"Oh my God," both hands suddenly clasped to her chin. "You're the Medes," arms rippling up into the air with excitement. It was as if, after a lifelong search, a personal crusade across snow-capped mountains, she'd found a member of this long lost tribe seated opposite her in her own dining room. She was at once beguiling, flattering and all-embracing: after all this Mede was about to be absorbed into the Davin family of nations.

"You look different?" I'd just returned from filming in Hungary. Winnie knew I'd been feeling low before I left for Budapest, my marriage recently over. A grim time. I told her of my '*coup de foudre*' For WKD *coup de foudre* was meat and three veg.

"Tell me more," she turned from the crowded table creating, instantly, a private confessional.

"Well, I'd just arrived on location for the first day of filming …" I waffled on.

"Get on with it, brevity, brevity, please." This from WKD the established Oxford University Press editor.

Dan and Winnie Davin, sculpted in bronze by Anthony Stones.

"... came round a corner, saw this dark-haired woman. *Bam!*"

"*Bam?*" leaning in closer.

"Yes, Winnie — *Wham, Bam, Kapow!*"

"Even *Kapow*? Wow!" Winnie chuckled. "Who is she?"

I explained she was the Italian costume designer on the movie.

"What's her name?" Winnie now nose-to-nose, frantic with interest, as if her own life depended on the answer. I told her and, without a second's hesitation, she threw her arms skywards in her characteristic gesture and announced loudly for all to hear:

"She'll be Dario's daughter. Her grandfather translated Chesterton into Italian!" Our confessional now blown into smithereens.

Two days later, back on location at Lake Balaton in Hungary, I asked my Italian if these and a multitude of other facts Winnie had told me, were true. By then I appeared to know more about her family than she did!

Mightily aggrieved, my inamorata grilled me.

"Yes, but how do you know?"

I stupidly answered "It's a long story. I'll tell you later." I never did, but that's another tale. Filming finished a few weeks later. It was a wrap. *Finis.*

"How's Nana?" Winnie asked brightly. I'd just arrived back in Oxford. I explained.

"Ah well, darling, win some, lose some," her crisp response. She'd known it was all on the rebound anyway and had knocked it on the head. Clever Winnie.

When Winnie was in charge of events she operated like a lightning conductor. Years after the 'confessional' she said to me, naming another European city I was about to work in, "While you're there you should look up Laura Buxton, you'll get on well."

When I arrived in that city, I contacted Laura and we arranged a meeting in a café. Over a coffee I politely enquired: "How do you know the Davins?" for Winnie had not explained. Laura said she'd met them only recently in Oxford. "I was sitting on my own in the Gardener's Arms. Do you know that pub?"

"Ah, yes," for it was a regular watering hole for the Davins, myself and other Oxford friends.

"I saw this handsome old man," Laura continued, "sitting by himself, drinking a pint and reading the *Times Literary Supplement*. He had such a fine head I decided to discreetly sketch him. Soon he put down the TLS, stood up to get another pint, but changed direction and came towards me. 'Would you care to join me?' the old man said to me ..."

L then stopped in her story and began to gently weep. "And I fell in love with him," she quietly explained. I was deeply moved by this beautiful young woman's story. But as I reached awkwardly across the table, to in some way comfort her, I could only think, "Clever Winnie." She'd known Laura would need to talk about "Her Dan". WKD had seen this all before; I'd merely, as I was headed that way, been elected emissary.

"You'll get on well."

*

"Is there anything you need, darling?" Dan in hospital, near the end. Winnie on the phone about to visit. I'd called to provide transport.

"What?" Dan had replied to her question.

"I'm coming to see you, shall I bring you anything?"

"What?" Dan repeated his question.

"Is there anything you need Dan?"

A Davin pause on the end of the line, then:

"Clarity," Dan said softly. Winnie recounted this story, triumphantly.

Rare though they were, Winnie did have her low moments.

"I think my mind is going." (It quite clearly wasn't)

"Rubbish, Winnie," I chipped in. "If your mind is going what about the rest of us? Don't you realise you're one of the treasures of the twentieth century?"

Winnie gave a reflective glance at the ceiling, followed by quick transmission. "Flatterer," she chuckled and patted my hand.

After Dan's passing (old soldiers …) I spent many happy hours in Winnie Davin's company. Watching television with her was a joy. She loved snooker on the box — playing every shot along with her favourites (Jimmy White, her hero) cheering them on when they knocked up a score and calling out instructions to them on screen when their game was not going the way she thought it should. As her deafness increased her interpretation of plots and dialogue in TV plays or films became ever more interesting and creative …

"Did he say …?"

"No Winnie, unfortunately, he said …"

She took to wearing a hearing aid.

"It was always more interesting before, Winnie."

"Shall I switch it off?" Gleeful, always quick to turn a disadvantage to her advantage.

"I have a cold, it may be bad for me if it becomes a chill," 'Doctor' Winifred Davin pronounced. A week later her daughter Delia phoned in London. "Winnie was rushed into hospital last night, it looks bad …"

At the hospital the prognosis was not good. The doctors said Winnie would not last the night. I was by her bed as Winnie flashed me a question with her big bright eyes.

"What are the odds?" her eyes seem to ask.

Winnie, who always insisted on straight answers, knew by my expression I was fudging it and turned her eyes away.

She did get through the night; the doctors and nurses all amazed. "She'll pull through," they now confidently announced. Winnie, the gambler, had won the jackpot against all odds. But a few hours later, she gently let go and left us. She'd won her final bet and calmly hung up her colours. There was to be no repeat performance … no re-run of the hurdle race for her.

A few weeks later I look down from Winnie's bedroom window into the garden that leads down to the Oxford Canal. The swans are nesting, as they have for many years. Suddenly, a miniature deer, a muntjac, leaps over the wall into the garden, landing just below the window. I am transfixed. I've never seen one before and now to see one here, in a suburban Oxford garden. Small and grey-coloured, it remains very still for a second or two, then bright-eyed and alert, sniffing at the air, is gone, as swiftly as it appeared, up and over into the next garden and away.

Winnie would have loved this, and Dan would also have grunted approval, I mused, still transfixed by this momentary sighting.

Many years before at the Gardener's Arms one of the assembled company had said:

"I saw the New Zealanders at Trieste. They were bathing from the rocks. Next to us rag-tag Pommie soldiers the Kiwis looked like Greek gods, so fit and bronzed and strong-looking." Dan smiled, his head rolled back, the silent laugh we all loved, then acknowledging me in the group at the table.

In Lambs Bookshop, London, with *Intimate Stranger* editor Janet Wilson at left, and Brigid Sandford Smith, one of Dan & Winnie's three daughters.

"Bruce's father would have been one of that lot."

Thank you, Dan.

"Look up Laura when you go to Paris, you'll have a lot in common, you should get on well."

Winnie the internet — the lightning rod.

Thanks, Winnie.

Like the two great performers they were, they'd exited the stage, leaving their audience still longing for more.

XI

They change their skies

IN THE MID-1990S I WAS DRIVING towards the plains of Thessaly in Greece with a friend from New Zealand who was researching a biography. We'd known one another since we were in our late teens and had shared memorable times in Greece on earlier trips. A mutual friend from the States sat in the rear passenger seat. Out of the blue my mate alongside me asked:

"What was your mother's maiden name?" As it was not a credit card safety check I thought his query odd, but nevertheless replied:

"Sutton." Then added: "That's a strange question, Vince. Are you by any chance drafting my obituary?"

Vincent didn't reply, nor did I grill him further, though in a quick sideways glance from the wheel of our fast-moving, snazzy purple hire car, I noted he blushed ever so slightly. We drove on to our destination, reaching it by early evening …

*

I'm in Rhyl, North Wales. It's 1960 and I'm dancing with a smartly dressed, ramrod-straight woman of eighty. She's my Welsh grandmother … my Nain. Earlier in the day I'd said to her:

"Happy birthday, Nain. How would you like to celebrate your eightieth?"

"You will take me dancing …"

That evening at a hotel on the sea front at Rhyl, with a Palm Court orchestra playing, I asked what she would like to drink.

"I shall drink Advocaat." And she did, downing several glasses during the evening in between being waltzed and foxtrotted around the ballroom by her 22-year-old grandson she'd met for the first time that very day.

I remember my mother in New Zealand saying to me in my teens: "Your Nain doesn't like Bruce as a name."

"Why?"

Mother smiled: "She thinks it's only a useful name for a big dog."

My Nain was very Welsh and very different to my other grandmother, whom I adored. Nana in New Zealand was warm-hearted in contrast to my formal, very 'cool' Nain. For instance, when I was a boy, Nana in New Zealand would literally let her hair down ... it was long and lustrous and fell to her waist. I would pass a big tortoiseshell comb gently, over and again, through my grandmother's beautiful strands. I adored this task ... one I could never imagine being set me by my elegant but stern Welsh Nain.

A year later, in 1962, my mother made her first return visit to the UK since emigrating to New Zealand in the mid-1930s. One day in north Wales during that trip we were walking up the graveyard path approaching Criccieth Church. I was leading, my mother behind me and my serious Nain bringing up the rear.

A woman called over the wall to me, in Welsh. Knowing only a few words and phrases of that language I probably looked bemused; in any case it was Nain who replied. Both the woman on the other side of the wall and my mother laughed. I turned to my Mum:

"What did that woman say?"

"She was telling you the church was locked."

"And what exactly did Nain reply?"

"She told that woman there was no point in addressing you for you are foreign," Mother smiled.

We walked back down the path away from the church.

"Nain," I called to her, "I'm your grandson, for goodness sake."

"You're still foreign." There was no vestige of humour in her observation.

Although my mother had three brothers and a sister, I'd not grown up with them around so didn't feel the same bond as I had with my New Zealand relatives. I did, however, become fond of two of my Welsh uncles and one great-uncle called Will Sam. I grew to like my mother's eldest brother, Len. He'd been a conjuror in the days of music hall, along with my aunt who'd been his assistant.

His stage name had been 'Leonard de Bear'. He did rather well and retired comfortably to North Wales when music hall finally died off with the advent of television. One favourite image that I was shown of him, taken at the peak of his career, was a black-and-white photo of him in full evening dress. On one arm, white against black, his sleeve was adorned with live white mice and alongside him stood his assistant, my sweet-natured and diminutive Aunt Marie. The sheer magic of his professional life lives for me in the memory of that single monochrome image. Len had worked with most of the stars of his music hall age and told wonderful stories about them. In particular, entertaining yarns about that legendary comedian, Max Miller. Another uncle, Harry, a less entertaining man, was a haberdasher and my Aunt Muriel had even less charm than my Nain. But Mother's youngest brother Cyril I really took to and he told me one story about my father which I treasure. During the Second World War Cyril had served in the Welsh Guards …

"We were in Italy and I heard that the New Zealanders were based near us. With a driver I took a vehicle to the New Zealand lines. I saw two Kiwi officers talking. Stepping out of the jeep I approached them. One had his back to me and when I asked if, by any chance, Bill Purchase was with them, the officer with his back to me turned and said calmly, as if the moment were completely day-to-day: 'Hello Cyril.' It was your dad, Bruce. We were able to talk for half an hour before I had to depart. I'd never before met your father and haven't since …" A serendipitous meeting in the theatre of war. Cyril emigrated to Canada in the 1960s and, apart from one brief meeting at Vancouver airport in the late '60s, we regrettably lost touch.

The drive to Thessaly mentioned earlier was part of the research that Vincent O'Sullivan, poet, academic, novelist, playwright, critic, editor and biographer, was making into the wartime experience of a distinguished New Zealander, John Mulgan, who'd fought alongside the Greeks in their resistance against German occupation. Mulgan was a heroic figure who died tragically young in Cairo, where he took his own life with a morphia overdose while commanding his group of resistance fighters. What we learnt on that trip to Thessaly was part, only part I imagine, of that horrific time. In Vincent's *Long Journey to the Border*, published in 2004, he acknowledged:

251

"... Barbara Caruso and Bruce Purchase were good companions in Thessaly and Roumelli ..." This was fitting, as the three of us have shared a lifetime of travel and friendship ... part of another long journey, with changing skies too ...

In October 1960 I stood shyly in the canteen at the Royal Academy of Dramatic Art. Auditions had taken place months before. This was the young Kiwi's first day of his two-year course. A man, slightly older than the me, approached:

"My name is Terence Rigby. Welcome to RADA."

A friendly gesture from a student who was about to complete his course. We have remained friends, but have worked together rarely, the first time in the successful BBC series of the 1960s, *Softly Softly*. Rigby was a regular. He has had a distinguished career and lives between New York and London. We worked together again in a major Shakespearean stage production for the National Theatre.

One recollection from that excellent, much-praised production. Rigby was rehearsing into the role of Buckingham in Shakespeare's *Richard III*. He'd just finished a scene and director Richard Eyre spoke to Terence:

"That's coming along ... Just one point, Terry ..."

Richard went on to tentatively suggest that on the line ..."He is not lying on a lewd love-bed" ... that 'lewd' should perhaps be pronounced lee-ewed and not as Terry had just said ... 'lood'. Terry, given the note, didn't bat an eyelid, but never changed his pronunciation. For the four-month tour we did of *Richard III*, in New York, Washington DC, St Paul, Denver, San Francisco and Los Angeles, no further reference was made to it by Richard Eyre or anyone else. That was until after our return from that long enjoyable tour in the States, when I phoned Terence at his London home ...

Terence R: Hello.

Bruce P: *(imitating Terry's idiosyncratic delivery)* Eee is not lyin' in a lood love-bed.
            (There followed a minute pause ... then:)

Terence R: Purchase ... you bastard.

He'd done it deliberately. When corrected by Richard Eyre, Terry had merely dug his heels in and had done it his way.

My time at RADA was rich and rewarding, spent as it was with a bevy of fellow students, many of whom went on to carve out fine careers.

I'm in Oxford. It's the late 1980s. I'm having a drink with friends in the Victoria Arms. It's my turn to buy the next round. Behind the bar is a delightful young woman called Lucy. She has been trying to get a job at Oxford University Press.

Bruce: Three pints please … oh, by the way, have you heard about that job you applied for at OUP?

Lucy: Yes, I've got it.

Bruce: Brilliant! Congratulations. Can I buy you a celebratory drink?

Lucy: No. The new landlord doesn't allow the staff to be bought drinks.

Bruce: How silly. What are you doing tomorrow? If you're free, let me buy you lunch.

We met at a favourite Chinese restaurant to celebrate her achievement. It was almost summer and her job didn't start until the autumn. Over lunch:

Bruce: Are you and John [her boyfriend] going to have a summer holiday together?

Lucy: No, I'm going to visit Russia, with my mother.

Bruce: Where are you planning to go?

Lucy: Moscow.

Bruce: Have you been to Russia before?

Lucy: Never … but my mother goes every summer.

Bruce: Any particular reason?

Lucy: My … my … grandfather lives there …

Bruce: Is he a diplomat?

Lucy: No.

Bruce: A businessman? Academic?

Lucy looked upwards before replying.

Lucy: No … he's a colonel in the KGB.

Bruce: Are you telling me that you are Kim Philby's granddaughter?

I was dumbfounded, but had guessed in one. She'd been, very trustingly, trying to find a way to tell me who her grandfather was. Her grandfather was an Englishman who, as a Soviet spy at the heart of the British Establishment, had finally fled to Russia many years before. She did meet him in Russia that summer and told me later about her reactions to that visit. Her grandfather, Kim Philby, died shortly afterwards in Moscow, never returning to the country of his birth. Lucy emigrated to Australia. She too, like her grandfather … changed her skies …

One personal loss was the death of a great friend from New Zealand. His name was Ken and he was, like me, a pupil at Auckland Grammar … but Ken was two years younger, therefore two years behind me. He was also keen on acting and two years after I was awarded a government bursary to study at RADA, he followed the same path as me to the UK and attended RADA. I had a theatrical agent, Elspeth Cochrane, and he was also taken onto her books. We only worked together twice … once on a single play (a boardroom thriller) at Coventry Rep and on the other occasion at New Zealand House in London's Haymarket … a programme based on the journals of Captain James Cook's travels to the South Pacific, where on board the *Endeavour* he re-discovered New Zealand and charted, for the first time by a European, its entire coastline. Ken and I were good mates. A tall rangy young man in his early twenties with a mop of red hair, he was a popular lad who always 'lit up a room' when he entered it.

Ken got a part in a film, cast in a role as a German officer, and sent me a postcard to say how filming had progressed and when he'd be back. "I'll ring you on my return" he signed off. But he didn't phone and it was our shared agent who broke the news a few days later when I visited her office in Knightsbridge.

"Sit down, Bruce. I take it you've not heard?"

"Heard? Heard what, Elspeth?"

"Ken Poitevin is dead." I sat in front of Elspeth's desk, pole-axed by the news.

His mother later told me he'd always promised himself that as soon as he started earning money he planned to have an operation on his ears, which stuck out slightly. He did have it on his return from filming in Europe, but what should have been a simple cosmetic operation went wrong and he died under the anaesthetic. Devastated by his death, his many friends were also angry that Ken had not shared his worry about his ears with them. They were, after all, no more 'sticky-out' than say ... Clark Gable's! Why hadn't he shared this self-consciousness about his appearance with us? We would have talked him out of it. We reflected upon what might have been as we stood in a North London graveyard that lay, that sad day, deep in snow that had fallen overnight.

Over the years I've continued to imagine what life might have been for my good young friend, the popular, intelligent and charming Ken Poitevin. What skies would Ken have experienced during what should have been a long, happy and successful life? Perhaps, for Ken, *'Quem Di diligunt adolescens moritur'* ... Whom the gods love die young ...

The two I now speak of were brothers, of Swiss extraction. They grew up in the north of England and though from lower middle-class backgrounds, attended Cambridge University, both on scholarships. Godfrey and Peter Lienhardt studied anthropology and became eminent in their chosen fields: Godfrey, the Dinka tribe of the Sudan and Peter, Persia. Both men were extremely witty and eccentric. Their careers came to full bloom at Oxford University, where I met them through Dan and Winnie Davin.

A favourite story about the Lienhardt brothers was told me with relish by Godfrey. Their mother was hanging out the washing on the line in the backyard of their simple terraced house in the north of England. A neighbour was likewise hanging out her washing too.

Mrs Lienhardt: (with a wooden peg in her mouth) Both my sons ... (peg from mouth to attach clothes to line ... a pause) ... have got scholarships to Cambridge University ...

Neighbour: (wooden peg in her mouth too) Aye ... (peg from mouth to line to attach clothes to washing line ... similarly, a brief pause ...) ... you can educate them till they're daft.

The neighbour was right. The two boys went to Cambridge, lost their north country accents, replacing their original childhood accent with an extraordinary strangulated upper-class version and became two very eccentric clever-clogs academics on the Oxford scene. One

255

day in an Oxford pub in the 1980s I approached their table carrying two pints of ale for them. As I reached the table …

Peter:	*(the taller of the two and somewhat concave of chest)* Oh, you're so big and strong. I think of myself as a bit of a wimp.
Godfrey:	(a smaller man with a rapier wit … in for the kill) Yes, Peter, you are a 'bit of a wimp'. Yesterday I saw you walking through St Giles and you were so stooped you looked like a camel.
Peter:	(a swift response) Yes, but I don't fart as much.

Another joyous memory is of Godfrey entering the Gardener's Arms in Oxford, dwarfed by the two ebony six-foot-six students of the Dinka tribe from the Sudan who accompanied him. The Dinkas were studying petro-chemical engineering. A memorable sight.

These two entertaining, though sometimes wasp-tongued brothers, held their own brilliantly in conversation at these gatherings with the Davins. Dan and Winnie and others gathered to exercise their wit and individual intelligence in the art of conversation … academics and writers for the most part, from all over the world. A heady mix of talk that for many years for me was both a challenge and a great pleasure to be part of.

On another occasion the sculptor Anthony Stones entered the bar. Godfrey, in clipped, Noel Coward-ish delivery, greeted him:

"And what have you been up to, Tony?"

Tony explained he'd been working in clay, long hard hours, on a life-size figure.

"Nonsense, Tony — a line of women gutting fish is hard work … what we do is pure indulgence."

Head of Bruce Purchase by Anthony Stones.

As Samuel Johnson, in *Johnson is Leaving*.

One character who occasionally joined this spirited mêlée was the academic, poet and novelist, John Wain, who wrote the one-man play about Sam Johnson for me.

For his services to literature Samuel Johnson received a royal pension, and Wain himself was also a beneficiary of a royal pension plus a CBE for his services to literature. The play John Wain wrote for me, though not of course a royal pension, is nonetheless a pension of sorts for Bruce Purchase, actor, too. A nice thought and one that I'm certain Wain had very much in mind when he wrote the play. I reflect upon this fact as I continue to perform John's monodrama and as I do so, get nearer in actual age to the character of Sam Johnson, as depicted in Wain's play. In fact the serious illness I experienced in 2007 curiously made it easier to essay the role when my own actual vulnerability in performance melded perfectly with the imagined vulnerability of Sam Johnson nearing the end of his life.

Wain, who died in 1994, was a good novelist (*Hurry on Down* was recently re-published a decade after his death), an excellent poet (professor of poetry at Oxford, 1973-78) and, like Samuel Johnson, was a real man of letters. His last books were his trilogy of novels, *Where the Rivers Meet* and his final creative work, *Johnson is Leaving*.

257

Dr Johnson and his doppelgänger at Strand-on-the-Green, Chiswick.
Jon Churchman photography..

John died on the very day I commenced rehearsing it, so he never saw me perform, only hearing me do a rehearsed reading, seated in Walter Pater's chair at Brasenose College in Oxford, a few weeks before his sudden death. But after my first performance at the Swan theatre in Stratford-Upon-Avon, John's eldest son Will said to me: "Dad would have been chuffed." Certainly this monodrama is an acute, perceptive and empathetic homage to the man of letters, Samuel Johnson and, as it is storytelling at its best, audiences of all ages enjoy and identify with it. Two recurring phrases of John's, in his own life, that I remember … one, whenever he offered up a toast, "Let's be lucky" and the other, when he was particularly cross about an individual …

"May a tram-car grow in his stomach!"
and "They pour cream down the sink in Oxford!"

*

Dan and Winnie Davin, two of my closest friends, advisers and guides in my life.

Dan:	Where are you filming?
Bruce:	On the Isle of Man.
Dan:	Do you know Bill Naughton? He lives there. You should look him up. I'll give you his address.

Dan then told me an extraordinary story about Naughton. Though they had never met, Dan (as a publisher at Oxford University Press) and Bill had a long correspondence about a book that Bill wished to write. Then, out of the blue one day, Dan received a short letter from Bill, which enclosed a large-ish cheque. "Thought the encl. might come in handy," Bill wrote.

"I was strapped for cash at the time," Dan explained, "but how did Naughton know …?"

"Did you publish his book, Dan?"

"No, in the end he never wrote it."

"And did you bank the cheque?"

"I did," Dan growled and grinned.

I was filming on the Isle of Man for BBC TV (an adaptation of Arnold Bennett's *Anna of the Five Towns*) and arranged to meet

Naughton. I had met him briefly many years before when I'd unsuccessfully auditioned for a role in his *Spring and Port Wine* at the Mermaid Theatre in London. The play *Alfie* (filmed with Michael Caine and again more recently with Jude Law) was another successful play written by the very productive and successful Bill Naughton.

On that sunny summer day in 1984, Bill awaited me at his front gate which led to his large property and insisted on walking alongside the car as I drove it down the long driveway to his big house, Bill talking all the while. It was an unnervingly jerky drive, as he would suddenly halt and then, equally unexpectedly, march on again at speed. Once I'd parked the car he insisted we walk in his rose garden. He had very deep-set eyes (hidden behind specs so they were impossible to discern) and quick darting movements. Bill started to grill me for all the tales I could muster up about our mutual colleague and friend, Bernard Miles, who ran the Mermaid and indeed created that theatre.

As I launched into anecdotes about Bernard, Bill, chuckling all the while, darted about the garden in such a staccato fashion, like a puppy, forever egging me on to tell him more. His sudden movements continued to faze me. After about half an hour of this carry-on he beckoned me to follow him around the side of his big modern bungalow to where, in a sun-filled outdoor alcove with a magnificent view of fields and the Irish Sea glinting in the distance, stood a comfortable-looking day-bed.

"Try lying down on it." I did so though I felt very self-conscious.

"Close your eyes," Bill said softly … and I must have fallen asleep immediately. This was very strange for it was only midday!

I awoke suddenly and glanced at my wristwatch. I estimated I must have dozed off for twenty minutes or so. Bill was nowhere to be seen but as I sat up and swung my legs off the day-bed, he reappeared.

"I fell asleep," I said foolishly.

"Thought you might," he replied enigmatically, then:

"Did you dream?"

"Yes, I did," I replied dazedly.

"Did you dream that you were skiing?"

"Yes I did ... but how ...?"

"Thought you had. Come and have a bite to eat."

He led me around a corner from the alcove to a table in the sun beautifully laid for three people. "Sit there," he cheerfully encouraged me. No sooner had my bum hit the seat when, as if by magic, his wife appeared from the house and I leapt to my feet again. I had never before met his wife, Erna, a handsome woman much younger than Bill. We commenced lunch and the strangeness of the day's events continued. The lunch was delicious and the wine excellent and both Erna and Bill were charming company. Having ascertained that Erna was from Austria I mentioned a curious coincidence in my life associated with Austria:

"My father at the end of the war was stationed for a time in Klagenfurt and it was in Klagenfurt where my step-daughter Josie learnt to ski, staying with Austrian friends. Josie learnt to ski very well and our friends always called her 'our little English champion'."

"Here's another coincidence." Bill smiled but his eyes were so deep set it was impossible to spot their expression. He gestured towards his wife.

"Erna was born in Klagenfurt."

One other odd moment happened over lunch. Out of the blue, Bill said:

"Have you seen Murray lately?"

"Murray ...?"

"Murray Sayle."

"I met him once in Paris in the early '60s but haven't seen him since. Nevertheless how did you know I'd ...?" But Bill crisply interjected: "I thought you'd know him. You should look him up again. He's lived for years now in Japan."

Over the years I'd often thought of journalist Murray Sayle. As a result of this exchange on that sunny terrace on the Isle of Man, Bill gave me the address in Japan and we did reconnect in 1990 when I worked in Tokyo.

At the end of that memorable luncheon Bill showed me his study. His current project was a book about dreams. When I was leaving, again, out of the blue, like so much that happened that day, Bill said, gently:

CHANGING SKIES

"Take care of yourself, Bruce, for the next few years will be very difficult for you."

I drove off, puzzled, musing also about the tale Dan Davin had told me ... but how right Bill Naughton was, for my marriage, out of a seemingly clear blue sky, ended a few months later and the grief associated with that tore my sky apart. Bill Naughton was certainly a kind of seer. His final years were spent looking out over the Irish Sea and skies, from his beautiful house high on the hills of the Isle of Man. I shall never forget that extraordinary, sun-drenched day.

Now a bleaker tale about another writer, though not entirely unamusing. In 1966 I was part of a splendid assemblage of actors at the Bristol Old Vic. It was the bicentenary celebration for that beautiful theatre. One evening I was invited to join a group for dinner and to my left was the writer Henry Williamson. Best known for his book *Tarka the Otter*, he was equally well known for his pre-war Fascist leanings and his friendship with Hitler and his vile cronies. The chance, I now describe, was too good to miss ... bolstered by good food and wine ... around about the sweet course, a glass of dessert wine in hand, I turned to Williamson and said:

"Mr Williamson?" He glanced in my direction. "When did you last meet Hitler?"

He looked at me as if I'd just crawled out from under a stone but being an English gentleman of his class and that period, answered me in a very correct, though understandably frozen, manner. His accent was definitely that of a toff.

"The last time I met A-dolf was a year or so before the outbreak of the war. He seemed depressed so I asked him what was the matter. A-dolf tried not to answer me but I pressed him further to get what was worrying him off his chest. He finally told me that things were going so badly ('bed-leh') in Europe and he didn't know what to do."

Williamson paused and looked steadily at me, his expression was unreadable. So, after a beat, I said:

"And then he made up his mind ...?"

"Yes," he drawled, "you might say that." He then cut me dead and we spoke not another word. My question had been impertinent, yes, but I'm ever so glad I asked it. I wonder what skies, what dreams

262

Williamson had wished before and during the war, for his good friend ... A-dolf?

That was something I never had the opportunity to ask ... only to imagine them dining, pleasantly, at All Souls College, Oxford, at a victory dinner after the war ... a celebration that thank God, never happened.

One intended victim of Williamson's 'chum' A-dolf, was my friend and colleague, Julius Gellner, who was my in-house advisor when I rehearsed the role of Othello at the Mermaid Theatre in 1971. A wise old guru, he was of enormous help to me when I approached that difficult part. Many years before he had directed *Othello*, with the powerful actor Frederick Valk in the title role, so he knew the piece well and was able to guide my young self in rehearsal. Julius, a Sudetenland-born German Jew had been captured while trying to cross the border into the safety of neutral Switzerland. He was guarded in a border-patrol hut by a young German soldier while the soldier's compatriots went off in search of suitable transport to whisk Gellner off to almost certain death.

Members of my Zander family took that cruel path to oblivion. In a book of names in the new Holocaust Museum in Berlin there are listed almost a 100 names of members of the Zander clan who were victims.

Julius (who was also a long-term advisor to that fine actor, Herbert Lom) told me what happened in that hut. The young German soldier sat opposite him with a pistol on the table in front of him. Julius began to talk quietly to the lad. He asked him where he'd been born, then what education he'd had; did he have siblings, friends at home, etc? He asked the soldier about his parents and what his father did. Finally, Julius said quietly:

"You must miss your family very much."

As Julius told it, after a long pause the German soldier got up and unlocked the outer door. Without a word to Gellner, he exited to a room that adjoined the one they were in. The soldier had left his pistol on the table. Julius exited through the unlocked door and without further incident safely crossed the border into Switzerland. He eventually arrived in Britain and lived out the rest of his life under English skies.

Alan Badel playing Michael Arlen and Bruce Purchase as Ernest Hemingway, on a set of New York's Algonquin Hotel for BBC TV *Exiles*.

"I often wonder what happened to that young lad," Julius said.
"Perhaps he was shot for his kindness towards you?"
"Yes."
Another wartime story that embraced a similar use of psychology involved the actor, Alan Badel, whose daughter Sarah was in my class at RADA. I worked often with Alan on television and admired him greatly. He was an actor *sans pareil*. During the war one of Badel's fellow commandos had been wounded and lay in an open area, some thirty yards from where Alan and his compatriots were hidden, sheltered from the heavy gunfire directed at them. Alan told the others he was going to rescue his wounded comrade.

"Don't be a fool," they said, "you'll be cut down."

But Badel took off his uniform and underwear and, naked, raised himself above the parapet of their hiding place. The firing ceased as he stood visible and naked to the enemy. Alan then walked slowly out to his wounded comrade, lifted him into his arms and returned to safety. During this time not a single shot was fired. A naked man … not just another enemy uniform to be shot at. Brilliant and brave.

With Vince O'Sullivan researching his book about John Mulgan and listening to the horrors of war in northern Greece, I was reminded of my first visit to Greece in 1967. Barbara Caruso had come from the US to journey with me from London by train and boat to Greece. We first had a stop-over in Firenze, and another on the Greek island of Corfu. Then onwards by ferry and coach to Athens where we were met by Vincent and his first wife, Tui. Our arrival in Athens coincided with the overthrow of the Greek government by 'the colonels,' as they became known. A military takeover. The four of us journeyed northwards to a mountain village to visit our friend, Kostas Argyropoulos, who lives and teaches in Athens but was born in the village of Plaka, high in the mountains near Karpenisi. He met us off our bus on the dry dusty valley road which seemed in the midst of nowhere. We trekked in the heat of the midday sun, up the steep path to Plaka, our luggage strapped to one mule and Barbara elegantly perched side-saddle on another, while Kostas, Vince, Tui and I went on foot. Dehydrated after the long climb, we were welcomed by Kostas' mother, who in the cool interior of her stone house offered each of us saucers filled with jam along with glasses of cool spring water to slake our thirst. A blissful welcome which was added to by a feast given us in the village square by the whole populace.

We learnt too of the suffering the folk in that village had to endure. During the bloody civil war that followed the Italian and German hostilities, the communist Greeks entered this idyllic mountain village and killed many they believed not on their side. Two victims included Kostas' uncle, who was the local Greek Orthodox priest and his father, the village schoolteacher. Both men were crucified … the uncle on the church door and Kostas' father on the door of the small school.

More recently, at a gathering of locals in his village, Kostas had to be physically restrained when he saw the man he believed responsible for that barbarity. While Kostas was held, the man allegedly responsible for the crimes was spirited away. "I would have killed him," Kostas said. As a New Zealander safely brought up far from the cruelty of the European conflicts I reflected, yet again, on the good fortune that time and place — way south in the Pacific — had afforded me.

Another man and his wife who suffered for their beliefs and with whom I was fortunate to share friendship, is Yang Sheni and his wife Gladys Yang, the daughter of English missionaries to China. These two ran the English Language Press in Beijing for many years. They were both imprisoned for a long time during the Red Guards period in China. Sheni had been an undergraduate at Oxford in the 1930s and had returned to his homeland. I met these two remarkable folk through the Davins in the 1980s. The Yangs were on a visit to Oxford, staying as honoured guests in a university apartment.

"Do go and visit Gladys and Sheni," Winnie Davin said to me. "Oh … and here's a tenner, take them a bottle of Scotch from us. They love whisky," she grinned. "You'll like them."

How right she was. My first meeting with this venerable pair was delightful. I turned up unannounced one evening and rang their bell. As instructed I was clutching Winnie Davin's gift of Scotch, wrapped in brown paper. Sheni opened the door and I opened my mouth to tell him who I was. However, Sheni spoke first: "Do come in," he said smoothly to the tall stranger, although I noted he glanced at the wrapped bottle clutched at my chest and must have instinctively known what I was carrying, and guessed I must be a friendly emissary. I followed him silently into their living room and, smooth as silk, he bade me sit on a sofa opposite his chair. As I did so, placing the gift on the table in front of me, I noted that a bottle of Scotch, half-consumed stood on the table plus two half-filled glasses of the amber nectar. As I sank into the sofa and made this observation, Gladys Yang glided into the room with a tray that held a single empty glass. She placed it neatly in front of me and, still wordlessly, still oh so smoothly, Sheni poured me a generous portion from his already open bottle. Gladys then sat and they both lifted their glasses, encouraging me to do the same. We smiled and Sheni then said:

"Now, tell us who you are." It was the beginning of a delightful friendship, especially with Sheni, for Gladys, though familiarly English, had a reserve about her which was hard to fathom or penetrate. Sheni by contrast was at all times ease personified.

Years later, after the trouble on Beijing's Tiananmen Square, I saw Sheni being interviewed on the BBC news about the violence and "these thugs who run my country". I panicked and decided to phone him at his home in Beijing. Incidentally, when referring to that city in English, he always referred to it by its former name, Peking. I tried phoning direct but couldn't get through but, knowing a trick or two about telephonic communication with China, phoned via Hong Kong and got through immediately. Sheni answered, speaking in English. He'd obviously already had a deluge of calls from other English-speaking friends from around the world.

"Hello," Sheni's familiar voice murmured.

"Hi, Sheni, it's Bruce."

"Hello, Bruce. How are you?"

"I'm okay, but more importantly … how are you?"

"Fine. Fine."

"Is this line being tapped, Sheni?"

"Of course."

"Then I'll keep this call brief … I'd just like to say that British Actors Equity and the Royal National Theatre send their support to you."

Sheni laughed heartily: "Thank you, Bruce."

"How's Gladys?"

"She's well …"

"Give her my best."

"Yes, I will. Thank you for phoning."

I'd hit the mark spot on, for, as I well knew, the Chinese authorities are always more impressed and affected by the mention of an organisation rather than an individual, sending support, although, of course, I had no authority to send such support from either my actor's union or the National Theatre! But every little helps and maybe that and many other calls Sheni received at the time kept him from harm, for Sheni was not arrested for the comments he'd made on British television.

Another friend from that part of the world, who was often a thorn in the side of his own country, was 'Rishy'. Son of a Rana of the Kingdom of Nepal, Rishikesh Shaha was an unwelcome democrat in that Royalist-led country. However his role made him an influential figure and Rishikesh wrote Nepal's modern constitution (incidentally abolishing the Ranas, which infuriated Rishy's father!) He was also, for a time, Nepal's representative to the United Nations.

His writings in English gave him added international standing. But Rishy's democratic beliefs often made him unpopular with the King of Nepal who would occasionally, mostly on a whim, lock him in jail. Like the Yangs of Beijing, Rishy's favourite tipple was also whisky and when in jail, incongruously, the King would send him gifts of Scotch. Even more strangely, if Rishikesh was invited to a party (say at a foreign embassy, maybe also attended by the King and Queen) the King would release my friend for the duration of the evening ... then it was straight back to jail again! This was the very King who died by his eldest son's hand, held — drug and booze-influenced — to the trigger of an automatic gun. No, the King had little to fear from Rishy's democratic beliefs, but much to fear from his own son.

Rishy was an inveterate gambler and on visits to London would always spend a lot of time in the casinos. He was often accompanied by an impressive woman, the irrepressible and irreplaceable New Zealander Meg Sheffield, though never along with her husband ... it was not a place the Scots-born writer Alex Guyan enjoyed. Meg and Alex had first met Rishikesh when Meg was seconded from the BBC to set up Educational Radio Broadcasting in Nepal and she and Alex were based in Kathmandu. Meg later switched to television and, until her early retirement, was a producer and director who made many remarkable educational films for the Open University. She filmed in many parts of the world and the works she left behind are a clear reminder to us of her particular talent and vision. Their home in Stony Stratford, especially after my divorce, became a second home for me and their loving support helped me to come through that lonely time and its aftermath.

Alex Guyan died in 1991, far too young, from cancer. Meg died seven years later to the day, from injuries received when, shortly after her retirement, she was knocked off her bike in New Zealand by a car driven by a teenager. Meg departed this life with so much she still intended to do ... the creation of a mud hut being one beautifully eccentric idea she had on her drawing board. Meg and Alex's daughter Kate Guyan is the very embodiment of them both and remains a beautiful bearer of the torch with which her parents lit up the world. She's a clever young woman; she won an Emmy in

New York for design and was my art director when I filmed a twelve-minute DVD promo for *Johnson is Leaving*.

It was the Mermaid Theatre's Bernard Miles who wrote:

> More and more frequently, there steals over one, the suspicion that the whole human story is a kind of play, a tragi-comedy in many episodes with the script still being written in the wings, the mammoth cast under-rehearsed, imperfectly made-up, unsure of their cues and dressed in the wrong clothes; the stage-management either very inexperienced, inebriated or blatantly incompetent; and the Great Director tearing his hair in the stalls. To be of some minute assistance to Him in pulling the show together, makes the whole thing seem abundantly worth while, and in any case, I daresay, it'll be all right on the night.

Yes, "the play's the thing" (*Hamlet*) ... and in life ... "all the men and women merely players." (*As You Like It*)

Shakespeare has always, in the playing of, been a joy and fun too.

The years 1980 through to '82 illustrate this feeling. The three years working that first time with the RSC were a joy, with a fine company gathered, that included Alan Howard, Sinead Cusack, David Suchet, Susan Fleetwood and Tom Wilkinson. Among others too numerous to mention was one of the wittiest and most intelligent men I've ever had the good fortune to work with and call a friend ... actor, humorist and writer *par excellence*, not a household name, but a star to the many who know him ... Trevor Baxter. He and I shared Dressing Room 2 at Stratford and his talent to make me laugh so heartily made the time there so much more agreeable, during that busy, sometimes stressful and exhausting time.

Shortly after the 1980 season began at Stratford-Upon-Avon, my wife Elspeth and our nine-year-old son, Reuben, had headed off for a holiday to New Zealand. I had booked it with my American Express card and had confided with Trevor, that, when the monthly account arrived in the post, I didn't have the funds to pay the debt. Then a miracle happened. On the day the Amex bill arrived in the post I opened another envelope and a residual cheque fell from it ... this for the sale of a television play I'd done a few years earlier and which, unbeknown to me, had been sold abroad. It covered my debt

As First Player in *Hamlet*. Royal Shakespeare Company, Stratford-Upon-Avon.

to American Express, with a bit left over. When I showed the cheque to Baxter he was quick to grasp this point:

"Good — there's forty quid left over for champagne."

During the next two years the company of Baxter was very rewarding. Trevor is a powerhouse of witty invention, for which I and the whole company were happy beneficiaries. First he created our dressing room, Dressing Room 2, not just our place to get into costume, but more importantly a Head of Department! This was formally announced on the company noticeboard. The RSC management went along with the joke and informed us of company matters. Then Baxter announced that Dressing Room 2 was private terrain. Anyone else wishing to enter it had first to speak to our dresser who, it was announced again formally on the noticeboard, was not only our dresser, but more importantly, our personal manager. Anyone who wished to enter this holy sanctum had first to apply via our representative, Alison, who had to be addressed as Mrs Kingsley and never as Alison ... no such impertinent over-familiarity allowed. It was further announced that upon his return from working in India, Mrs Kingsley's husband would take up his new post as Dressing Room 2's 'gardener', and complete for us an elegant rock garden on the roof that led out from DR 2. This was fiction too, of course. Mrs Kingsley's husband Ben was, as announced, "at present in India ... working on some little film." The little film was Richard Attenborough's *Gandhi* and Mrs Kingsley's husband, Ben, was playing the title role. This would soon make him an Oscar winner, a rich man and eventually a Knight of the Realm ... *Sir* Ben Kingsley. The fantasy rock garden on the roof, was never completed.

Best jape of all in that season — which included fine productions of *As You Like It* (me as the wicked Duke), *Romeo and Juliet* (me as Prologue/Duke), *Hamlet* (ditto, as First Player), *Richard III* (Hastings), *Richard II* (Northumberland) — was Trevor Baxter's invention of a fictional family ... 'wife, Edie', plus a 'son' and 'daughter'. He would regale us with tales of his 'family'. This invariably took place on the company terrace overlooking the picturesque Avon, with its elegant swans and passing riverboat traffic. These inventions always amused us. His 'daughter' was said to be a lesbian police officer, his 'wife,'

As Leonarto in BBC TV's *Much Ado About Nothing*.

Edie, very eccentric, as indeed was his 'son' too. Over a period of a few months his yarns continued to convulse and transfix us ... to the extent that the whole company almost began to believe these characters actually existed. Then a very strange thing happened. Trevor, the inventor of 'his family' received a letter in the post ... from his 'wife' Edie. He showed me the letter and Trevor was untypically thrown by this unexpected missive.

"Who in the company has written it, do you think?"

We tried to guess, but without success.

The 'voice' of Edie in this long letter, was so reminiscent of the character Trevor had invented, it was truly unnerving. In her letter 'Edie' mentioned many things we'd all become familiar with, but most unnerving of all Edie announced she would meet her 'husband', Trevor, in a well known local Stratford tea and coffee place in Sheep Street, a short walk from the theatre. Edie nominated the time and the date, which lay a few weeks ahead.

Trevor became quite frantic, trying to guess who was playing this double joke. His paranoia became quite infectious, first rubbing off on me, then the whole company (except for the actual perpetrator of the gag, of course) as he confided this information to them.

On the day of the announced meeting, a Saturday at 11 a.m., many of the actors in the company had taken up all the booths on the top floor of this café. Crowding every seat, except one left free for 'Edie', sat the likes of Sinead Cusack, Alan Howard, David (TV's Poirot) Suchet, Richard Pasco, Barbara Leigh Hunt, Susan Fleetwood and many others. We were all nervous, not knowing who would walk in, impersonating the fictional Edie. Literally, as the clock struck eleven, a tall, thin, eccentrically-dressed woman entered swiftly and without hesitation made a bee-line for the vacant seat opposite her 'husband' T Baxter. She planted a gruesome lipstick-printed kiss on Baxter's cheek and loudly ordered a doughnut and coffee. She then set about talking at such a pace about herself and 'the family'. Baxter's face was a study. All our faces were studies in amazement. We were gob-smacked. She only stayed for about ten raucous minutes and by then she'd talked, splashed her coffee about in all directions, gobbled her doughnut, talked, talked and talked. 'Edie Baxter' left as suddenly and dramatically as she'd arrived, shouting over her shoulder as she exited, that she had to get a train back to London, to attend upon 'the children'.

I have never, and will probably never again, see a bunch of leading actors, familiar with the craft of make-believe, look so stunned. No-one in the room believed they'd ever seen this individual before, so it wasn't a case of us all thinking 'Oh, of course it's So and So'. We rose and walked back to the theatre to perform a matinée of *As You Like It*, still dazed by what we'd witnessed. It was a very surreal matinée that day as we all had only one thing on our mind … Who was that extraordinary woman?

The perpetrator of this double bluff finally owned up. No one had guessed it was our stage manager. Edie had been played by one of actor Graeme Crowden's daughters, who in fact I had known as a young girl years before when Graeme played Prospero in *The Tempest* at the Mermaid Theatre. I was also in the cast of that production, directed by Dr Jonathan Miller, but I hadn't recognised her on that amazing day. Hers was truly an exemplary performance — bold and brash.

"But God, I was nervous … performing in front of you lot," she told me when I met her again a few years later.

Unfortunately, not one of us there that day had the wit to bring a camera.

It took Trevor time to recover from this double bluff, 'the biter bit' … but recover he did.

The last character to be mentioned from the changing skies of my memory is also every bit as indefatigable as anyone I've ever met and she too lived out most of her life under different skies to those where she was born. The remarkable Mrs Patricia Moss of Osney Island, in the city of dreaming spires, Oxford, was, for twenty wonderful years, a close confidante and friend. Born in India in 1924, she was truly an essential manifestation of the British Raj. Daughter, grand-daughter and great-granddaughter of serving officers in the Indian Army, Patricia, often referred to as the 'Duchess of Osney', was an extraordinary woman. P Moss, as she called herself, always looked elegant … somewhat like a galleon under full sail. Comfortably off, but not rich, Patricia (as I called her) was one of the most generous and warm-hearted human beings anyone could ever meet. She was also, like my mother, one of the finest hostesses I've ever known … her dinners, lunches and parties were stylish in a way rarely experienced and which money alone can never buy. One aspect that made her achievements so remarkable was that Patricia was very infirm as a result of rheumatic fever that nearly killed her as a child in India. "P Moss, get up and do something," was an oft-heard familiar phrase of hers. Another, when referring to herself: "This old bag."

I first met La Duchesse d'Osney when I went to look at a house near hers which I had a mind to buy. Patricia was the key-holder. I'd driven from the Cotswolds and found myself outside the front door to what I imagined was a simple terraced house on Osney Island. Mrs P Moss opened the door, warmly greeted me and invited me in. Upon entering I realized what a spacious house it really was and so very beautifully furnished, in a way I came to realize was uniquely her style.

After selling our Cotswold base, my wife and I did buy the house, and with a team of mates gutted the property and, from our own design, rebuilt it. It became for a time — too short — also a wonderful home. Mrs Patricia Moss very generously offered me the use of her local builder's merchant account, which meant Elspeth and I were able to save many thousands of pounds on building expenditure. I was very proud of our achievement but three years later, because of our divorce, we sold up to buy separate dwellings. Financially we made a healthy profit, though not an emotional one. Our parting of the ways left me cautious for some twenty years about the prospect of another permanent commitment until, quite recently in fact, a surprising new relationship occurred, allowing me to view my past with more relaxed hindsight.

It would be nonsense to say that nothing good came out of those twenty years, for many good friendships and several delightful liaisons buttressed me along the way … Dan and Winnie Davin were two such friends and many others I have mentioned in this book; and not the least of these, the friendship P Moss and I enjoyed. For this remarkable woman became like a mother to me and much of what was achieved over those twenty years had to do with her unswerving loyal support. And when she was quite clearly dying, after an accident, she did manage to utter:

"…a surprising new relationship occurred"
… with Sara Hebblethwaite.

"But what fun we've had darling. Such fun!"

Nº 55 West Street, Osney Island, Oxford, for twenty glorious years, was an epicentre of good times enjoyed by me and many others too.

"I'd like to leave you something," she once said.

"Patricia … you don't need to leave me anything."

But she insisted: "Choose," she said grandly. 'Grand' she did ever so well. She was rather like the Queen Mother!

"All right … that little watercolour on the wall there." I have it on my wall now, to remind me, though no reminder of the good times shared is really required.

One incident at Patricia's home which amused me was when the Bishop of New Guinea, an Aussie, was invited for lunch. In full regalia, a huge crucifix at his breast, he insisted, when I offered him a glass of champagne: "Only one glass, because I'm driving." He quaffed another three. During the first course, which was delicious smoked trout, I proffered white wine. "Only one glass. You see I'm driving." Another three! Then the main course, pheasant, and I gestured in his direction with a bottle of red. "Only one please, for I'm driving back to London after lunch." He enthusiastically drank three glasses of the claret. Then, the dessert — "Only one," he slightly slurred, though he knocked back three. Finally I went to pour him yet another Beaume de Venise … "No, no, that's my water glass," he asserted, somewhat testily (it wasn't). Not to be put down as some nincompoop, a mere waiter in his befuddled eyes, I riposted: "Then perhaps you'll allow me to turn your water into wine."

I'm glad I didn't accept his later kind offer of a lift back to London in his car, for though keen to reach Heaven's Gate and particularly in such celestial company, I deemed it a little soon for such adventure.

Graham Greene's last words, reported by his long-term lover, Cloetta: "Do you think it [the journey] will be interesting?" may like many reported last lines, be apocryphal.

Highlights of friendships, often involving travel, spring to mind ... the many delightful visits to stay at Villa Stella on the Balearic island of Menorca, in the Mediterranean, with my hosts Sebastian Black and Judi Binney ... these visits, first with my family, then with other friends, spanning thirty years. Travels too in the company of Vincent O'Sullivan and Barbara Caruso to Greece as mentioned, but also to Ireland, Italy, France, the States, New Zealand ... this 'Jules et Jim-like' triumvirate, have shared laughter, good conversation, food and wine ... under many changing skies. More to come perhaps? Much to be grateful for.

In summing up I identify with that quote from Horace: *Caelum non animum mutant qui trans mare current.*

... ...

'They change their skies, not their souls, who rush across the seas.'

... ...

Horace

Acknowledgments

I THANK Gay Menefy, whose idea it was for me to write this book and whose practical encouragement has made it possible. David Arbury of Thames assisted me with the history of our home town. Information about Maoridom in the Coromandel was generously provided by Professor Judith Binney of Auckland University. For the structure and sequence of the book I owe many thanks to Sebastian Black of Auckland.

I thank my family: my brother Grenville; my sister-in-law Ann; their children, Cameron, Anthony and Eleanor; my cousin Rosalie and my other cousins and my great-nephews Noah, Sol, Ryan and Oliver. I also thank my 'adopted' family: Richard, Jane, Ben, Toby and James, Kate, Amy, and Peter Hebblethwaite. Lastly, I cannot forget my many friends who have encouraged me in this project.

Photo by Jon Churchman, 2007.

278

Index

Bruce with Sara Hebblethwaite at his most recent exhibition, London 2007.

With Burn Gorman in Mike Hodges' stage production of *Shooting Stars*.

As the concierge in *Shooting Stars.*

From *Dr Who*: pirate captain Bruce at left.